Routledge Revivals

The Industrial History of England

Gibbins' *Industrial History of England* gives a thorough outline of England's economic and industrial history from the Romans to the early 20th Century. As well as considering the economic and industrial aspects of English life, this study also presents social, political and military aspects of different time periods to give a fuller picture of how England's industry progressed through the years. Originally published in 1890, this text has been reprinted several times with this edition published in 1912. This title will be of interest to students of British and industrial history.

The Industrial History of England

Henry De Beltgens

Routledge
Taylor & Francis Group
Routledge Revivals

First published in 1890
By Methuen & Co.

This edition first published in 2015 by Routledge
2 Park Square, Milton Park, Abingdon, Oxon, OX14 4RN
and by Routledge
711 Third Avenue, New York, NY 10017

Routledge is an imprint of the Taylor & Francis Group, an informa business

Publisher's Note
The publisher has gone to great lengths to ensure the quality of this reprint but points out that some imperfections in the original copies may be apparent.

Disclaimer
The publisher has made every effort to trace copyright holders and welcomes correspondence from those they have been unable to contact.

A Library of Congress record exists under LC control number: 15010482

ISBN 13: 978-1-138-18596-8 (hbk)
ISBN 13: 978-1-315-64413-4 (ebk)
ISBN 13: 978-1-138-18597-5 (pbk)

THE INDUSTRIAL HISTORY OF ENGLAND

BY

H. DE B. GIBBINS, LITT.D., M.A.

SOMETIME SCHOLAR OF WADHAM COLLEGE, OXFORD
AND UNIVERSITY (COBDEN) PRIZEMAN
IN POLITICAL ECONOMY

WITH MAPS

EIGHTEENTH EDITION
REVISED AND ENLARGED

METHUEN & CO. LTD.
36 ESSEX STREET W.C.
LONDON

First Published	*July*	*1890*
Second Edition	*December*	*1892*
Third Edition	*October*	*1892*
Fourth Edition	*February*	*1895*
Fifth Edition	*January*	*1897*
Sixth Edition	*December*	*1897*
Seventh Edition	*October*	*1900*
Eighth Edition	*February*	*1902*
Ninth Edition	*October*	*1903*
Tenth Edition	*February*	*1904*
Eleventh Edition	*March*	*1906*
Twelfth Edition	*October*	*1906*
Thirteenth Edition	*June*	*1907*
Fourteenth Edition	*December*	*1907*
Fifteenth Edition	*October*	*1908*
Sixteenth Edition	*July*	*1910*
Seventeenth Edition	*July*	*1911*
Eighteenth Edition, Revised	*January*	*1912*

PREFACE

THIS little book is an attempt to relate in a short, concise, and simple form the main outlines of England's economic and industrial history. It is meant to serve as an introduction to a fuller study of the subject and as a preliminary sketch which the reader can afterwards, if he wishes, fill in for himself from larger volumes dealing with special periods. At the same time it is hoped that this outline may succeed in giving not only to the student but to the ordinary reader a general view of a side of history too frequently neglected, but of the utmost importance to a proper understanding of the story of the English nation. I have endeavoured, as far as possible in the brief limits of a work like this, to connect economic and industrial questions with social, political, and military movements, believing as I do that only in some such mutual relation as this can historical events obtain their full significance.

The paramount necessity of simplicity and conciseness in an outline of this kind has compelled me to omit or mention very briefly many points which those who are familiar with my subject might well expect to be included. I have not, for instance, given elaborate statistical figures or voluminous footnotes upon the actual condition of our trade at various periods. Nor have I given more than an outline of the old and new Poor Laws, of financial measures, or of Banking ; and with much reluctance I have omitted a discussion of Colonial Trade. But all these points, except perhaps the last, may be reserved by a student till he comes to much larger works ; though a proper economic history of our Colonies yet remains to be written. Such as it is, however, I trust that this general view of the broad outlines of the growth of our wealth and industry in their relation to the general history of England may have its uses.

I have preferred not to weary my reader by constant references to authorities in footnotes, but have acknowledged my obligations to the various authorities consulted in an appendix, where suggestions for further reading will be found.

PREFACE TO THE EIGHTEENTH EDITION

SINCE the original publication of this book in 1890, twenty-one years have elapsed, and the author, whose untimely death all scholars deplore, was able to embody various corrections which made this book harmonize more completely with his larger work *Industry in England*. On certain points he was led to modify his opinions—a course inevitable in a book covering so large a ground.

In the Preface to the Fifth Edition he wrote: "It has been said that I write with a prejudice against the owners of land: but this is not the case. The landed gentry of England happen for some centuries to have held the predominant power in the State and in society, and used it, not unnaturally, in many cases to further their own interests. It is the duty of an historian to point this out, but it need not therefore be thought that he had any special bias against the class. Any other class would certainly have done the same, as, for instance, mill-owners did among their own *employees* at the beginning of this century, and as, in all probability, the working classes will do when a further extension of democratic government shall have given them the opportunity.

"It is a fault of human nature that it can rarely be trusted with irresponsible power, and unless the influence of one class of society is counterbalanced more or less by that of another, there will always be a tendency to some injustice. I trust that my readers will bear this in mind when reading the following pages, and will believe that I intend no unfairness to the landed gentry of England, who have done much to promote the glory and stability of their country."

The present, or eighteenth edition, has been carefully revised by Miss M. E. Hirst, M.A., and in addition to such revision she has written a new chapter (Chapter VIII.) which treats of the New Age of Industrial Expansion. *The Industrial History of England* is thus continued from the point at which the author left it and is carried up to the year 1911.

CONTENTS

PERIOD I

ENGLAND BEFORE THE NORMAN CONQUEST

PAGE

CHAP. I. INTRODUCTORY—THE ROMANS AND THEIR SUCCESSORS—TRADE 1

„ II. THE LAND: ITS OWNERS AND CULTIVATORS . 5

PERIOD II

FROM THE NORMAN CONQUEST TO THE REIGN OF HENRY III. (1066–1216 A.D.)

CHAP. I. DOMESDAY BOOK AND THE MANORS . . 10

„ II. THE TOWNS AND THE GILDS . . . 22

„ III. MANUFACTURES AND TRADE: ELEVENTH TO THIRTEENTH CENTURIES . . . 31

PERIOD III

FROM THE THIRTEENTH TO THE END OF THE FIFTEENTH CENTURY, INCLUDING THE GREAT PLAGUE (1216–1500)

CHAP. I. AGRICULTURE IN MEDIÆVAL ENGLAND . . 40

„ II. THE WOOLLEN TRADE AND MANUFACTURES . 47

„ III. THE TOWNS, INDUSTRIAL VILLAGES, AND FAIRS 57

„ IV. THE GREAT PLAGUE AND ITS ECONOMIC EFFECTS . 67

„ V. THE PEASANTS' REVOLT OF 1381, AND THE SUBSEQUENT PROSPERITY OF THE WORKING CLASSES 75

PERIOD IV

FROM THE SIXTEENTH CENTURY TO THE EVE OF THE INDUSTRIAL REVOLUTION (1509–1760)

		PAGE
CHAP. I.	THE MISDEEDS OF HENRY VIII., AND ECONOMIC CHANGES IN THE SIXTEENTH CENTURY .	83
,, II.	THE GROWTH OF FOREIGN TRADE . .	91
,, III.	ELIZABETHAN ENGLAND . . .	100
,, IV.	PROGRESS OF AGRICULTURE IN THE SEVENTEENTH AND EIGHTEENTH CENTURIES . .	109
,, V.	COMMERCE AND WAR IN THE SEVENTEENTH AND EIGHTEENTH CENTURIES . . .	121
,, VI.	MANUFACTURES AND MINING . . .	132

PERIOD V

THE INDUSTRIAL REVOLUTION AND MODERN ENGLAND

CHAP. I.	THE EVE OF THE REVOLUTION . . .	144
,, II.	THE EPOCH OF THE GREAT INVENTIONS .	157
,, III.	WARS, POLITICS, AND INDUSTRY . .	167
,, IV.	THE FACTORY SYSTEM AND ITS RESULTS .	176
,, V.	THE CONDITION OF THE WORKING CLASSES .	187
,, VI.	THE RISE AND DEPRESSION OF MODERN AGRICULTURE	198
,, VII.	MODERN INDUSTRIAL ENGLAND . . .	211
,, VIII.	THE NEW AGE, 1897-1911 . . .	223

NOTE ON AUTHORITIES FOR INDUSTRIAL HISTORY .	241
NOTES	243
INDEX	253

THE INDUSTRIAL HISTORY OF ENGLAND

PERIOD I

ENGLAND BEFORE THE NORMAN CONQUEST

CHAPTER I

INTRODUCTORY—THE ROMANS AND THEIR SUCCESSORS—TRADE

§ 1. ALTHOUGH the industrial history of England does not properly begin until the settlement made by the Norman Conquest, it is nevertheless impossible to omit some reference to the previous economic condition of the country. As everybody knows, the Romans were the first to invade Britain, although it had been known, probably for centuries previously, to the Phenicians and Carthaginians who used to sail here for its tin and lead. The Romans, however, first colonized the country and began to develop its resources; and they succeeded in introducing various industries and in opening up a considerable commerce.

Under Roman sway Britain reached a high level of prosperity, and there is abundant evidence of this fact from Roman writers. They speak of the rich natural productions of Britain, of its numerous flocks and herds, of its minerals, of its various commercial facilities, and of the revenues derived from these sources.

We know that there were no less than fifty-nine cities in Britain in the middle of the third century A.D., and the population was probably fairly large, though we have no certain statistics upon this point.[1] Large quantities of corn were exported from the land, as many as 800 vessels being sent on one occasion to procure corn for the Roman cities in Germany. This shows a fairly advanced agriculture. Tin also was another important export, as indeed it has always been; and British slaves were constantly sent to the market at Rome. In the country itself great material works, such as walled towns, paved roads, aqueducts, and great public buildings were undertaken, and remained to testify to the greatness of their builders long after their name had become a distant memory. The military system of the Romans helped to produce industrial results, for the Roman soldiers took a prominent part in road-making, building dykes, working mines, and the great engineering operations that marked the Roman rule. The chief towns very largely owed their origin to their importance as military stations; and most of them, such as York, London, Chester, Lincoln, Bath, and Colchester, have continued ever since to be considerable centres of population, though of course with occasional fluctuations. When, however, the Romans finally left Britain (in A.D. 410), both trade and agriculture began to sink; the towns decayed; and for centuries England became the battle-ground of various predatory tribes from the Continent, who gradually effected a settlement, first in many kingdoms, but finally in one, and became known as "the English," or the Anglo-Saxon nationality (A.D. 827).

§ 2. **Trade in the Anglo-Saxon period**—But although Egbert became Lord of the Saxons in 827, it was not till

[1] See note 1, p. 243, on Population of Roman Britain.

the reign of Edgar (958–975) that England became one united kingdom, and indeed throughout this period internal war was almost constant, and naturally prevented any great growth of home industry or foreign trade. The home industry, such as it was, was almost entirely agricultural, under a system of which I shall speak in the next chapter. The separate communities living in the country villages or small towns were very much disinclined for mutual intercourse, and endeavoured as far as possible to be each a self-sufficing economic whole, getting their food and clothing, coarse and rough as it generally was, from their own flocks and herds, or from their own land in the mark or manor.[1] Hence only the simplest domestic arts and manufactures were carried on.

§ 3. **Internal Trade. Money**—But, however much a community may desire to be self-sufficing, it cannot be so entirely. Differences of soil, mineral wealth, and other advantages cause one community to require what another has in abundance. Salt, for instance, was largely in request for salting meat for the winter, and it cannot be universally procured in England. Hence local markets arose, at first always on the neutral boundary between two marks,[2] the place of the market being marked by the boundary stone, the origin of the later "market cross." These markets at first took place only at stated times during the year. Shrines and burial-places of noted men were the most frequented spots for such annual fairs. Thus, *e.g.*, the origin of Glasgow may be traced from the burial-place of St Ninian (A.D. 570). There seems to have been a well-defined, though small, trading class; but, at any rate at first, most people of different occupations met

[1] See next chapter.

[2] See note 2, p. 243, on Markets on Boundaries.

at well-known, convenient places, and bartered without the assistance of any kind of middlemen.

Mere barter, however, is tedious and cumbersome; and although, up to the time of Alfred (A.D. 870), a large proportion, though not the whole, of English internal trade was carried on in this fashion, the use of metals for exchange begins to become common in the ninth century; and in A.D. 900 regular money payments by tenants are found recorded. And when we come to the levy of the Danegeld (A.D. 991)—the tax raised by Ethelred as a bribe to the Danes—it is clear that money coinage must have been widely diffused and in general circulation.

§ 4. **Foreign Trade**—Trade of all kinds had suffered a severe blow when the Romans quitted Britain, but during the Anglo-Saxon period English merchants still did a certain amount of foreign trade. They were encouraged too in this by a doom, of Danish origin,[1] which provided that "if a merchant thrived so that he fared thrice over the sea by his own means, then was he of thane-right worthy," which gave him a comparatively high rank. The settlement of German merchants in London, pointing to some continental trade, also dates from the time of Ethelred the Unready (about A.D. 1000). Much of this foreign trade lay in the treasures of precious metals and embroideries, which were imported for use in monasteries. It is interesting, by the way, to note that St Dunstan (who died in 988) encouraged handicraft work in metals, especially in ironwork. The exports from England were chiefly wool—which we shall afterwards see becomes of great importance—some agricultural produce, and also, as before, lead and tin. English merchants we know went to Marseilles, and others frequented the great French fairs of Rouen and St Denis in the ninth century; while,

[1] See note 3, p. 243, on Danish Influence on Commerce.

rather earlier, we have a most interesting document, our first treaty of commerce in fact, dated A.D. 796, by which Karl the Great, or Charlemagne, as some people call him, grants protection to certain English traders from Mercia. And in King Alfred's days one English bishop even "penetrated prosperously" to India with the king's gifts to the shrine of St Thomas.

§ 5. **General Summary**—Taking a general view of the period between the Saxon Conquest and the Norman Conquest, we see that crafts and manufactures were few and simple, being confined as far as possible to separate and isolated communities. Fine arts, and works in metal and embroideries were limited to the monasteries, which also imported them. The immense mineral wealth of the island in iron and coal was untouched. Trade was small, though undoubtedly developing. The mass of the population was engaged in agriculture, and every man had, so to speak, a stake in the land, belonging to a manor or parish. A landless man was altogether outside the pale of social life. The owners of the land, and the method of its cultivation, will occupy us in the next chapter.

CHAPTER II

THE LAND: ITS OWNERS AND CULTIVATORS

§ 1. **The Mark**—We have just said that the population of England as a whole was almost entirely engaged in agriculture; and indeed for some centuries onward this industry was by far the most important in the country. Now, it is impossible to understand the conditions of this industry without first glancing at the tenure of land as existing about this time. It has been thought, but it is not at all certain, that in very early times before the tribes afterwards called English had crossed over to England, or perhaps even before they had arrived in Europe, all land was held in common by various communities of people, perhaps at first with only a few families in each. The land occupied by this community (whether it was a whole tribe or a few families) had probably been cleared away from the original forests or wastes, and was certainly separated from all other communities by a fixed boundary or *mark*,[1] whence the whole land thus separated off was called a mark. Within this mark was the primitive village or "township," where each member of the community had his house, and where each had a common share in the land. This land was of three kinds—(1) The *forest*, or *waste* land, from which the mark had been originally cleared, useful for rough natural pasture, but uncultivated. (2) The *pasture* land, sometimes enclosed and sometimes open, in which each mark-man looked after his own hay, and stacked it for the winter, and which was divided into allotments for each member. (3) The *arable* land, which also was divided into allotments for each mark-man. To settle any question relating to the division and use of the land, or to any other business of common importance, the members of the mark, or mark-men, met in a common council called the *mark-moot*, an institution of which relics survived for many centuries. This council, and the mark generally, formed the political, social, and economic unit of the early English tribes. How far it actually existed when these tribes occupied England it is difficult to say, and it is probable that it had already undergone considerable transformation towards what is called the *manorial*

[1] For a criticism of the mark theory see *Industry in England*, pp. 47–61.

system. But this much is certain, that in England, as in Germany, traces of communal life still remain. Our commons, still numerous in spite of hundreds of enclosures, and the names of places ending in *ing*, which termination frequently implies a primitive family settlement, are evidences which remain among us to-day. And it is only comparatively recently that the "common fields," yearly divided among the commoners of a parish, together with the "three-field system," which this allotment involved, have disappeared from our English agriculture.

§ 2. **The Manor**—But when we come to the time when the Anglo-Saxons had made a final settlement, and were ruled by one king, we find a different system prevailing —*i.e.* the manorial system. The word "manor" is a Norman name for the Saxon "township," or community, and it differs from the mark in this: the mark [1] was a group of households organized and governed on a common, democratic basis, while in the manor we find an autocratic organization and government, whereby a group of *tenants* acknowledge the superior position and authority of a "lord of the manor." But although "manor" is a Norman name, the change from the old mark system had taken place long before the Norman Conquest, and even if perhaps occasional independent communities still existed, they were completely abolished under the Norman rule. The great feature of the manor was, that it was subject to a "lord," who owned absolutely a certain portion of the land therein, and had rights of rent (paid in services, or food, or money, or in all three) over the rest of the land. It is probable that the lord of the manor had gained his position under a promise of aiding and protecting his humbler brethren; but, even in later

[1] *i.e.* supposing it ever existed.

times, he had to acknowledge certain rights belonging to them.

§ 3. **Combined Agriculture**—In the manor, just as in the earlier stage, all agriculture was carried on collectively by the tenants of the manor. Men gathered together their oxen to form the usual team of eight wherewith to drag the plough, pastured their cattle in common, and employed a common swineherd or shepherd for their pigs and sheep.

The distinctive feature of this combined agriculture was the three-field system. All the arable land near a village was divided into three strips, and was sown in the following manner :—A field was sown with wheat or rye in the autumn of one year ; but owing to the slowness of primitive farming this crop would not be reaped in time for autumn sowing the next year, so the sowing took place in the following spring, the next crop being oats or barley ; after this crop the land lay fallow for a year. Hence, of these three strips, every year one had wheat or rye, another oats or barley, while the third was fallow. The land of each individual was necessarily scattered between the various plots of his neighbours, so that each might have a fair share in land of good quality. This style of agriculture, of course, produced very meagre results, but it seems to have been sufficient for the simple wants of the occupiers of that epoch.

§ 4. **The Feudal System**—In the next period we shall see this manorial system consolidated and organized under the Norman rule, and so may defer a full description of a typical manor till then. Here we may say that the manor is closely connected with the *feudal* system, which, it must be remembered, had begun a considerable time before the Norman Conquest. For the manor afforded a convenient political and social unit for the estimation of feudal services, and the lord of the manor became more and more a feudal chief. But it must be understood that the manorial system was not the same as the feudal system, though it helped to prepare the way for it; and eventually the lords of the manors became nominally the protectors, but really the masters of the village husbandmen dwelling around them. The lord professed to take them under his protection if they surrendered their independence to him, and it was probably owing to the frequent incursions of the Danes that the system grew as it did. In Canute's reign we find it in full force, for at this time the kingdom was divided into great military districts, or *earldoms*, the "earl" being responsible to the king and receiving the profits of his district. When William the Norman conquered England he did not, as is often supposed, impose a feudal system upon the people. The system was there already, developed from the old manors, and all William I. did was to reorganize it, and give the English people Norman instead of Anglo-Saxon or Danish lords.

NOTE.—The theory of the mark (which is now regarded as very doubtful) is dealt with more fully in ch. iv. of my *Industry in England*, where also the evidences of communal village life are discussed; and I must refer my readers to this for more recent views.

PERIOD II

FROM THE NORMAN CONQUEST TO THE REIGN OF HENRY III. (A.D. 1066-1216)

CHAPTER I

DOMESDAY BOOK AND THE MANORS

§ 1. **Domesday Book**—It was very natural that, when William the Norman conquered England, he should wish to ascertain the capabilities of his kingdom both in regard to military defence and for taxation; and that he should endeavour to gain a comprehensive idea of the results of his conquest. So he ordered a grand survey of the kingdom to be made, and sent commissioners into each district to make it. These officials were bidden to inquire about all the estates in the realm—who held them, what was the value of each, how many men occupied it and how many cattle each supported. The results of this survey form our earliest and most reliable statistics for English industrial history; and it is to be regretted that no general table or analysis of this great work has yet been made, or that historians do not use it more copiously for gaining a knowledge of the social and economic conditions of the time. For this latter purpose it is absolutely unrivalled.[1]

§ 2. **Economic condition of the country as shown in Domesday**—From it we may gather the following few facts

[1] For recent works on Domesday Book, see p. 242.

as to the economic condition of England about the time of the Norman Conquest. The population numbered about 2,000,000, three-fourths of whom lived by agricultural labour, the remaining fourth being townsfolk, gentry, and churchmen. The East and South, especially the county of Kent, were the best tilled, richest, and most populous parts of the country. "The downs and wolds gave fine pasturage for sheep, the copses and woods formed fattening grounds for swine, and the hollows at the downs' foot, the river flats, and the low, gravel hills, were the best and easiest land to plough and crop. Far the largest part of the country was forest—*i.e.* uncleared and undrained moor, wood, or fen."[1] The chief towns were London, Canterbury, Chester, Lincoln, Oxford, York, Hereford, and Winchester; but these were trading centres rather than seats of manufacturing industry. A small foreign export trade was done in wool and lead, the imports being chiefly articles of luxury. There were 9250 villages or manors in the land; in these about three-fifths of each is waste—*i.e.* untilled, common land—one-fifth pasture, and one-fifth arable.

§ 3. **The Manors and their owners**—Now each of these manors after the Norman Conquest was held by a "lord," who held it more or less remotely from the king. For it is the distinguishing feature of the Conquest, that William the Norman made himself the supreme landlord of the country, so that all land was held under him. He himself of course held a good many manors, which were farmed by his bailiffs, and for each of these manors he was the lord. But the majority of the manors were held by his followers, the Norman nobles, and nearly all of them had several manors apiece. Now it was impossible for a noble to look after all his manors himself, and they

[1] V. *Industry in England*, p. 69.

found it was not always the best plan to put their bailiffs in to work them; so they used to sublet some of their manors to other tenants, often to Englishmen who had submitted to the Norman Conquest. The nobles who held the land direct from the king were called *tenants in chief*,[1] the tenants to whom they sublet it were called *tenants in mesne*.[2] If a noble let a manor to a tenant in mesne the tenant then took his place, and became the *lord* of the manor. Thus, then, we have some manors owned directly by the king, others by the great nobles, and others again by tenants in mesne. For instance, in the part of Domesday relating to Oxfordshire, we find that one Milo Crispin, a tenant in chief, held several manors from the king, but also let some of them to sub-tenants, that of Cuxham, *e.g.*, being let to one Alured, who was therefore its lord. So in Warwickshire the manor of Estone (now Aston) was one of those belonging to William Fitz-Ansculf, but he had let it to Godmund, an Englishman, who was then "lord of the manor of Estone."

§ 4. **The inhabitants of the manors**—Besides the lord himself (whether king, noble, or sub-tenant), with his personal retainers, and generally a parish priest or some monks, there were three other classes of inhabitants. (1) First came the *villeins*, who formed 38 per cent. of the whole population recorded in Domesday, and who held their land in virgates, a *virgate* being some thirty acres of arable land, scattered of course in plots (cf. p. 20) among the common fields of the manor, together with a house and messuage in the village. These villeins were often called *virgarii* (or *yardlings*), from this term virgate. (2) Below the villeins came the *cottars*, or *bordars*, a class distinct from and below the former, who probably held

[1] Or, *in capite*.

[2] *i.e.* sub-tenants.

only some five or ten acres of land and a cottage, and did not even possess a plough, much less a team of oxen, apiece, but had to combine among themselves for the purpose of ploughing. They form 32 per cent. of the Domesday population. Finally came (3) *the slaves*, who were much smaller in numbers than is commonly supposed, forming only 9 per cent. of the Domesday population. Less than a century after the Conquest these disappear and merge into the cottars.

§ 5. **The condition of these inhabitants**—The chief feature of the social condition of these classes of people was that they were subject to a lord. They each depended upon a superior, and no man could be either lordless or landless; for all persons in *villeinage*, which included everyone below the lord of the manor, were subject to a master, and bound to the land, except, of course, "free tenants" (p. 15). But even against their lord the villeins had certain rights which had to be recognized. They had, moreover, many comforts and little responsibility, except to pay their dues to their lord. Moreover, it was possible for a villein to purchase a remission of his services, and become a "free tenant." Or he might become such by residing in a town for a year and a day, and being a member of a town gild, as long as during that period he was unclaimed by his lord. And in course of time the villein's position came to be this—he owed his lord the customary services (see p. 14) whereby his lord's land was cultivated; but his lord could not refuse him his customary rights in return—"his house and lands, and rights of wood and hay"—and in relation to everyone but his lord he was a perfectly free citizen. His condition tended to improve, and up to the time of the Great Plague (1348) a large number of villeins had become actually free, having commuted their services for money payments. What these services were we shall now explain. But finally, we wish to point out that the state of villeinage and of serfage was practically the same thing in two aspects; the first implying the fact that the villein was bound to the soil, the second that he was subject to a master. A serf was not a slave; and, as we saw above, *slaves* became extinct soon after the Norman Conquest.

§ 6. **Services due to the lord from his tenants in villeinage**—Under the manorial system rent was paid in a very different manner from that in which it is paid to-day, for it was a rent not so much of money, though that was employed, as of services. The services thus rendered by tenants in villeinage, whether villeins or cottars, may be divided into *week-work*, and *boon-days* or work on special days. The week-work consisted of ploughing or reaping, or doing some other agricultural work for the lord of the manor for two or three days in the week, or at fixed times, such as at harvest; while *boon-day* work was rendered at times not fixed, but whenever the lord of the manor might require it, though the number of boon-days in a year was limited. When, however, the villein or cottar had performed these liabilities, he was quite free to do work on his own land, or for that matter on any one else's land, as indeed the cottars frequently did, for they had not much land of their own, and so often had time and labour to spare. It was from this cottar class with time to spare that a distinct wage-earning class, like our modern labourers, arose, who lived almost entirely by wages. We shall hear more of them later on; but at the time of the Conquest they hardly existed.

§ 7. **Money payments and rents**—It was also usual for a tenant, besides rendering these servile services, to pay his lord a small rent either in money or kind, generally in both. Thus on Cuxham manor we find a villein (or serf) paying his lord ½*d.* on November 12th every year and 1*d.* whenever he brews. He also pays, in kind, 1 quarter of seed-wheat at Michaelmas; 1 peck of wheat, 4 bushels of oats, and 3 hens on 12th November; also 1 cock and 2 hens, and 2*d.* worth of bread every Christmas. His *services* are—to plough and till ½ acre of the lord's land, to give 3 days' labour at harvest, and other days when required by the bailiff. This was the rent for about 12 or 15 acres of land (half a virgate), and upon a calculation of the worth of labour and provisions at that time (end of thirteenth century) comes to about 6*d.* an acre for his land, and 3*s.* a year for his house and the land about it (*curtilage*).

§ 8. **Free Tenants. Soke-men**—So far I have been speaking only about tenants in villeinage. But in the Domesday Book we find another class of tenants, called *free*, who had to pay a rent fixed in amount, either in money or kind, and sometimes in labour. This rent was fixed and unalterable in amount, and they were masters of their own actions as soon as it was paid. They were not, like the villeins, bound to the soil, but could transfer their holdings or even quit the manor if they liked. They were, however, subject to their lord's jurisdiction in matters of law, and hence were called *soke-men* (from *soke* or *soc*=jurisdiction exercised by a lord). They also were bound to give military service when called upon, which the villeinage tenants had not to give. If they had any services to render, these were generally commuted into money payments; and here we may observe, that there was a constant tendency from the Conquest to the time of the Great Plague (1348) towards this commutation. Villeins also could, and did frequently, commute their labour rents for money rents.

In Domesday, we find that the Eastern and East-central counties were those in which "free" tenants or soke-men were most prevalent. There they form from 27 to 45 per cent. of the inhabitants of those parts, though, taking all England into view, they only form 4 per cent. of the total population. The number of free tenants, however, was constantly increasing, even among tenants in villeinage, for the lord often found it more useful to have money, and was willing to allow commutation of services; or again, he might prefer not to cultivate *all* his own land (his *demesne*), but to let it for a fixed money rent to a villein to do what he could with it; and thus the villein became a free man, while the lord was sure of a fixed sum from his land every year, whether the harvest were good or bad.

§ 9. **Illustrations of old manors.** (1) **Estone**—To make clear what I have said in this chapter, it will perhaps be well to give two illustrations drawn from the Domesday Book (eleventh century) and from bailiffs' accounts of a later period (end of thirteenth century).

First we will take a manor in Warwickshire in the Domesday Survey (1089)—Estone, now Aston, near Birmingham. It was one of a number belonging to William, the son of Ansculf, who was tenant in chief, but had let it to one Godmund, a sub-tenant in mesne. The Survey runs: "William Fitz-Ansculf holds of the King Estone, and Godmund of him. There are 8 hides.[1] The arable employs 20 ploughs; in the demesne the arable employs 6 ploughs, but now there are no ploughs. There are 30 villeins with a priest, and 1 bondsman, and 12 bordars [*i.e.* cottars]. They have 18 ploughs. A mill pays 3

[1] A *hide* varied in size, and was (after the Conquest) equal to a *carucate*, which might be anything from 80 to 120 or 180 acres. Perhaps 120 is a fair average, though some say 80.

shillings. The woodland is 3 miles long and half a mile broad. It was worth £4; now 100 shillings."

Here we have a good example of a manor held by a sub-tenant, and containing all the three classes mentioned in § 4 of this chapter—villeins, cottars, and slaves (*i.e.* bondsmen). The whole manor must have been about 5000 acres, of which 1000 were probably arable land, which was of course parcelled out in strips among the villeins, the lord, and the priest. As there were only 18 ploughs among 30 villeins, it is evident some of them at least had to use a plough and oxen in common. The demesne land does not seem to have been well cultivated by Godmund the lord, for there were no ploughs on it, though it was large enough to employ six. Perhaps Godmund, being an Englishman, had been fighting the Normans in the days of Harold, and had let it go out of cultivation, or perhaps the former owner had died in the war, and Godmund had rented the land from the Norman noble to whom William gave it.

§ 10. **Cuxham Manor in the eleventh and thirteenth centuries**—Our second illustration can be described at two periods of its existence—at the time of Domesday and 200 years later. It was only a small manor of some 490 acres, and was held by a sub-tenant from a Norman tenant in chief, Milo Crispin. It is found in the Oxfordshire Domesday, in the list of lands belonging to Milo Crispin. The Survey says: "Alured [the sub-tenant] now holds 5 hides for a manor in Cuxham. Land to 4 ploughs; now in the demesne, 2 ploughs and 4 bondsmen. And 7 villeins with 4 bordars have 3 ploughs. There are 3 mills of 18 shillings; and 18 acres of meadow. It was worth £3, now £6." Here, again, our three classes of villeins, cottars or bordars, and slaves are represented. The manor was evidently a good one, for though smaller than Estone it was worth more, and has three mills and good meadow land as well. Now, by the end of the thirteenth century this manor had passed into the hands of Merton College, Oxford, which then represented the lord, but farmed it by means of a bailiff. Professor Thorold Rogers gives us a description of it,[1] drawn from the annual accounts of this bailiff, which he has examined along with a number of others from other manors. We find one or two changes have taken place, for the bondsmen have entirely disappeared, as indeed they did in less than a century after the Conquest all through the land. The number of villeins and bordars has increased. There are now 13 villeins and 8 cottars, and 1 free tenant. There is also a prior, who holds land (6 acres) in the manor but does not live in it; also two other tenants, who do not live in the manor, but hold "a quarter of a knight's fee" (here some 40 or 50 acres)—a knight's fee comprising an area of land varying from 2 hides to 4 or even 6 hides, but in any case worth some £20. As the Cuxham land was good, the quantity necessary for the valuation of a fee would probably be only the small hide or carucate of 80 acres, and the quarter of it of course 20 acres or a little more. The 13 serfs hold 170 acres, but the 8 cottars only 30 acres, including their tenements. The free tenant holds $12\frac{3}{4}$ acres, and Merton College as lord of the manor some 240 acres of demesne. There are now two mills instead of three, one belonging to the prior, and the other to another tenant. There were altogether, counting the families of the villeins and cottars, but not the two tenants of military fees, about 60 or 70 inhabitants, the most important being the college bailiff and the miller.

§ 11. **Description of a manor village**—Now in both these country manors, as in all others, the central feature

[1] In his *Six Centuries of Work and Wages.*

would be the dwelling of the lord, or manor-house. It was substantially built, and served as a court-house for the annual sittings of the *court baron* and *court leet.*[1] If the lord did not live in it, his bailiff did so, and then the lord would come once or twice a year to hold these courts. Near the manor-house generally stood the church, often large for the size of the village, because the nave was frequently used as a town-hall for meetings or for markets. Then there would be the house of the priest, possibly in the demesne ; and after these two the most important building was the mill, which, if there was a stream, would be placed on its banks in order to use the water-power. The rest of the tenants generally inhabited the principal street or road of the village, near the stream, if one ran through the place. The houses of these villages were poor and dirty, not always made of stone, and never (till the fifteenth century) of brick, but built of posts wattled and plastered with clay or mud, with an upper storey of poles reached by a ladder. The articles of furniture would be very coarse and few, being necessarily of home manufacture ; a few rafters or poles overhead, a bacon-rack, and agricultural tools being the most conspicuous objects. Chimneys were unknown, except in the manor-houses, and so too were windows, and the floor was of bare earth. Outside the door was the "mixen," a collection of every kind of manure and refuse, which must have rendered the village street alike unsavoury, unsightly and unwholesome. But though their life was rude and rough, it seems that the villagers were fairly happy, and, considering all things, about as well off as are their descendants now.

§ 12. **The kinds of land in a manor**—Before concluding this chapter, it is necessary, in order to complete our

[1] See note 4, p. 243, on Manorial Courts.

sketch of the manorial system from the time of the Conquest onwards, to understand how the land was divided up. We may say that there were seven kinds of land altogether. (1) First came the lord's land round about the manor-house, the *demesne* land, which was strictly his own, and generally cultivated by himself or his bailiff. All other land held by tenants was called *land in villeinage*. (2) Next came the arable land of the village held by the tenants in *common fields*. Now these fields were all divided up into many strips, and tenants held their strips generally in quite different places, all mixed up anyhow (cf. diagram, where the tenants are marked A, B. C, etc.). The lord and the parson might also have a few strips in these fields. There were at least three fields, in order to allow the rotation of crops mentioned before (p. 8). Each tenant held his strip only till harvest, after which all fences and divisions were taken away, and the cattle turned out to feed on the stubble. (3) Thirdly came the *common pasture*, for all the tenants. But each tenant was restricted or stinted in the number of cattle that he might pasture, lest he should put on too many, and thus not leave enough food for his neighbours' cattle. Sometimes, however, we find pasture without stint, as in Port Meadow at Oxford to this day. (4) Then comes the *forest* or *woodland*, as in Estone, which belonged to the lord, who owned all the timber. But the tenants had rights, such as the right of lopping and topping certain trees, collecting fallen branches for fuel; and the right of "pannage"—*i.e.* of turning cattle, especially swine, into the woods to pick up what food they could. (5) There was also in most manors what is called the *waste*—*i.e.* uncultivated—land, affording rough pasture, and on which the tenants had the right of cutting turf and bracken for fuel and fodder. Then near the stream there would

THE KING (supreme landlord)

TENANT IN CHIEF, owning various manors.

A SUB-TENANT, or tenant in mesne, the lord of the manor below.

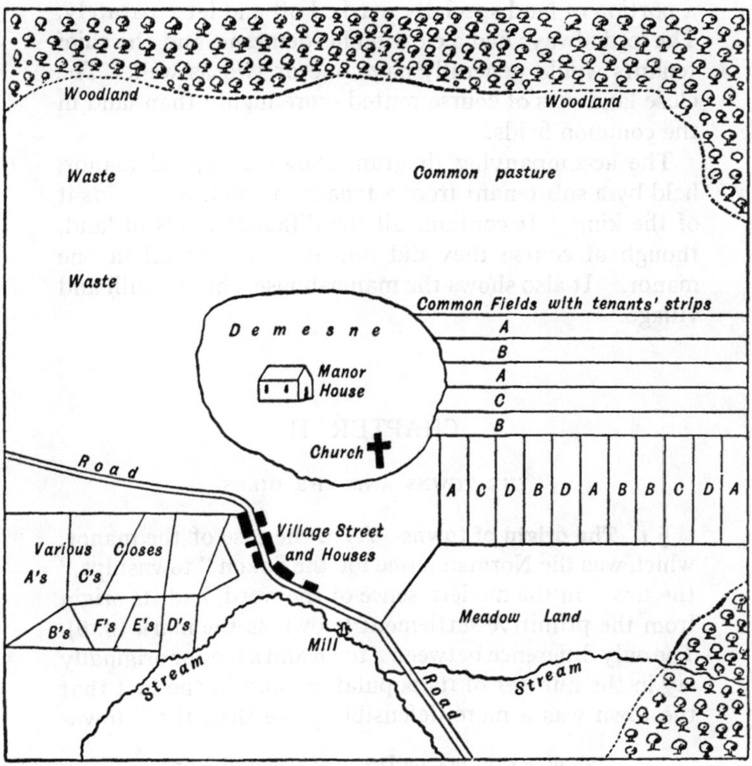

perhaps be some (6) *Meadow land*, as at Cuxham ; but this always belonged to the lord, and if he let it out, he always charged an extra rent (say eightpence instead of sixpence an acre), for it was very valuable as affording a good supply of hay for the winter. Lastly, if the tenant could afford it, and wanted to have other land besides the common fields, where he could let his cattle lie, or to cultivate the ground more carefully, he could occupy (7) a *close*, or a portion of land specially marked off and let separately. The lord always had a close on his demesne, and the chief tenants would generally have one or two as well. The close land was of course rented more highly than land in the common fields.

The accompanying diagram shows a typical manor, held by a sub-tenant from a tenant in chief, who holds it of the king. It contains all the different kinds of land, though of course they did not always exist all in one manor. It also shows the manor-house, church, mill and village.[1]

CHAPTER II

THE TOWNS AND THE GILDS

§ 1. **The origin of towns**—As in the case of the manor, which was the Norman name for the Saxon " townships," the town, in the modern sense of the word, had its origin from the primitive settlement known as the mark (p. 6). The only difference between a town and a manor originally lay in the number of its population, and in the fact that the town was a more defensible place than the " town-

[1] See note 5, p. 244, on Decay of Manorial System.

ship," or rural manor, probably having a mound or moat surrounding it, instead of the hedges which ran round the villages. In itself it was merely a manor or group of manors ; as Professor Freeman puts it, "one part of the district where men lived closer together than elsewhere." The town had at first a constitution like that of a primitive village in the mark, but its inhabitants had gradually gained certain rights and functions of a special nature. These rights and privileges had been received from the lord of the manor on which the town had grown up ; for towns, especially provincial towns, were at first only dependent manors, which gained safety and solidity under the protection of some great noble, prelate, or the king himself, who finally would grant the town thus formed a charter.

§ 2. **Rise of towns in England**—Towns first became important in England towards the end of the Saxon period. Saxon England had never been a settlement of towns, but of villages and townships, or manors. But gradually towns did grow up, though differing widely in the circumstances and manner of their rise. Some grew up in the fortified camps of the invaders themselves, as being in a secure position ; some arose from a later occupation of the once sacked and deserted Roman towns. Many grew silently in the shadow of a great abbey or monastery. Of this class was Oxford, which first came into being round the monasteries of St Frideswide and Osney. Others clustered round the country houses of some Saxon king or earl. Several important boroughs owed their rise to the convenience of their site as a port or a trading centre. This was the origin of the growth of Bristol, whose rise resulted directly from trade ; and London of course had always been a port of high commercial rank. A few other towns, like Scarborough and Grimsby, were at first small havens for fishermen. But all the English towns were far less flourishing before the arrival of the Normans than they afterwards became.

§ 3. **Towns in Domesday : London**—If, now, we once more go back to our great authority, the survey made by William the Norman, we find that the status of these towns or boroughs is clearly recognized, though they are regarded as held by the lord of the manor "in demesne," or in default of a lord, as part of the king's demesne. Thus Northampton at that time was a town in the king's demesne ; Beverley was held in demesne by the Archbishop of York. It was possible, too, that one town might belong to several lords, because it spread over, or was an aggregate of, several manors or townships. Thus Leicester seems to have included four manors, which were thus held in demesne by four lords—one by the king, another by the Bishop of Lincoln, another by a noble, Simon de Senlis, and the fourth by Ivo of Grantmesnil, the sheriff. In later times it was held under one lord, Count Robert of Meulan.

Now, in the Domesday Book there is mention made of forty-one provincial cities or boroughs, most of them being the county towns of the present day. There are also ten fortified towns of greater importance than the others. They are Canterbury, York, Nottingham, Oxford, Hereford, Leicester, Lincoln, Stafford, Chester, and Colchester. London was a town apart, as it had always been, and was the only town which had a civic constitution, being regulated by a port-reeve and a bishop, and having a kind of charter, though afterwards the privileges of this charter were much increased. London was of course a great port and trading centre, and had many foreign merchants in it. It was then, as well as in subsequent centuries, the centre of English national life, and the voice of its citizens counted for something in national affairs. The other great ports of England at that time were Bristol, Southampton, and Norwich, and as trade grew and prospered, many other ports rose into prominence (see p. 64).

§ 4. **Special privileges of towns**—Even at the time of the Conquest most towns, though small, were of sufficient importance to have a certain status of their own, with definite privileges. The most important of these was the right of composition for taxation, *i.e.* the right of paying a fixed sum, or rent, to the Crown, instead of the various tallages, taxes, and imposts that might be required of other places. This fixed sum, or composition, was called the *firma burgi*, and by the time of the Conquest was nearly always paid in money. Previously it had been paid both in money and kind, for we find Oxford paying to Edward the Confessor six sectaries of honey as well as £20 in coin ; while to William the Norman it paid £60 as an inclusive lump sum. By the end of the Norman period all the towns had secured the *firma burgi*, and the right of assessing it themselves, instead of being assessed by the sheriff ; they had the right also of choosing a mayor of their own, instead of the king's bailiff or *reeve*. They had, moreover, their own tribunals, a charter for their customs, and special rules of local administration, and, generally speaking, gained entire judicial and commercial freedom.

§ 5. **How the towns obtained their charters**—It is interesting to see what circumstances helped forward this emancipation of the towns from the rights possessed by the nobles and the abbeys, or by the king. The chief cause of the readiness of the nobles and kings to grant charters during this period (from the Conquest to Henry III.) was their lack of ready money. Everyone knows how fiercely the nobles fought against each other in Stephen's reign, and how enthusiastically they rushed to the Crusades under Richard I. They could not indulge their love of fighting, which in their eyes was their main duty, without money to pay for their fatal extravagances in this direction, and to get money they frequently parted with their manorial rights over the towns that had grown up on their estates. Especially was this the case when a noble, or king, was taken prisoner, and wanted the means of his ransom. In this way Portsmouth and Norwich gained their charters by paying part of Richard I.'s ransom (1194). Again, Rye and Winchelsea gained theirs by supplying the same king (in 1191) with two ships for one of his Eastern crusades. Many other instances might be quoted from the cases of nobles who also gave charters when setting out upon these extraordinary religious and sentimental expeditions. Indeed, the Crusades had a very marked influence in this way upon the growth of English towns. Someone had to pay for the wars in which the aristocracy delighted, and it is well to remember the fact that the expenses of all our wars—and they have been both numerous and costly—have been defrayed by the industrial portion of the community. And the glories and cruelties of that savage age of so-called knightly chivalry, which has been idealized and gilded by romancers and history-mongers, with its tournaments and torture-chambers, were paid for by that despised industrial population of the towns and manors which contained the real life and wealth of mediæval England.

§ 6. **The gilds and the towns. Various kinds of gilds**—But besides the indirect effect of the Crusades, there was another powerful factor in the growth and emancipation of the towns after the Conquest. I refer to the *merchant* *gilds*, which were becoming more and more prominent all through this period, though the height of their power was reached in the fourteenth century. These merchant gilds were one out of four other kinds of gilds, all of which seem to have been similar in origin. The earliest gilds are found in Saxon times, and were very much what we understand by clubs. At first they were associations of men for more or less religious and charitable purposes, and formed a sort of artificial family, whose members were bound by the bond not of kinship, but of an oath ; while the gild-feast, held once a month in the common hall, replaced the family gatherings of kinsfolk. These gilds were found both in towns and manors, but chiefly in the former, where men were brought more closely together. Besides (1) the *religious* gilds, we find in Saxon times (2) the *frith* gilds, formed for mutual assistance in case of violence, wrong, or false accusation, or in any legal affairs. But this class of gilds died out after the Conquest. The most important were (3) the *merchant* gilds mentioned above, which existed certainly in Edward the Confessor's time, being called in Saxon *ceapemanne* gilds, and they were recognized at the time of the Conquest, for they are recorded in Domesday here and there as possessing lands. The merchant members of these gilds had various privileges, such as a monopoly of the local trade of a town, and freedom from certain imposts. They had a higher rank than the members of the (4) *craft* gilds. These last were associations of handicraftsmen, or artisans, and were separate from the merchant gilds, though also of great importance. If a town was large enough, each craft or manufacture had a gild of its own, though in smaller towns members of various crafts would form only one gild. Such gilds were found, too, not only in towns but in country villages, as is known, *e.g.*, in the case of some

Norfolk villages, and remains of their halls in villages have been found. Their gild feasts are probably represented to this day in the parish feasts, survivals of ancient custom.

§ 7. **How the Merchant Gilds helped the growth of towns**—Now it was only natural that the existence of these powerful associations in the growing boroughs should secure an increasing extent of cohesion and unity among the townsmen. Moreover, the craft and merchant gilds had a very important privilege, which could make many men anxious to join their ranks, namely, that membership in a gild for a year and a day made a tenant in villeinage a free man, as were all the members of a gild. Thus the gilds included all the free tenants in a town, and in becoming a merchant gild the body of free citizens, who formed the only influential portion of a town, began to enlarge their municipal powers. It became their special endeavour to obtain from the king or from their lord wider commercial privileges, grants of coinage, of holding fairs, and of exemption from tolls. Then they asked for freedom of justice and of self-government; and more especially did the gilds, as representing practically the town, buy up the *firma burgi*, or fixed tax, and thus became their own assessors, and finally bought a charter, as we have seen, from a king or noble in need of ready money. And so gradually, and by other steps which are not always clear, the emancipation of the towns was won by the gilds; the boroughs became free from their lords' restrictions and dues; till by the end of the twelfth century chartered towns, which were very few at the time of the Conquest, became the general rule.

§ 8. **How the Craft Gilds helped industry**—So far we have specially noted the work of the merchant gilds, which, as it were, built up the constitution and freedom of the towns.

We must now look for a moment at the work of the artisans' gilds, or craft gilds, which afterwards became very important. These gilds are found not only in London, but in provincial towns. The London weavers are mentioned as a craft gild in the time of Henry I. (A.D. 1100), and most of these gilds seemed to have existed already for a long period. The Goldsmiths' Gild claimed to have possessed land before the Norman Conquest, and it was fairly powerful in the days of Henry II. (A.D. 1154), for he found it convenient to try and suppress it. But it did not receive the public recognition of a charter till the fourteenth century. They arose, of course, first in the towns, and originally seem to have consisted of a small body of the leading men of a particular craft, to whom was confided the regulation of a particular industry, probably as soon as that industry was thought of sufficient importance to be regulated. The gild tried to secure good work on the part of its members, and attempted to suppress the production of wares by irresponsible persons who were not members of the craft. Their fundamental principle was, that a member should work not only for his own private advantage, but for the reputation and good of his trade; hence bad work was punished, and it is curious to note that night-work is prohibited as leading to poor work. The gild took care to secure a supply of competent workmen for the future by training young people in its particular industry, and hence arose the *apprentice system*, which at first, at any rate, had considerable advantages.

The gild, moreover, exercised a moral control over its members, and secured their good behaviour, thus forming an effective branch of the social police. On the other hand, it had many of the characteristics of a benefit society, providing against sickness and death among those belonging to it, as indeed all gilds did.

These institutions, however, did not only belong to the towns, but were found in country districts also; thus we hear of the carpenters' and masons' rural gilds in the reign of Edward III. Even the peasant labourers, according to Professor Thorold Rogers, possessed these associations, which in all cases served many of the functions of the modern trade unions. Later on (1381) we shall come to a very remarkable instance of the power of these peasants' unions in the matter of Tyler's rebellion.

§ 9. **Life in the towns of this time**—The inhabitants of the towns were of all classes of society. There was the noble who held the castle, or the abbot and monks in the monastery, with their retainers and personal dependants; there were the busy merchants, active both in the management of their trade and of civic affairs; and there were artisans and master workmen in different crafts. There were free tenants, or *tenants in socage*, including all the burgesses, or burgage-tenants, as they were called; and there was the lower class of villeins, which, however, always tended to rise into free men as they were admitted into the gilds. "To and fro went our forefathers in the quiet, quaint, narrow streets, or worked at some handicraft in their houses, or exposed their goods round the market-cross. And in those old streets and houses, in the town-mead and market-place, amid the murmur of the mill beside the stream, and the notes of the bell that sounded its summons to the crowded assembly of the town-mote, in merchant gild and craft gild, was growing up that sturdy, industrial life, unheeded and unnoticed by knight or baron, that silently and surely was building up the slow structure of England's wealth and freedom."[1]

[1] V. *Industry in England*, p. 96; and Green, *History*, i. 212.

CHAPTER III

MANUFACTURES AND TRADE: ELEVENTH TO THIRTEENTH CENTURIES

§ 1. **Economic effects of the Feudal System**—We shall find that for some time after the Norman Conquest English industry does not develop very rapidly, and that for obvious reasons. The feud that existed between Norman and Saxon—although perhaps partially allayed by Henry I.'s marriage to an English wife—and the social disorder that accompanied this feeling, hardly tended to that quiet and security that are necessary for a healthy industrial life. The frightful disorders that occurred during the fierce struggle for the kingdom between Stephen of Blois and the Empress Maud, and the equally frightful ravages and extortions of their contending barons, must have been serious drawbacks to any progress. As the old annalist remarks—"They fought among themselves with deadly hatred; they spoiled the fairest lands with fire and rapine; in what had been the most fertile of counties they destroyed almost all the provision of bread."[1] But this mighty struggle fortunately ended in ruining many of the barons who took part in it, and in the desirable destruction of most of their abodes of plunder. And the accession of Henry II. (1154) marks a period of amalgamation between Englishmen and Normans, not only in social life, but in commercial traffic and intercourse.

But even when we come to look at the feudal system in a time of peace, we see that it did not tend to any great growth of industry. For it encouraged rather than diminished that spirit of isolation and self-sufficiency

[1] Quoted by Green, *History*, i. 155.

which was so marked a feature of the earlier manors and townships, where, again, little scope was afforded to individual enterprise, from the fact that the consent of the lord of a manor or town was often necessary for the most ordinary purposes of industrial life. It is true, as we have seen, that when the noble owner was in pecuniary difficulties the towns profited thereby to obtain their charters; and perhaps we may not find it altogether a matter for regret that the barons, through their internecine struggles, thus unwittingly helped on the industry of the land. It may be admitted also, that though the isolation of communities consequent upon the prevalent manorial system did not encourage trade and traffic between separate communities, it yet tended to diffuse a knowledge of domestic manufactures throughout the land generally, because each place had largely to provide for itself.

The constant taxation, however, entailed by the feudal system in the shape of tallages, aids, and fines, both to king and nobles, made it difficult for the lower classes to accumulate capital, more especially as in the civil wars they were constantly plundered of it openly. The upper classes merely squandered it in fighting. Agriculture suffered similarly; for the villeins, however well off, were bound to the land, especially in the earlier period soon after the Conquest, and before commutation of services for money rents became so common as it did subsequently; nor could they leave their manor without incurring a distinct loss, both of social status and—what is more important—of the means of livelihood. The systems of constant services to the lord of the manor, and of the collective methods of cultivation, were also drawbacks to good agriculture. Again, in trade, prices were settled by authority, competition was unduly checked, and merchants had to pay heavy fines for royal "protection."

§ 2. **Foreign Trade. The Crusades**—But, on the other hand, the Norman Conquest, which combined the Kingdom of England with the Duchy of Normandy in close political relations, gave abundant opportunities for commerce, both with France and the Continent, and foreign trade certainly received a stimulus from this fact. It was further developed by the Crusades. The most obvious effect of these remarkable expeditions for a visionary success was the opening up of Trade Routes throughout Europe to the shores of the Mediterranean Sea, and to the East in general. They produced also a considerable redistribution of wealth in England itself, for the knights and nobles that set out for the Holy Land often mortgaged their lands and never redeemed them, or they perished and their lands lapsed to the crown, or to some monastery that took the place of a trustee for the absent owner. The growth of towns also, as we saw, is directly attributable to the privileges and freedom secured at this time by supplying money to a crusading lord. As to foreign trade, our chief authority at this time is the old chronicler, Henry of Huntingdon, whose history was published about A.D. 1155. Like most historians, even of the present day, he says very little about so insignificant a matter as trade; but the single sentence which he devotes to it is probably of as great value as any other part of his book. From it we gather that our trade with Germany was extensive, and that we exported lead and tin among the metals; fish and meat and fat cattle (which seems to point to some improvement in our pastoral economy); and, most important of all, fine wool, though at that time the English could not weave it properly for themselves. Our imports, however, are very limited, comprising none of the necessities of life, and few of its luxuries beyond silver and foreign furs. Other imports were fine woven cloths, used for the dresses of the nobility; and, after the Crusades began, of rich Eastern stuffs and spices, which were in great demand, and commanded a high price. So too did iron, which was necessary for agricultural purposes, as Englishmen had not yet discovered their rich stores of this metal, but had to get it from the lands on the Baltic shore. Generally speaking, we may say that our imports consisted of articles of greater intrinsic value and scarcity than our exports, and thus were fewer in number, though of course balancing in total value, as imports and exports always must.

§ 3. **The trading clauses in the Great Charter**—One great proof of the existence of a fair amount of foreign trade is seen in the clauses which were inserted in the Great Charter (1215), by the influence of the trading class. One enactment secures to foreign merchants freedom of journeying and of trade throughout the realm, and another orders a uniformity of weights and measures to be enforced throughout the whole kingdom. The growth of home industry in the towns is seen in the enactment which secures to the towns the enjoyment of their municipal privileges, their freedom from arbitrary taxation, and the regulation of their own trade. The forfeiture of a freeman, even upon conviction of felony, was never to include his wares, if he were a merchant. The exactions of forced labour by the royal officers was also forbidden, and this must have been a great boon to the agricultural population. There is also a clause which endeavours to restrict usury exacted by the Jews, a clause which points to the usual characteristics of the Hebrew race, and which shows their growing importance in economic England. We will therefore briefly mention the facts concerning them at this period.

§ 4. **The Jews in England: their economic position**—The first appearance of the Jews in England may practically be reckoned as occurring at the time of the Norman Conquest, for immediately after 1066 they came in large numbers from Rouen, Caen, and other Norman towns. They stood in the peculiar position of being the personal property, or "chattels," of the king, and a special officer governed their settlements in various towns. These settlements were called Jewries, of which those at London, Lincoln, Bury St Edmund's, and Oxford were at one time fairly considerable. They were protected by the king, and of course paid him for their protection. Their general financial skill was acknowledged by all, and William II. employed them to farm the revenues of vacant sees, while barons often employed them as stewards of their estates. They were also the leading if not the only capitalists of that time, and must have assisted merchants considerably in their enterprises, of course upon the usual commission. After the death of Henry I. the security which they had enjoyed was much weakened, in proportion as the royal power declined in the civil wars, and in the twelfth and thirteenth centuries they were in a precarious position. Stephen and Matilda openly robbed them; Henry II. (in 1187) demanded one-fourth of their chattels, and Richard I. obtained large sums from them for his crusading extravagances. From 1144 to 1189, riots directed against them became common, and the Jewries of many towns were pillaged. In 1194 Richard I. placed their commercial transactions more thoroughly under local officers of the crown. John exploited them to great advantage, and levied heavy tallages upon them, and Henry III. did very much the same. They were expelled from the kingdom in 1290, and before this had greatly sunk from their previous position as the financiers of the crown, to that of petty money-lenders to the poor at gross usury. What concerns us more immediately to notice in this early period of English history, is their temporary usefulness as capitalists in trading transactions, at a time when capital was not easily accumulated or kept in safety.[1]

§ 5. **Manufactures in this period: Flemish weavers**—We now turn from the subject of trade and finance to that of manufacturing industry. On doing so, we find that the chief industry is that of weaving coarse woollen cloth. An industry so necessary as this, and one too that can be carried on in a simple state of society with such ease, as a domestic manufacture, would naturally always exist, even from the most uncivilized times. This had been the case in England. But it is noticeable that although Henry of Huntingdon mentions the export of "fine wool" as one of the chief English exports, and although England had always been in a specially favourable position for growing wool, her manufacture of it had not developed to any great extent. Nevertheless it was practised as a domestic industry in every rural and urban community, and at this period already had its gilds—a sure sign of growth. Indeed one of the oldest *craft* gilds was that of the London weavers, of which we find mention in the time of Henry I. (A.D. 1100). And in this reign, too, we first hear of the arrival of Flemish immigrants in this country, who helped largely both then and subsequently in the development of the woollen manufacture. Some Flemings had come over indeed in the days of William the Norman, having been driven from Flanders by an incursion of the sea, and had settled at Carlisle. But Henry I., as we read in

[1] See note 6, p. 244, on their return.

Higden's Chronicle, transferred them to Pembrokeshire in A.D. 1111: "Flandrenses, tempore regis Henrici primi, ad occidentalem Walliæ partem, apud Haverford, sunt translati." Traces of them remained till a comparatively recent period, and the names of the village of *Flemingston*, and of the road called the *Via Flandrica*, running over the crest of the Precelly mountains, afford striking evidence of their settlement there, as also does the name *Tucking Mill* (*i.e.* Cloth-making mill, from German and Flemish *tuch*, "a cloth"). Norfolk also had from early times been the seat of the woollen industry, and had had similar influxes of Flemish weavers. They do not, however, become important till the reign of Edward III., when we shall find that English cloth manufacture begins to develop considerably. In this period, all we can say is that England was more famed for the wool that it grew than for the cloth which it manufactured therefrom, and it had yet to learn most of its improvements from lessons taught by foreigners.

§ 6. **Economic appearance of England in this Period. Population**—The England of the Domesday Book was very different from anything which we can now conceive, nor did its industrial condition change much during the next century or two. The population was probably under 2,000,000 in all; for in Domesday Book only 283,342 able-bodied men are enumerated. These multiplied by five, to include women and children, give 1,400,000 of general population, and allowing for omissions we shall find two millions rather over than under the mark. Nor indeed could the agricultural and industrial state of the country have supported more. This population was chiefly located in the Southern and Eastern counties, for the North of England, and especially Yorkshire, had been laid waste by the Conqueror, in consequence of its revolt in 1068. The whole country between York and the Tees was ravaged, and the famine which ensued is said to have carried off 100,000 victims. Indeed, for half-a-century the land "lay bare of cultivation and of men" for sixty miles northward of York, and for centuries more never fully recovered from this terrible visitation. The Domesday Book records district after district, and manor after manor, in Yorkshire as "waste." In the East and North-west of England, now the most densely populated parts of the country, all was fen, moorland, and forest, peopled only by wild animals and lawless men. Till the seventeenth century, in fact, Lancashire and the West Riding of Yorkshire were the poorest counties in England. The fens of East Anglia were reclaimed only in 1634. The main ports were London for general trade; Southampton, for the French trade in wines; Norwich for the export wool trade with Flanders, and for imports from the Baltic; and on the west coast Bristol, which had always been the centre for the western trade in Severn salmon and hides. At one time, too, it was the great port for the trade of English slaves who were taken to Ireland, but William the Norman checked that traffic, though it lingered till Henry II. conquered Ireland. For internal trade *market towns*, or villages as we should call them, were gradually springing up. They were nearly always held in demesne by the lord of the manor, who claimed the tolls, though in after years the town bought them of him. Some of these markets had existed from Saxon times, as is seen by the prefix "Chipping" (=*chepinge*, A.S. a market), as in Chipping Norton, Chippingham, and Chepstowe; others date from a later period, and are known by the prefix "Market," as *e.g.* Market Bosworth. But these market towns were very small, and indeed only some

To face p 38

DARK GREEN: Density of population greater.
RED BROWN: Forest. YELLOW: Marsh.

The chief colour is *Green* to show that whole country was chiefly agricultural. Part of Yorks *Pale* to show it was waste.

The ten chief towns: 1—York.* 4—Norwich.* 2—Bristol.* 5—Coventry.* 3—Lincoln.*

6—Oxford. 8—Nottingham. 7—Colchester. 9—Winchester.

And 10—London.

* Population over 5000.

half-dozen towns in the kingdom had a population above 5000 inhabitants. These were London, York, Bristol, Coventry, Norwich, and Lincoln.

§ 7. **General condition of the Period**—Speaking generally for the whole period after the Conquest, we may say that, though the economic condition of England was by no means unprosperous, industrial development was necessarily slow. The disputes between Stephen and Maud, and the civil wars of their partisans, the enormous drain upon the resources of the country caused by Richard I.'s expenses in carrying on Crusades when he should have been ruling his kingdom, and the equally enormous taxes and bribes paid by the worthless John to the Papal See, could not fail seriously to check national industry. It is no wonder that in John's reign, at the beginning of the thirteenth century, we hear of great discontent throughout all the land, of much misery and poverty, especially in the towns, and of a general feeling of revolt. That miserable monarch was only saved from deposition by his opportune death.

Yet with all these evils the economic condition of England, although depressed, was by no means absolutely unhealthy ; and the following reign (Henry III., 1216–1272), with its comparative peace and leisure, afforded, as we shall see, sufficient opportunity to enable the people to regain a position of general opulence and prosperity. This time of quiet progress and industrial growth forms a fitting occasion for the marking out of a new epoch.

PERIOD III

FROM THE THIRTEENTH TO THE END OF THE FIFTEENTH CENTURY, INCLUDING THE GREAT PLAGUE (1216-1500)

CHAPTER I

AGRICULTURE IN MEDIÆVAL ENGLAND

§ 1. Introductory. Rise of a wage-earning class—The long reign of Henry III., although occasionally troubled by internal dissensions among the barons, was upon the whole a prosperous and peaceful time for the people in general, and more especially for those whom historians are pleased to call the lower classes. For by this time a remarkable change had begun to affect the condition of the serfs or villeins, a change already alluded to before, by which the villeins became free tenants, subject to a fixed rent for their holdings. This rent was rapidly becoming a payment in money and not in labour, for, as we saw, the lords of the manors were frequently in want of cash, and were ready to sell many of their privileges. The change was at first gradual, but by the time of the Great Plague (1348), money rents were becoming the rule rather than the exception; and though labour rents were not quite obsolete, it was an ill-advised attempt to extort them again that was the prime cause of Wat Tyler's insurrection (1381). Before the Plague, in fact, villeinage in the old sense had become almost extinct, and the peasants, both great and small, had achieved practical freedom. The richer villeins had developed into small farmers; while the poorer villeins, and especially the cottars, had formed a separate class of agricultural labourers, not indeed entirely without land, but depending for their livelihood upon wages paid for helping to cultivate the land of others. The rise of this class, that lived by wages and not by tilling their own land, was due to the fact that cottars and others, not having enough land of their own to occupy their whole time, were free to hire themselves to those who had a larger quantity of land. Especially would they become labourers at a fixed wage for the lord of a manor when he had commuted his rights to the unpaid services of all his tenants for a fixed money rent. Of course this change came gradually, but its effect is seen subsequently in the difficulties as to wages expressed in the Statute of Labourers, difficulties which first became serious after the Great Plague.

§ 2. **Agriculture the chief occupation of the people**—Throughout the whole of this period the vast majority of the population were continuously engaged in agricultural pursuits, and this was rendered necessary owing to the very low rate of production consequent upon the primitive methods of agriculture. The production of corn was only about four, or sometimes eight, bushels per acre, and this naturally had the effect of keeping down the population, at this time still only between 1,500,000 and 2,000,000. It is a remarkable fact that even the inhabitants of the towns used at harvest-time to go out into the country to get agricultural work, and people often migrated from one district to another for the same purpose, just as Irish agricultural labourers of to-day are accustomed to cross over to England for the harvesting.

Some attention was being paid to sheep farming, and a noticeable increase in this branch of industry took place in the beginning of the fourteenth century. One order of monks in particular, the Cistercians, used to grow large quantities of wool; and indeed England had almost a monopoly in the wool trade with Flanders, for even Spanish wool could not be utilized without an admixture of English. But the great increase of sheep farming occurs rather later, at the beginning of the sixteenth century.

§ 3. **Methods of cultivation. The capitalist landlord and his bailiff. The "stock and land" lease**—The agriculture of the early part of this period is described to us by Walter de Henley, who wrote a book on husbandry some time before 1250. It cannot be said that our agriculture was at this time at a high level, for, as we have seen, the production of wheat (*e.g.*) was exceedingly low, not being more than four to eight bushels per acre. If we look at a typical manor, we shall find that the arable lands in it were divided pretty equally between the landlord and the tenants of the manor; and before the Great Plague the landlord was not merely a rent-receiving master, but a capitalist land-owner, who cultivated his land by means of his bailiff, subject to his personal supervision. These bailiffs kept very accurate accounts, and we are thereby greatly helped in our investigations in this period. The average rent paid by tenants from the thirteenth to the sixteenth century was sixpence per acre. In many cases, especially on lands owned by monasteries, the land was held on the "stock and land" lease system, by which the landlord let a certain quantity of stock with the land, for which the tenant, at the expiration of his lease, had to account either in money or kind. A relic of this kind of lease existed even in the eighteenth century, for Arthur Young occasionally mentions the practice of the landlord letting cows to dairy farmers. In mediæval times the person to whom cows were leased for dairy purposes was the *deye*—*i.e.* dairyman or dairymaid. The stock and land lease plan was favourable to the tenant, for it supplied his preliminary want of capital, and if he was fortunate allowed him often to make considerable profits, and even eventually purchase an estate for himself.

§ 4. **The tenant's communal land and closes**—It must always be remembered, however, that the arable land in a manor was "communal"—*i.e.* each tenant held a certain number of furrows or strips in a common field, the separate divisions being merely marked by a piece of unploughed land, where the grass was allowed to grow. The ownership of these several strips was limited to certain months of the year, generally from Lady Day to Michaelmas, and for the remainder of the year the land was common pasture. This simple and rudimentary system was utterly unsuited to any advanced agriculture. The tenants, however, also possessed "closes," some for corn, others for pasture and hay. The rent of a close was always higher than that of communal land, being eightpence instead of sixpence per acre. Besides the communal arable land, and his close, the husbandman also had access to two or three kinds of common or pasture—(1) a common close for oxen, kine, or other stock, pasture in which is stinted both for landlord and tenant; (2) the open ("champaign" or "champion") country, where the cattle go daily before the herdsmen; (3) the lord's out-woods, moors, and heaths, where the tenants are stinted but the lord is not. Thus the tenant had valuable pasture rights, besides the land he actually rented. But the system of holding arable land in strips was very cumbrous and caused many disputes, since often a tenant would hold a short lease on one strip and a longer lease on another; or confusion of ownership would arise; while in many ways tenure was made insecure, and no encouragement was given to advanced agriculture.

§ 5. **Ploughing**—As regards the cultivation of the land, it was generally ploughed three times a year. Ordinary ploughing took place in the autumn, the second ploughing in April, the third at midsummer. The furrows were, according to Walter de Henley, a foot apart, and the plough was not to go more than two fingers deep. The ploughing and much other work was done by oxen, as being cheaper than horses. The hoeing was undertaken by women, who also worked at harvest-time in the fields. In *Peres the Plowman's Crede* (about A.D. 1394) we have a description of a small farmer ploughing while his wife leads the oxen. "His wife walked by him with a long goad, in a cutted cote cutted full high" (l. 433).

An average yield of six bushels per acre is what Walter de Henley thinks necessary to secure profitable farming.

§ 6. **Stock, Pigs and Poultry**—As to stock, the amount kept was generally rather large, and the agriculturist of the thirteenth century was fully alive to the importance of keeping it; for Walter de Henley advised stocking land to the full extent it would bear. Oxen, as we saw, were kept for the plough and draft; but not much stock was fatted for the table, especially as it could not be kept in the winter. There was no attempt to improve breeds of cattle, for the scarcity of winter food (winter roots being unknown till much later), and the general want of means for resisting the severities of the winter helped to keep all breeds much upon the same level. On the other hand, swine were kept in large numbers, and every peasant had his pig in his sty, and, indeed, probably lived on salt pork most of the winter. Care was taken with the different breeds. The whole of the parish swine were generally put in summer under the charge of one swine-herd, who was paid both by tenants and the lord of the manor. The keeping of poultry, too, was at that time universal, so much so that they were very rarely bought by anyone, and when sold were almost absurdly cheap. This habit of keeping fowls, ducks, and geese must have materially helped the peasant in ekeing out his wages, or in paying that portion of his rent which was paid in kind ; as *e.g.* in the case of the Cuxham tenant (p. 15) who had to pay his lord six fowls in all during the year.

§ 7. **Sheep**—This animal is so important in English agriculture that we must devote a special paragraph to it alone. For the sheep was, in the earlier periods of English industrial history, the mainstay of the British farmer, chiefly, of course, owing to the quantity of wool required for export. England had, up to a comparatively recent period, almost a monopoly of the raw wool trade, her only rival being Spain. There were, as mentioned before, a great number of breeds of sheep, and much care was taken to improve them. The fleece however was light, being only as an average 1 lb. 7¾ oz., according to Professor Rogers, and the animal was small. The reason of this was that the attempts of the husbandman to improve his breeds were baffled by the hardships of the mediæval winter, and by the prevalence of disease, especially the rot and scab. It is probable that the average loss on the flocks was 20 per cent. a year. They were generally kept under cover from November to April, and fed on coarse hay, wheat, and oat straw, or pea and vetch haulm; but no winter roots were available.

§ 8. **Increase of sheep farming**—A great increase of sheep farming took place after the Great Plague (1348), and this from two causes. The rapid increase of woollen manufactures promoted by Edward III. rendered wool growing more profitable, while at the same time the scarcity of labour, occasioned by the ravages of the Black Death, and the consequently higher wages demanded, naturally attracted the farmer to an industry which was at once very profitable, and required but little paid labour. So, after the Plague, we find a tendency among large agriculturists to turn ploughed fields into permanent pasture, or, at any rate, to use the same land for pasture and for crops, instead of turning portions of the "waste" into arable land. Consequently from the beginning of the fifteenth century we notice that the agricultural population decreases in proportion as sheep farming increases; and the steady change may be traced in numerous preventive statutes till we come (in 1536) to those of Henry VIII. about decayed towns, especially in the Midlands and the Isle of Wight, culminating in the excitements of 1549. Another cause that, in Henry VIII.'s time, had a distinct influence in promoting sheep farming, was the lack of capital that made itself felt, owing to the general impoverishment of England in his wasteful reign, and which naturally turned farmers to an industry that required little capital, but gave quick returns.

§ 9. **Consequent increase of enclosures**—One consequence of this more extensive sheep farming was the great increase in enclosures made by the landlords in the sixteenth century. So great were these encroachments and enclosures in north-east Norfolk, that they led, in 1549, to a rebellion against the enclosing system, headed by Ket; but, though more marked, perhaps, in Henry VIII.'s reign, the practice of sheep farming had been growing steadily in the previous century. Fortescue, the Lord Chancellor of Henry VI. (in the middle of the fifteenth century), refers to its growth and the prosperity it caused in rural districts—a prosperity, however, that must have been confined only to the great land-owners. We receive other confirmation of this from various statutes designed to prevent the rural population from flowing into the towns, as, for example, the Acts of 1 and 9 Richard II. (1377 and 1385), of 17 Richard II. (1394), promoting the export of corn in hopes of making arable land more valuable. Another Act was passed in 1489 (4 Henry VII.) to keep the rural population from the towns. But the growth of sheep farming is also connected with a great economic and industrial development in England, the rise and progress of cloth manufactures and of the weaving industry generally, and to this we must now devote our next chapter.

CHAPTER II

THE WOOLLEN TRADE AND MANUFACTURES

§ 1. **England's monopoly of wool**—In the Middle Ages England was the only wool-producing country in the North of Europe. Spain grew wool also, but it could not be used alone for every kind of fabric, and besides it was more difficult to transport wool from Spain to Flanders, the seat of the manufacture of that article, than it was to send it across the narrow German Ocean, where swarms of light craft plied constantly between Flanders and the eastern ports of England. Hence England had a practical monopoly of the wool trade, which was due not only to its favourable climate and soil, but also to the fact that even at the worst periods of civil war—and they did not last for long—our island was incomparably more peaceful than the countries of Western Europe. From the thirteenth to the seventeenth century, the farmers of Western Europe could not possibly have kept sheep, the most defenceless and tender of domestic animals, amid the wars that were continually devastating their homesteads; nor, as a matter of fact, did they do so. But in England, especially after the twelfth century, nearly everybody in the realm, from the king to the villein, was concerned in agriculture, and was interested therefore in maintaining peace. Even when the great landlords, after the Plague of 1348, gave up the cultivation of their arable land, they went in, as we saw, for sheep farming, and enclosed large tracts of land for that purpose. Hence the export trade in wool became more and more important, and there was always a continual demand for English wool to supply the busy looms of the great manufacturing towns in Flanders.

§ 2. **Wool and Politics**—The most convincing proof of the importance of the wool trade is seen in England's diplomatic relations with Flanders, which, by the way, afford an interesting example of the necessity of taking economic factors into account in dealing with national history. Flanders was the great manufacturing country of Europe at that time. England supplied its raw material in vast quantities, and nine-tenths of English wool went to the looms of Bruges and Ghent. A stoppage of this export from England used to throw half the population of the Flemish towns out of work. The immense transactions that even then took place, are seen from the fact that a single company of Florentine merchants would contract with the Cistercian monks of England for the whole year's supply of the wool produced on their vast sheep-ranges on the Yorkshire moorlands; for the Cistercian order were among the foremost wool-growers in the country. Now, it is a curious and significant fact that when Edward I., Edward III., and Henry V. premeditated an attack on France, they generally took care to gain the friendship of Flanders first,[1] so as to use that country as a base from which to enter France, or at least as a useful ally; and secondly, they paid a large proportion of the expenses of their French expeditions by means of a wool-tax in England. Thus, when Edward III. opened his campaign against France in 1340, he did so from Flanders, with special help afforded by a Flemish alliance. This king also received annually £60,000 from the wool-tax alone, and on special occasions even more. Again, it was a grant of 6*s.* 8*d.* on each sack of wool exported that enabled Edward I. in 1275 to fill his treasury for his subsequent invasion of Wales. The same king in 1297 got the means for equipping an expedition against France, *via* Flanders, in the same way. Similarly Henry V. took care to cultivate the friendship of the Flemish and their rulers before setting out to gain the French crown, and paid for his expedition by raising taxes on wool and hides. The enormous revenues also which from the thirteenth to the fifteenth century were exacted from England by the Papal Court, and by the Italian ecclesiastics quartered on English benefices, were transmitted in the shape of wool to Flanders, and sold by the Lombard exchangers, who transmitted the money thus realized to Italy. The extent of these revenues may be gathered from the fact that the Parlia-

[1] See note 7, p. 244, on Flanders and England.

ment of 1343, in a petition against Papal appointments to English ecclesiastical vacancies, asserted that—"The Pope's revenue from England alone is larger than that of any Prince in Christendom." And at this very time the deaneries of Lichfield, Salisbury, and York, and the archdeaconry of Canterbury, were all held by Italian dignitaries, while the Pope's collector sent from London 20,000 marks a year to his master at Rome. Now, these impositions were paid out of the proceeds of English wool. It is interesting, too, to find that taxes for King Edward III. were calculated, not in money, but in sacks of wool. In one year the Parliament granted him 20,000 sacks ; in another year 30,000 sacks. In 1339 the barons granted him "the tenth sheep, fleece, and lamb." Early in the fifteenth century £30,000 out of the £40,000 revenue from customs and taxes came from wool alone. Once more, as in the days of the Crusades, we are able to see how the Hundred Years' War with France, and the exactions of Rome, were paid for by the industrial portion of the community, while underneath the glamour of the victories of Edward III. and Henry V. lies the prosaic but powerful wool-sack.[1]

§ 3. **Prices and brands of English wool**—Having now seen the importance of wool as a factor in English industry and political history, we must proceed to study more closely the facts of the woollen trade, and the manufacture of woollen cloth. The chief growers of wool were the Cistercian monks, who owned huge flocks of sheep. The wool grown near Leominster, in Herefordshire, was the finest of all, and, generally speaking, that grown in Wiltshire, Essex, Sussex, Hampshire, Oxfordshire, Cambridge and Warwickshire, was the best. The poorest came from the North of England, and from

[1] See note 8, p. 245, on Other Sources of Income.

the Southern downs. There were a number of different breeds of sheep, for care was taken to improve the breed, and it would seem that forty-four different brands of English wool, ranging in value from £13 to £2, 10*s.* the sack (of 364 lbs.), were recognized both in the home and foreign markets, as mentioned in a Parliamentary petition of 1454. The average price of wool from 1260–1400 was 2*s.* 1¾*d.* per clove of 7 lbs.—*i.e.* a little over threepence a pound, sometimes fourpence. In the middle of this period (1350) the average annual export, according to Misselden, in the *Circle of Commerce*, was about 11,648,000 lbs., representing a value of some £180,683 yearly.

§ 4. **English manufactures**—Now, although I have spoken of Flanders as the manufacturing centre for Europe, it must not be supposed that England could not manufacture any of the large quantity of wool which it grew. Undoubtedly the people of the Netherlands were at that time the great manufacturers of the world, and were acquainted with arts and processes to which the English were strangers, while for a long time the English could not weave fine cloths ; but, nevertheless, there was a considerable manufacturing industry, chiefly of coarse cloths, an industry very widely spread, and carried on in people's own cottages under the domestic system. The chief kinds of cloth made were hempen, linen, and woollen coverings, such as would be used for sacks, dairy-cloths, woolpacks, sails of windmills, and similar purposes. The great textile centres were Norfolk and Suffolk, where, indeed, manufacturing industries had existed long before the earliest records. An idea of their importance may be given from the fact that, in the assessment for the wool-tax of 1341, Norfolk was counted by far the wealthiest countyin England after Middlesex (including London).

There was also a cloth industry of importance in the West of England, the chief centres being Westbury, Sherborne, and Salisbury. The linen of Aylsham was also celebrated.

§ 5. **Foreign manufacture of fine goods**—But we find rich people used to purchase fine cloths from abroad—*e.g.* linen from Liège and Flanders generally, and velvet and silk goods from Genoa and Venice—although there was certainly a silk industry in London, carried on chiefly by women, and protected by an Act of 1454. In the England of which we are now speaking, the textile industries were prevented from attaining a full development from the fact that, though general, they were strictly local; and, moreover, those who practised them did not look upon their handicraft as their sole means of livelihood, but even till the eighteenth century were generally engaged in agriculture as well. The cause of this is connected with the isolation and self-sufficiency of separate communities, previously noted. An evidence of the consequent inferiority of English to Flemish cloth is given by the fact that an Act of 1261 attempts to prohibit the import of spun stuff and the export of wool. Needless to say it was useless. The prices of cloth at this period are interesting, as showing the great difference between the fine (*i.e.* foreign) and coarse (home) cloths. The average price of linen is 4*d.* an ell, being as low as 2*d.* and as high as 8½*d.* Inferior woollens sold at 1*s.* 7½*d.* a yard, "russet" at 1*s.* 4*d.*, blanketing at 1*s.* On the other hand, scarlet cloth (foreign) rises to the enormous price of 15*s.* a yard. Cloth for liveries varied from 2*s.* 1*d.* to 1*s.* per yard. Speaking generally for the period 1260–1400, we may give the average price of the best quality at 3*s.* 3½*d.* a yard from 1260–1350, and 3*s.* 5½*d.* from 1350–1400; while cloth of the second quality fetched 1*s.* 4½*d.* in the first period, and 1*s.* 11¼*d.* in the second.

§ 6. **Flemish settlers teach the English weavers. Norwich**—It is to Edward III., very largely, that the development of English textile industry is due. It is true that, long before, Henry II. had endeavoured to stimulate English manufacture by establishing a "cloth fair" in the churchyard of St Bartholomew. But English industry had developed slowly till the days of Edward, partly, no doubt, owing to the continual disorder of the preceding reigns. Stimulated, probably, by his wife Philippa's connexion with Flanders, he encouraged Flemish weavers to settle in England, chiefly in the Eastern counties, though we hear of two Flemings from Brabant settling in York in 1331; and about this time one John Kemp, also a Fleming, removed from Norwich, and founded in Westmoreland the manufacture of the famous "Kendal green." The chief centre, however, of the foreign weavers was naturally Norwich, the Manchester of those days, with a population of some 6000, and the chief industry was that of worsted cloths, so named from the place of manufacture, Worstead. When we speak of worsted cloths, we mean those plain, unpretending fabrics that probably never went beyond a plain weave or a four-shaft twill. The yarn was very largely spun on the rock or distaff, by means of a primitive whorl or spindle, while the loom was but a small improvement on that in which Penelope wove her famous web. There was a great demand among religious orders for sayes and the like, of good quality; plain worsteds were generally worn by the public.

§ 7. **The worsted industry**—Whether the growth of the worsted cloth industry was connected or not with this particular Flemish immigration we cannot determine.

The manufacture was confirmed to the town of Worstead by a patent of 1313, and in 1328, also, Edward III. issued a letter patent on behalf of the cloth workers in worsted in the county of Norfolk. The manufacture was already so extensive and important that the next year a special "aulnager" (or cloth searcher) was appointed to inspect the worsted stuffs of Norwich and district, and held his office for twenty years. In 1348, however, on the petition of the worsted weavers and merchants themselves, the patent was revoked, and the aulnager removed. But in 1410, when Norwich gained a new charter, the power of "aulnage" was once more given, at its own request, to its mayor and sheriffs, or their deputies.

§ 8. **Gilds in the cloth trade**—In the previous period we referred to the origin and growth of the craft gilds, and it is interesting to note their importance in connexion with the woollen industry at this time. As a separate craft, that of the weaver cannot be traced back beyond the early part of the twelfth century; in the middle of the twelfth century, however, gilds of weavers are found established in several of the larger English towns. At first they were in voluntary association, though acting independently of each other, but it became the policy of the government in the fourteenth century to extend the gild organization over the whole country, and thus to bring craftsmen together in organized bodies. Elaborate regulations were drawn up for their governance by Parliament, or by municipalities. Now, in London at this date (1300), and probably at Norwich and other large towns, the woollen industry was divided into four or five branches, the weavers and burellers, the dyers and fullers, and the tailors (*cissores*). The weavers and burellers were united in the same gild, the dyers and fullers in another, while the tailors formed a third gild of their own. But they were all very conscious that they had interests in common, and they were accustomed to act together in matters affecting the industry as a whole, such as, *e.g.*, ordering cloth made in the city to be dyed and fulled in that city, and not sent out to some other town.

§ 9. **The dyeing of cloth**—The dyeing and fulling industry, however, could not have flourished much in England at this time, for English cloths were mostly sent to be fulled and dyed in the Netherlands; and indeed we cannot consider dyeing as a really English industry till the days of James I., where it will be duly mentioned. At the same time it was not unknown, for we have scarlet, russet, and black cloths of English make in the fourteenth century. But the industry was chiefly carried on in the Netherlands, owing to the progress there made in the cultivation of madder, which forms the basis of so many different dyes. This plant has never been at any time largely cultivated in England, and, moreover, the Dutch for several centuries possessed the sole secret of a process of pulverizing the root in order to prepare it for use. Such being the case, there is no wonder that they far excelled the English in the art of dyeing.

§ 10. **The great transition in English industry**—From the time of this first Flemish immigration in the fourteenth century, we perceive the beginning of an important modification in our home industries. Hitherto England had been almost exclusively a purely agricultural country, growing large quantities of wool, exporting it as raw material, and importing manufactured goods in exchange. But from this period the export of wool gradually declines, while on the other hand our home manufactures increase, until at length they in turn are exported. In fact, manufactured cloth, and not raw wool, becomes the basis of our national wealth, and finally the export is forbidden altogether, so that we may have the more for the looms at home.

A proof of the growing importance of manufacture in this period is the noticeable lack of labourers and the high wages they get, as set forth in the Act 7 Henry IV. (*i.e.* 1406), which points to an increase of weavers in all parts of the kingdom, that takes labourers from other employments.

§ 11. **The manufacturing class and politics**—The growing importance of the manufacturing class which was now rapidly springing up, can be clearly traced in the politics of the Tudor period. In spite of two great drawbacks the cloth manufacture was growing. It had naturally been severely checked for a generation or so by the awful national disaster of the Great Plague, which occurred so soon after Edward II. had helped to found it in England, and which for the time utterly paralysed English industry in all its branches. It had been checked again by the long and useless wars which Edward III. and his successors carried on against France, at enormous cost and with no practical results, but which of course were paid for out of the proceeds of our national industries. But after these two checks it developed steadily, even during the Wars of the Roses; for these wars were carried on almost exclusively by the barons and their retainers, in a series of battles hardly any of which were of any magnitude, exaggerated though they have been both by contemporary and later historians. These wars had the ultimate effect of causing the feudal aristocracy to destroy itself in a suicidal conflict, and thus helped to increase the influence of the middle class—*i.e.* the merchants and manufacturers—as a factor in political life. And thus it became the policy of the Tudor sovereigns, who were gifted with a certain amount of native shrewdness, to hasten the decaying power of the feudal lords by simultaneously supporting, and being supported by, the middle class, and to the alliance thus made between the crown and the industrial portion of the community we owe a rapid increase of the commercial prosperity which laid the foundations of the greatness of the Elizabethan age, and of the great mercantile enterprises that succeeded it.

CHAPTER III

THE TOWNS, INDUSTRIAL VILLAGES, AND FAIRS

§ 1. **The chief manufacturing towns**—During the period between the Norman Conquest and the middle of the thirteenth century, the towns, as we saw, had been gradually growing in importance, gaining fresh privileges, and becoming almost, in some cases quite, independent of the lord or king, by the grant of a charter. Moreover they had grown from the mere trading centres of ancient times into seats of specialized industries, regulated and organized by the craft gilds. This new feature of the industrial or manufacturing aspect of certain towns is well shown in a compilation, dated about 1250, and quoted by Professor Rogers in *Six Centuries of Work and Wages*, which gives a list of English towns and their chief products. Hardly any of the manufacturing towns mentioned are in the North of England, but mostly in the East and South.

[TABLE

The following table gives the name of the town, and its manufacture or articles of sale.

TOWN	PRODUCT	TOWN	PRODUCT
(1) *Textile Manufactures*		(5) *Markets*	
Lincoln	Scarlet cloth.	Ripon	Horses.
Bligh	Blanket.	Nottingham	Oxen.
Beverley	Burnet cloth.	Gloucester	Iron.
Colchester	Russet ,,	Bristol	Leather and Hides.
Shaftesbury	Linen fabrics.	Coventry	Soap.
Lewes	,,	Northampton	Saddlery.
Aylesbury	,,	Doncaster	Horse-girths.
Warwick	Cord.	Chester	Skins and Furs.
Bridport	Cord and Hempen fabrics.	Shrewsbury	,,
		Corfe	Marble.
		Cornwall towns	Tin.
(2) *Bakeries*			
Wycombe	Fine bread.	(6) *Fishing Towns*	
Hungerford	,,		
St Albans	,,	Grimsby	Cod.
		Rye	Whiting.
(3) *Cutlery*		Yarmouth	Herrings.
Maxtead	Knives.	Berwick	Salmon.
Wilton	Needles.		
Leicester	Razors.	(7) *Ports*	
(4) *Breweries*		Norwich	
		Southampton	
Banbury	Brewing.		——
Hitchin	,,		
Ely	,,	Dunwich	Mills.

This list is obviously incomplete, for it omits towns like Sheffield and Winchester, both of which were important as manufacturing towns from very early times, though the woollen manufactures of the latter were soon outstripped by those of Hull, York, Beverley, Lincoln, and especially Norwich. But such as it is the list is curious, chiefly as showing how manufactures have long since deserted their original abodes, and have been transferred to towns of quite recent origin.

§ 2. **Staple towns and the merchants**—It will have been

observed that by the time this list was compiled, most towns were either the seat of a certain manufacture, or the market where such manufactures were sold. Now, in the days of Edward I. and Edward II. (1272–1327), several such towns were specially singled out and granted the privilege of selling a particular product, the *staple* of the district, and were hence called *staple towns.* Besides a number of towns in England, staples were fixed at certain foreign ports for the sale of English goods. At first Antwerp was selected as the staple town for our produce, and afterwards St Omer. A staple was also set up at Calais when we took it (1347), but at the loss of that town in 1558 it was transferred to Bruges. The staple system thus begun by the first two Edwards, was established upon a firm legal basis by Edward III. The statute 27 Edward III. c. 9 (1354), enumerates all the staple towns of England, and sets forth the ancient customs payable upon staple goods. It enacts that only merchants of a particular staple—*i.e.* those engaged in a particular trade like wool or hides—may export these goods, and that each staple should be governed by its own mayor and constables. Now, although regulations like these are opposed to our modern ideas of free competition, they were to a certain extent useful in the Middle Ages, because the existence of staple towns facilitated the collection of custom duties, and also secured in some degree the good quality of the goods made in, or exported from, a town. For special officers were appointed to mark them if of the proper quality and reject them if inferior. The system also had the important *political* result of bringing into prominence the merchants as a class, and of increasing their influence. So much were they a special class, that the sovereign always negotiated with them separately. Thus in 1339, when Edward III. was as usual fighting against France, and, also as usual, in great want of money, he was liberally supplied with loans by Sir William de la Pole, a rich merchant of Hull, who acted on behalf of himself, and many other merchants. Sir Richard Whittington performed similar services for Henry IV. and Henry V.

§ 3. **Markets**—Another class of towns were the country market towns, many of which exist in agricultural districts to-day, in much the same fashion as they did six centuries ago. The control and regulation of the town market was at first in the hands of the lord of the manor, but by this period it had been bought by the corporation or by the merchant gild, or by both, and was now one of the most valued of municipal privileges. The market-place was always some large open space within the city walls, such as, for instance, exists very noticeably in Nottingham to this day. London had several such spaces, of which the names Cornhill, Cheapside, the Poultry, still remain. The capital was indeed a perpetual market, though of course provincial towns only held a market on one or two days of the week. It is curious to notice how these days have persisted to modern times. The Wednesday and Saturday market of Oxford has existed for at least six centuries, if not more. The control of these markets was undertaken by the corporation for various purposes. The first of these was to prevent frauds and adulteration of goods, and for this purpose special officers were appointed, as in the staple towns, or like the "aulnager" of Norwich mentioned before (p. 54). This was possible in a time when industry was limited, and the competitive idea was as yet unborn, and one cannot help thinking that it must have been of great use to purchasers. The second object of the regulators of the market was to keep prices at a "natural level," and to regulate the cost of manufactured articles. The price of provisions in especial was a subject of much regulation, but our forefathers were not very successful in this point, laudable though their object was.[1]

§ 4. **The great fairs**—Now, besides the weekly markets there were held annually in various parts of the kingdom large fairs, which often lasted many days, and which form a most important and interesting economic feature of the time. They were necessary for two reasons: (1) because the ordinary trader could not and did not exist in the small villages, in which it must be remembered most of the population lived, nor could he even find sufficient customers in a town of that time, for very few contained over 5000 inhabitants; (2) because the inhabitants of the villages and towns could find in the fairs a wider market for their goods, and more variety for their purchases. The result was that these fairs were frequented by all classes of the population, from noble and prelate to the villein, and hardly a family in England did not at one time of the year or another send a representative, or at least give a commission to a friend, to get goods at some celebrated fair. They afforded an opportunity for commercial intercourse between inhabitants of all parts of England, and with traders from all parts of Europe. They were, moreover, a necessity arising from the economic conditions of a time when transit of goods was comparatively slow, and when ordinary people disliked travelling frequently or far beyond the limits of their own district. The spirit of isolation which is so marked a feature of the mediæval town or village encouraged this feeling, and except the trading class few people travelled about, and those who did so were regarded with suspicion. Till the epoch of modern railways, in fact, fairs were a

[1] See note 9, p. 245, on Assize of Bread and Ale.

necessity, though now the rapidity of locomotion and the facility with which goods can be ordered and despatched, have annihilated their utility and rendered their relics a nuisance. But even in the present day there are plenty of people to be found in rural districts who have rarely, and sometimes never, been a dozen miles from their native village.

§ 5. **The fairs of Winchester and Stourbridge**—Fairs were held in every part of the country at various parts of the year. Thus there was a fair at Leeds, which for several centuries served as a centre where the wool-growers of Yorkshire and Lancashire met English and foreign merchants from Hull and other eastern ports, and sold them the raw material that was to be worked up in the looms of Flanders. But there were a few great fairs that eclipsed all others in magnitude and importance, and of these two deserve special mention, those at Winchester and Stourbridge. (1) That at *Winchester* was founded in the reign of William the Norman, who granted the Bishop of Winchester leave to hold a fair on St Giles' Hill, for one day in the year. Henry II., however, granted a charter for a fair of sixteen days. During this time the great common was covered with booths and tents, and divided into streets called after the name of the goods sold therein, as, *e.g.*, "The Drapery," "The Pottery," "The Spicery." Tolls were levied on every bridge and roadway to the fair, and brought in a large revenue. The fair was of importance till the fourteenth century, for in the *Vision of Peres the Plowman*, Covetousness tells how

> "To Wye and to Winchester I went to the fair."

But it declined from the time of Edward III., chiefly owing to the fact that the woollen trade of Norwich and other eastern towns had become far more important, while on the other hand Southampton was found to be a more convenient spot for the Venetian traders' fleet (p. 93) to do business.

(2) *Stourbridge Fair*—But the greatest of all English fairs, and that which kept its reputation and importance the longest, was the Fair of Stourbridge, near Cambridge.[1] It was of European renown, and lasted for a whole month, from the end of August to the end of September. Its importance was due to the fact that it was within easy reach of the ports of the east coast, which at that time were very accessible and much frequented. Hither came the Venetian, and Genoese merchants, with stores of Eastern produce—silks and velvets, cotton, and precious stones. The Flemish merchants brought the fine linens and cloths of Bruges, Liège, and Ghent, and other manufacturing towns. Frenchmen and Spaniards were present with their wines; Norwegian sailors with tar and pitch; and the mighty traders of the Hanse towns exposed to sale furs and amber for the rich, iron and copper for the farmers, flax for their wives; while homely fustian, buckram, wax, herrings, and canvas mingled incongruously in their booths with strange, far-off Eastern spices and ornaments. And in return the English farmers—or traders on their behalf—carried to the fair hundreds of huge wool-sacks, wherewith to clothe the nations of Europe; or barley for the Flemish breweries, with corn and horses and cattle also. Lead was brought from the mines of Derbyshire, and tin from Cornwall; even some iron from Sussex, but this was accounted inferior to the imported metal. All these wares were, as at Winchester, exposed in stalls and tents in long streets, some named after the various nations that congregated

[1] See note 10, p. 246, on Stourbridge Fair.

there, and others after the kind of goods on sale. This vast fair lasted down to the eighteenth century in unabated vigour, and was at that time described by Daniel Defoe, in a work now easily accessible to all,[1] which contains a most interesting description of all the proceedings of this busy month. It is not much more than a hundred years since the Lancashire merchants alone used to send their goods to Stourbridge, upon a thousand pack-horses, but now the pack-horses and fairs have gone, and the telegraph and railway have taken their place.

§ 6. **English mediæval ports**—In the last paragraph mention was made of the east coast having ports of great prominence in this period. It will be convenient here to notice what were the chief ports of England, and to remark how few of them have retained their old importance. The chief port was of course London, which has always held an exceptional position, and the other principal ports were on the east and south coast. Southampton was from early times the chief southern harbour, and next to it Dartmouth, Plymouth, Sandwich, and Winchelsea, Weymouth, Shoreham, Dover, and Margate. They were connected with the trade in French and Spanish goods. On the western coast Bristol was almost the only port much frequented, and was the centre and harbour for the western fisheries, and also a place of export for hides and the cloth manufactures of the western towns. In the fifteenth century Bristol fishermen penetrated through the Hebrides to the Shetland and Orkney Islands and the northern fisheries, where they found that the Scarborough men had long preceded them. On the eastern coast, indeed, Scarborough was one of the most enterprising ports. Boston, Hull, Lynn, Harwich, Yar-

[1] *Tour through the Eastern Counties* (Cassell's National Library, 3*d*.).

mouth, and Colchester were also very flourishing, and were concerned in the Flemish and Baltic trade. Farther north Newcastle was the centre for the coasting trade in coal, and Berwick was a fisherman's harbour. But the southern and eastern ports were the most frequented, as being suitable to the light and shallow craft that did a coasting trade, or ran across to the Continent in smooth weather.

§ 7. **The temporary decay of manufacturing towns**—We have now noticed the chief markets, fairs, ports, and manufacturing towns of mediæval England, and it will be seen that commercial prosperity was certainly developing. So too were home manufacturing industries, but their growth brought about a curious effect in the decay of certain towns, and the rise of industrial villages in rural districts. To the decay of towns we find frequent reference in the Statutes of Henry VII. and his successor —*i.e.* from 1490 or 1500 onwards. This decay was due to two causes: (1) to the growth of sheep farming, mentioned above (p. 45), and (2) to the fact that the industrial disabilities imposed upon dwellers in towns, in consequence of the corporate privileges of the gilds, now far exceeded the advantages of residence there. The days of usefulness for the gilds had gone past; their restrictions were now only felt to cramp the rising manufacturing industries. Hence we find the manufacturers of the Tudor period were leaving the towns and seeking open villages instead, where they could develop their trade free from the vexatious restrictions of old-fashioned corporations. Of course laws were passed to check this tendency, and to confine particular industries to particular towns. Thus, in Norfolk, no one was to "dye, shear, or calendar cloth" anywhere but in the town of Norwich (Act of 14 and 15 Henry VIII.); no one in the northern counties was to make "worsted coverlets" except in York (Act of 33 and 34 Henry VIII.).

§ 8. **Growth of industrial villages. The germs of the modern factory system** — Such protective enactments were, however, as protective enactments must generally be, utterly in vain. Henry VII. tried to remedy the supposed evil by limiting the privileges of interference of the gilds, but even this step was useless. Manufactures were slowly and surely transferred to various villages, and in several industries a kind of modern factory system can be traced at this time. Master manufacturers, weary of municipal and gild-made restrictions, organized in country places little communities solely for industrial purposes, and so arranged as to afford greater scope for the combination and division of labour. The system of apprenticeship was a powerful element in this scheme, and supplied ready labour for these small factories. The goods were made not as formerly only for local use, but for the purposes of trade and profit throughout the kingdom. The master was bound to his workmen rather more closely than the mill-owner of the present day to his "hands," for the spirit of personal sympathy and obligation still survived in these small labour communities. But the germs of the modern system were there; for this new system was not that of domestic or cottage industry, as had been the rule in previous periods, but a system of congregated labour organized upon a capitalistic basis by one man—the organizer, head, and owner of the industrial village—the master clothier. Among the famous master clothiers of the woollen industry, we read of Cuthbert of Kendal, Hodgkins of Halifax, Brian of Manchester, each of whom "kept a great number of servants at work—carders, spinners, weavers, dyers, shearers, and others." Perhaps the greatest of them was John Winchcombe, or "Jack of Newbury," as he was called, of whom it is recorded that a hundred looms always worked in his house, and he was rich enough to send a hundred of his journeymen to Flodden Field, in 1513. His kerseys were famous all over Europe. It was from communities such as these that the villages of Manchester, Bolton, Leeds, Halifax, and Bury took their rise, and afterwards developed into the great factory towns of to-day. But these workshops, large though they seemed then, were utterly insignificant compared with the huge factories of to-day, where the workmen are numbered in thousands, and are, to the capitalist-employer or joint-stock company that owns the mill, merely a mass of human machines, more intelligent though not so durable as other machines, and possessed of an unpleasant tendency to go out "on strike," for reasons that naturally appear to their employer insufficient and subversive of the whole industrial system. However, the industrial system is not subverted, though the workmen can hardly be said to be upon the same pleasant footing with their employers as they used to be in the old industrial village.

CHAPTER IV

THE GREAT PLAGUE AND ITS ECONOMIC EFFECTS

§ 1. **Material progress of the country**—In the preceding chapters we have attempted to give an idea of the state of industry and commerce in England in the Middle Ages. We now come to a most important landmark in the history of the social and industrial condition of the people—viz. the Great Plague of 1348 and subsequent years. Almost two centuries had elapsed since the death of Stephen (1154), and the cessation of those great civil conflicts which harried England in his reign. These two centuries had witnessed on the whole a continuous growth of material prosperity. The wealth of the country had increased; the towns had developed and had aided the growth of a prosperous mercantile and industrial middle class, who regulated their own affairs in their gilds, and also had a voice in municipal management. The country at large was mainly devoted to agricultural and pastoral pursuits, and the mass of the people were engaged in tilling the ground or feeding cattle. The mass of the people too were now better fed and better clothed than those of a similar class on the Continent, and a great proof of their general prosperity is to be found in the nature of their food. It is a significant economic fact that wheaten bread was then, and has generally since been, the staple food of the English labourer. In most other lands, bread made from rye and other cereals was generally good enough for the working classes. If rye failed they had nothing to fall back upon, and thus famines were frequent. But the English labourer always had some other cereal besides wheat in reserve.

§ 2. **Social changes. The villeins and wage-paid labourers**—Besides the growth of material prosperity in these two centuries, we find that the commutation of villeinage services into money payments to the lord of the manor—a tendency frequently commented upon—had been growing apace. This commutation had been going on for a long time, in fact ever since the Conquest, if not before, and the villeins in general had freed themselves not only from labour-dues, but from the vexatious customary fines or "amercements" which they had to pay to the lord of the manor on certain social occasions—such as the marriage of a daughter, or the education of a son for the Church. But of course this freedom was not complete, though it is important to notice its growth, for we shall see that it formed the occasion of a great class struggle some years after the Great Plague.

There is another feature which is also of importance, and which had come more and more into prominence during the past two centuries. I refer to the increase in the numbers of those who lived upon the labour of their hands, and were employed and paid wages like labourers of the present day. It has been mentioned before that they arose from the cottar class, who had not enough land to occupy their whole time, and who were therefore ready to sell their labour to an employer. These two features, the commutation of labour-dues for money payments, and the rise of a wage-paid labouring class, are closely connected, for it was natural that, when the lord of a manor had agreed to receive money from his tenants in villeinage instead of labour, he should have to obtain other labour from elsewhere and pay for it in the money thus received by commutation. The tendency of these social changes was greatly in favour of the villeins, whose social condition had steadily improved, and whose tenancy in villeinage was more and more becoming a "free" tenancy. Neither were the villeins, whether comparatively well-to-do yeomen or agricultural labourers, so much bound to the manor as formerly, for in proportion as their labour services were no longer necessary, their lord would let them leave the manor and seek employment, or take up some manufacturing industry, elsewhere. It had always been possible for the villeins (or serfs) to do this on payment of a small fine (*capitagium*), and it is certain that as money payments became increasingly the fashion, the lord would not object to receiving this further payment, unless perchance he would require a good deal of labour done upon his own land.

§ 3. **The Famine and the Plague**—The position of the labouring class had been further improved by the effects of the famines which occurred in A.D. 1315–16. Of course they suffered great hardships and their numbers were considerably thinned, but at the same time this loss of life and diminution in their numbers caused their services to become more valuable in proportion to their scarcity, and they gained a rise of some 20 per cent. in wages. From this date till the coming of the Great Plague, some thirty years later, they and the rest of the English people enjoyed a period of great prosperity. It was on the whole a "merry England" on which the Great Plague suddenly broke. The prosperity of the people was reflected in the splendour and brilliancy of the court and aristocracy, and the national pride had been increased by the recent victory of Crecy, and by the other successes in the French war, which brought not only glory but occasionally wealth, in the shape of heavy ransoms. But in 1348 the prosperity and pride of the nation was overwhelmed with gloom. The Great Plague came with sudden and mysterious steps from Asia to Italy, and thence to Western Europe and England, carried some say by travelling merchants, or borne with its infection on the wings of the wind. It arrived in England at the two great ports of Bristol and Southampton in August 1348, and thence spread all over the land. Its ravages were frightful. Whole districts were depopulated, and about one-third of the people perished. Norwich and London, being busy and crowded towns, suffered especially from the pestilence, and though the numbers of the dead have been grossly exaggerated by the panic of contemporaries and the credulity of modern historians,[1] there can be no doubt that the loss of life was enormous.

§ 4. **The effects of the Plague on wages**—The most immediate consequence of the Plague was a marked scarcity in the number of labourers available. For being of the poorest class they naturally succumbed more readily to famine and sickness. This scarcity of labour naturally resulted in higher wages. The land-owners began to fear that their lands would not be cultivated properly, and were content to buy labour at higher prices than would have been given at a time when the necessity of the labourer to the capitalist was more obscured. Hence the wages of labourers rose far above the customary rates. In harvest-work, for example, the rise was nearly 60 per cent., and what is more it remained so for a long period ; the rise in agricultural wages generally was 50 per cent. So it was also in the case of artisans' wages, in the case of carpenters, masons, and others. It seems the upper classes and the capitalists of that day very strongly objected to paying high wages, as they naturally do. The king himself felt deeply upon the point. Without waiting for Parliament to meet, Edward III. issued a proclamation ordering that no man should either demand or pay the higher rates of wages, but should abide by the old rate. He forbade labourers to leave the land to which they were attached, and assigned heavy penalties to the runaways. Parliament assembled in 1349 and eagerly ratified this proclamation,

[1] It was asserted by the fourteenth-century chroniclers, and has often been repeated since, that nearly 60,000 people died in Norwich alone. As a matter of fact, the whole county of Norfolk, including that city, hardly contained 30,000 people.

in the laws known as the *Statutes of Labourers.* But the demand for labour was so great that such legislative endeavours to prevent its proper payment were fortunately ineffective. Runaways not only found shelter, but also good employment and high wages. Parliament fulminated its threats in vain; and in vain increased its penalties, by a later Statute of 1360 ordering those who asked more than the old wages to be imprisoned, and, if they were fugitives, to be branded with hot irons. For once the labourer was able to meet the capitalist on equal terms.

§ 5. **Prices of provisions**—Now, although there was a great rise in the price of labour, the price of the labourers' food did not rise in proportion. The price of provisions, indeed, was but little affected, for food did not require much manual labour in its production, and hence the rise of wages would not be much felt here. What *did* rise was the price of all articles that required much labour in their production, or the cost of which depended entirely upon human labour. The price of fish, for instance, is determined almost entirely by the cost of the fisherman's labour, and the cost of transit. Consequently we should under these circumstances expect a great rise in the price of fish, and such indeed was the case. So, too, there was an enormous increase in the prices of tiles, wheels, canvas, lead, ironwork, and all agricultural materials, these being articles whose value depends chiefly upon the amount of labour spent over them, and upon the cost of that labour. Hence, both peasant and artisan gained higher wages, while the cost of living remained for them much the same; and those who suffered most were the owners of large estates, who had to pay more for the labour which worked these estates, and more too for the implements used in working them.

§ 6. **Effects of the Plague upon the land-owners**—The fact that the larger land-owners found the cost of working their land doubled or even trebled caused important economic changes. Before the Plague the cost of harvesting upon an ordinary estate, quoted by Professor Rogers, was £3, 13*s*. 9*d*. : afterwards it rose to £12, 19*s*. 10*d*. Moreover, the landlord had to consent to receive lower rents, for many tenants could not work their farms profitably with the old rents, and the new prices for labour and implements. And, as rent is paid out of the profits of agriculture, it was obvious even to the landlord that smaller profits meant lower rents. Now, in this state of things, the landlord had two courses open to him. He could turn off the tenant and cultivate all his land himself ; or he could try and exist upon the smaller income gained from lower rents. It was obviously impossible for him to cultivate all his land himself, for he would have to employ a large number of bailiffs for his various manors, and trust to their honesty to do their best for him. Moreover, he would have to pay his bailiffs, while after all his tenants paid him something, though less than formerly. So he decided to allow his tenants to pay him a smaller rent. What is more, he decided under the circumstances to give up farming altogether, and let even the lands which he had reserved for his own cultivation. The landlords, in fact, had not apparently either the ability or the inclination to superintend agriculture under these changed conditions, and gave up trying to work their land themselves. So that one great result of the Plague was that landlords to a large extent gave up capitalist farming upon their own account, and let their tenants cultivate the soil, and also pay them for continuing to do so.

§ 7. **Rise of the tenant farmer or yeoman class**—The

natural effect of this change on the part of the landowners was that the small peasant farmers greatly increased in numbers. The circumstances of the time favoured them, for the rise in the price of labour was not so severely felt by them, since they could and did use the unpaid labour of their families upon their holdings. Then, when they had tided over the immediate results of the Plague, they took larger holdings as they grew richer. They were helped in this by the stock and land lease system already referred to (p. 42), which gave them the use of a larger quantity of agricultural capital than they could otherwise have commanded. But when the tenant farmer's wealth increased he found himself able, as a rule, to keep his own stock.

§ 8. **The emancipation of the villeins**—The gradual amelioration of the conditions of villeinage or serfage received a forcible impetus from the Great Plague. Those villeins who had not already become free tenants, and especially those who lived on wages, shared in the advantages now gained by all who had labour to sell. Their labour was more valuable, and they were able with their higher wages to buy from their lord a commutation of those exactions which interfered with their personal freedom of action, with their right to sell their labour to other employers, or with their endeavours to reach a better social position. Serfage or villeinage gradually became practically extinct after the Plague,[1] though the landowners, backed up by the lawyers, interposed many obstacles in the path of emancipation, and a great Revolt was necessary to enable the villeins to show their power. This Revolt and its success must now engage our attention.

[1] See note 11, p. 246, on Survivals.

CHAPTER V

THE PEASANTS' REVOLT OF 1381, AND THE SUBSEQUENT PROSPERITY OF THE WORKING CLASSES

§ 1. **New social doctrines**—By no means the least important among the effects of the Great Plague was the spirit of independence which it helped to raise in the breasts of the villeins and labourers, more especially as they now gained some consciousness of the power of labour, and of its value as a prime necessity in the economic life of the nation. There was indeed a revolutionary spirit in the air in the last quarter of the fourteenth century, and the villeins could not help breathing it. The social teaching of the author of *Peres the Plowman*, with his outspoken denunciation of those who are called the upper classes ; the bold religious teaching of Wiklif and the wandering friars, and the marked political assertion of the rights of Parliament by the "Good Parliament" of 1376, were all manifestations of this spirit. It was natural, too, that, feeling their power as they did, the villeins should become restive when they heard from the followers of Wiklif that, as it was lawful to withdraw tithes from priests who lived in sin, so "servants and tenants may withdraw their services and rents from their lords that live openly a cursed life."

§ 2. **The coming of the Friars. Wiklif**—Such indeed was the teaching that Wiklif promulgated, and it was carried throughout all England by that great association of wandering friars which he founded under the title of the "poor priests." These men were like the mendicant friars who had come to England a century before [1] to work in the poorer parts of the English towns; only Wiklif's priests generally wandered out into the isolated and remote country villages, and spread abroad the independent doctrines and the revolutionary spirit of the times. Spending their lives in moving about among the "upland folk," as the country people were called, clad in coarse, undyed brown woollen garments, they won the confidence of the peasants, and what is more, helped them to combine in very effectual trade unions. They acted as treasurers for the common funds of these peasants' unions, and served as messengers between those in different parts of the country, having passwords and a secret language of their own. Their preaching was similar to that of the celebrated priest of Kent, John Ball, who for twenty years before the great rising (1360-80) openly spoke words like these: "Good people, things will never be well in England so long as there be villeins and gentlemen. By what right are they whom we call lords greater than we? On what grounds have they deserved it? Why do they hold us in serfage? They have leisure and fine houses: we have pain and labour, and the wind and rain in the fields. And yet it is of us and our toil that these men hold their estate." These searching questions as to the rights of the lords, and the bold but true statement that it was the villeins and labouring classes who supported—and paid for—their high estate, came closely home to the peasants. They were encouraged too by the independent religious views of the Lollards, and it is said that half England held their views. And this independence of social and religious tenets was hardly calculated to make the villeins bear

[1] The Black Friars of Dominic came in 1221, and the Grey Friars of Francis in 1224.

with equanimity the exactions of their lords after the Great Plague.

§ 3. **The renewed exactions of the landlords**—For it must be remembered that the Great Plague did not immediately emancipate the villeins, or cause the land-owners to give up farming on their own account. The process, of course, took a few years, and in these few years the land-owners made desperate efforts to avoid paying higher wages than formerly for labour. As it had now become costly, they insisted more severely upon the performance by their tenants of such labour-dues as were not yet commuted for money payments. They even tried to make those tenants who had emerged from a condition of villeinage to a free tenancy, return back to villeinage again, with all its old labour-dues and casual services. If a man could not prove by legal documentary evidence that he held his land in a free tenancy, the land-owner might pretend he was a villein tenant, and subject to all a villein's services, although these services might long ago have been commuted for a money rent without any legal formality. There is much reason to believe, more-over, that they abused their power of inflicting "amercements," or fines, upon their tenants in the manor courts for trivial breaches of duty. So at least Wiklif and the author of *Peres the Plowman* tell us. The villeins naturally resisted this attempt to make a retrograde movement, which would force them back into the old bondage from which they had redeemed themselves; the free tenants supported them, for they knew their turn would come next if the serfs failed; and the labouring classes eagerly joined the movement also, in hopes of getting rid of the vexatious Statutes of Labourers.

§ 4. **The Peasants' Revolt**[1]—The crisis came in 1381, and was perhaps precipitated by the oppressive manner in which the poll-tax was collected. But the poll-tax itself was not the real cause of the revolt. The rising had long been foreseen, and arrangements had been duly made among the peasants' unions by the poor priests, their agents and messengers, who formed the connecting links between all the labour organizations of the land. A sudden rising took place, as unanimous as it was unanticipated, throughout all England, from Scarborough to Kent and Devon. Almost simultaneously the peasants showed their combined strength, and a large body of them under Wat Tyler marched upon London. It is well known how they met the young King Richard II. at Mile-end, and demanded of him the petition which shows the real meaning of the movement: " We will that you free us for ever, us and our lands," they asked; " and that we be never named or held as villeins." " I grant it," said the king, with regal diplomacy, and the peasants believed him. But they very soon learned how vain a thing it is to put one's trust in princes, for after the peasant armies in the various parts of England had quieted down, and the Essex men, among others, claimed the fulfilment of his royal promise, Richard openly broke faith. " Villeins you were," said the king, " and villeins you are. In bondage shall you abide, and that not your old bondage, but a worse!" Fortunately this never happened. Although suppressed, the rising was practically successful, for it had shown the power of the combination of labour, in the great strife between labour and capital. A few of the ringleaders were imprisoned and executed, among them being several priests. The

[1] For other views of this Revolt see my *Industry in England*, ch. xii.

authorities of course blustered, and swore they would never give in. Equally of course they did give in; no further attempts were made to exact labour-dues or *corvées*; and within a generation or so villeinage or serfage became practically extinct[1]; and the villeins became known as copyholders or tenants by custom.

§ 5. **The Condition of the English labourer**—After this great insurrection came what has been termed the golden age of the English labourer, and it lasted all through the fifteenth century. Food was cheap and abundant; wages were amply sufficient. True, the employers of labour still tried, by various petitions and Acts (*e.g.* 7 Henry IV., 4 Henry V., 23 Henry VI., 11 Henry VII.), to enforce the Statute of Labourers, but they were practically unsuccessful, and prosperity was progressive and continuous till the evil days of Henry VIII. The wages of a good agricultural labourer, before the Plague, had been £2, 7*s.* 10*d.* per year as an average, including the labour of his wife and child; after the Plague his wages would be £3, 15*s.*, and the cost of his living certainly not more than £3, 4*s.* 9*d.* An artisan, working 300 days a year, would get, say, £3, 18*s.* 1½*d.* before 1348, and after that date £5, 15*s.* 7*d.*, which was so far above the cost of maintenance as to give him a very comfortable position. His working day, too, was not excessive, while the fixed rents of the time were very low. These low rents were also one great cause of the prosperity of the new yeoman, or tenant farmer class (p. 73) that had arisen after the collapse of the capitalist land-owners in consequence of the Plague. This class remained for at least two centuries the backbone of English agriculture.

§ 6. **Drawbacks**—There were, however, a few drawbacks in this "golden age," as various critics have told

[1] For survivals see note 11, p. 246.

us. The ordinary hardships of human life were in many respects greater than they are now—disease was more deadly, and the risks of life more numerous [1]; but from this very fact the extremes of poverty and wealth were less widely distinguished and less acutely felt; and, although it cannot be asserted that people did not occasionally die of want in very bad times, yet the grinding and hopeless poverty just above the verge of actual starvation, so often prevalent in the present time, did not belong to mediæval life. The chief hardships to be encountered were in the winter, for, owing to the absence of winter roots, stock could only be kept in limited quantities, and the only meat procurable was that which had been previously salted. It is certain that much of mediæval disease is traceable to the excessive use of salted provisions. The houses, also, were rudely built of mud, clay, or even wattled material, for brick-making was a lost art, and stone was only used for the manor-houses and the dwellings of the wealthy. But food was abundant and cheap. The cost of living was not more than one-tenth of what it is at the present day. Three pounds of beef could be bought for a penny; a pig cost about fourpence; beer was only a halfpenny a gallon. Employment was fairly constant and regular, and in addition to their wages, labourers still possessed the valuable old manorial common rights of common pasture and forest.

§ 7. **The close of the Middle Ages**—So things went on happily after the Great Revolt, and in the days of the fourth and fifth Henries. The brilliant, but useless, French victories of the latter monarch were paid for partly by the prosperous middle and lower classes, and

[1] The question is more fully treated in *Industry in England*, ch. xii. (end).

partly by the French themselves; and very costly they were. England was still mainly agricultural, but manufactures were growing. Though wool was still exported, much was being worked up in the towns and villages. Artisans earned about 3*s*. a week, which would certainly be worth more than 30*s*. a week at present. Industry, as will be remembered, was organized in the craft gilds, and apparently the gild system was a success till its restrictions in towns began to cramp the growing manufactures. The fifteenth century was a period of prosperity and content, in spite of both civil and foreign wars; and even the wasteful reign of Henry VI., with its unsuccessful war with France, and huge subsidies to Rome, though it made the Government unpopular and caused widespread national discontent and occasional insurrections in Kent and Wiltshire, did not materially injure the general prosperity. The king himself, however, was nearly bankrupt. The Wars of the Roses which followed (1455–86) did not affect the country at large, being fought in a series of much exaggerated skirmishes by small bodies of nobles and their followers. They ended in the very desirable consummation of the ruin of the remnants of the feudal aristocracy, and at the same time opened a further path for the influence of the industrial classes, whose favour Henry VII. had the wisdom to court, and in return was supported by them in his policy of weakening the power of the great barons. He encouraged commerce,[1] and aided the prosperity of his kingdom, thereby amassing for his own treasury considerable wealth. In his reign the feudal system was dying out, the nation prospered, and the Middle Ages came to a close in a wealthy and industrious England (A.D. 1500).

[1] Cf. note 7, p. 244.

But before the next century was completed part of the nation was impoverished, the labourers were degraded and despoiled, and a long legacy of pauperism and misery was bequeathed to the country by the wastefulness and extravagance of Henry VIII.

PERIOD IV

FROM THE SIXTEENTH CENTURY TO THE EVE OF THE INDUSTRIAL REVOLUTION (1509-1760)

CHAPTER I

THE MISDEEDS OF HENRY VIII., AND ECONOMIC CHANGES IN THE SIXTEENTH CENTURY

§ 1. **Henry VIII.'s wastefulness**—Henry VIII. came to the throne in 1509. He succeeded to a full treasury left by his thrifty father, and replenished by contributions from the general prosperity of the country at the close of the fifteenth century. But he soon dissipated the whole of these accumulations. He spent a great deal of money in subsidizing the needy Emperor of Germany, Maximilian, and in interfering in foreign affairs which were better left alone, in the hope of winning for himself a military reputation. His Continental wars and alliances cost him dear, or rather they cost the English people dear, for they gave him liberal grants of money (as *e.g.* in 1513) before he set out on his fruitless expeditions. But even in time of peace his expenditure was equally extravagant. The cost of his household establishments, and those of his children, was simply enormous ; for the establishments of Mary, Edward, and even Elizabeth were each more costly than the whole annual charge of his father's household. His extravagance was monumental, though where his money went he could not himself discover. Wolsey said of him, " Rather than miss any part of his will, he will endanger one-half of his kingdom." As a matter of fact he succeeded in impoverishing the whole of it.

§ 2. **The dissolution of the monasteries**—He soon wasted the carefully accumulated treasures of his father, and sought for further supplies. They were gained at first by increased taxation, but as this money was spent in the French wars, Henry was soon in difficulties again. Then he tried another expedient. The monasteries suggested themselves to him as an easy prey, and he knew that an attack upon them would not displease the growing Protestant party in the country. These institutions were in many cases not fulfilling their ancient functions properly, and were often far from being the homes of religious virtue. So excuses were easily found, and in 1536 the smaller monasteries with an income below £200 a year were suppressed, and in 1539 the larger ones were similarly treated. About 1000 houses were suppressed, the *annual* income of which was £161,000, equivalent to more than two millions sterling of our present money. Half-a-dozen bishoprics and a few grammar schools were founded out of the proceeds of this spoliation, in order to blind the eyes of the people at large. But with these paltry exceptions the whole of that vast capital and revenue was granted to courtiers and favourites, sold at nominal prices, or gambled away by the king and his satellites.

§ 3. **Results of the suppression**—Although the mass of the people did not protest very vigorously against this piece of royal robbery, many of them witnessed with silent dismay the destruction of ancient institutions that had formed so integral a part of the national life. A few even expressed their discontent in open insurrection, and risings took place in Lincolnshire and Yorkshire,[1] but these

[1] *e.g.* " The Pilgrimage of Grace," 1536.

were put down. The economic disturbances which resulted were not so clearly seen, but were far more severe. They were acute enough from the mere fact of so much wealth having suddenly changed hands and being spent with reckless prodigality. It is said that one-fifth, or even one-third, of the land in the kingdom was held by the monasteries, and it was now transferred from the holding of the Church into the hands of a new set of nobles and landed gentry, created from the dependants and time-servers of Henry's court. These were enriched, but the former tenants of the monasteries and the poorer class of labourers suffered greatly. Hence serious results followed. Nearly all monastic lands were held by tenants upon the "stock and land lease" system, spoken of before; but, when these monastic lands were suddenly transferred into the clutches of Henry's new and needy nobility, the stock was confiscated and sold off, while the money rent was raised. The new owners did not care for the slow, though really lucrative, system of providing the tenant with a certain amount of stock for his land, but simply wished to get all the money they could without delay. The result was that the poorer tenants were almost ruined, and it seems probable that pauperism was greatly increased. What small amount of pauperism had previously existed had been sufficiently relieved by the monasteries, who, owing their wealth to charitable offerings, could not well refuse charity to those that needed it; but on their dissolution pauperism had no longer such relief, and very soon we shall see it became necessary to provide that relief by law. With the dissolution the history of English legal pauperism may be said to begin, although of course other causes contributed to its growth. But among these causes the spoliation of the monasteries had no unimportant place.

§ 4. **The issuing of base coin**—Four years after the dissolution, Henry was in difficulties again. He dared not ask his Parliament for further supplies so soon after his last piece of plunder, so he betook himself to a still more wicked kind of robbery. In 1543 he began to debase the currency, and repeated this criminal action in 1545 and 1546. This debasement forms a landmark in English industrial history as disastrous as the other landmark of the Great Plague. Its effect was not felt immediately, but it was none the less real. The chief point that concerned the labourer was that prices rapidly rose, but that, as is always the case, the rise of wages did not coincide with this inflation, and when they did rise they did not do so in a fair proportion. The necessaries of life rose in proportion of one to two and one-half ; wages, when they finally rose, only in the proportion of one to one and one-half. When too late it was recognized that the issue of base money was the cause of dearth in the realm, and Latimer lamented the fact in his sermons. Meanwhile, the mischief had been done.

§ 5. **The confiscation of the gild lands**—What Henry did with his gains thus obtained by underhand robbery cannot be accurately discovered. But it soon went, for he again required a supply of money.

One other method of robbing the industrial classes still remained, and though Henry died, his ministers were not slow to take advantage of it. This step was the confiscation of the gild lands, planned by Henry VIII. but finally carried out by his son's guardian, Somerset. These lands had been acquired by the craft gilds both in town and country, partly by bequests from members, and partly by purchase from the funds of the gilds. The revenues of these lands were used for lending, without usury, to poorer members of the gilds, for apprenticing poor children, for widows' pensions, and, above all, for the relief of destitute members of the craft. Thus the labourer of that time had in the funds of the gild a kind of insurance money, while the gild itself fulfilled all the functions of a benefit society. Now, Henry VIII. got an Act passed for the confiscation of this and other property, but died before his scheme was carried out. It was then Somerset who procured the Act for perpetrating this offence—on the plea that these lands were associated with superstitious uses. Only the property of the London gilds was left untouched. The gilds had relieved pauperism in the Middle Ages, assisted in steadying the price of labour, and formed a centre for associations that fulfilled a want now only partially supplied by modern trade unions. Their abolition was a heavy blow to the English labourer.

Why this abolition was not more generally resented is a point of some interest. In the first place, the religious gilds and craft gilds were suppressed together on the plea above mentioned, and thus the difference between them was confused. Then again, the London gilds were spared because of their power, and thus it was made their interest not to interfere with the destruction of their provincial brethren. The nobles were bought off with presents gained from the funds of the gilds. Moreover, the *craft* gilds in the country towns were becoming close corporations, whose advantages were often monopolized by a few powerful members. This led, as we saw, to the manufacture of cloth being spread from the towns into industrial villages in the rural districts, where perhaps the mass of the population, not perceiving the full significance of the act, did not object to a measure which struck a blow at the town "mysteries." But, nevertheless, a great deal of discontent was aroused. Somerset became very unpopular, and insurrections broke out in many parts of the country, the most dangerous being in Cornwall, Devonshire, and in the West. They were caused not only by this spoliation but by agrarian discontent as well, but German and Italian mercenaries were introduced to put them down, and the protests of the people were everywhere choked in their blood.

§ 6. **The agrarian situation**—Such were the acts instigated or actually performed by that miserable monarch, whom nevertheless not a few people who write history seek to glorify. Possibly they do so in ignorance of the facts. This much is certain, that Henry VIII.'s reign witnessed growing pauperism in a country which had been a few years previously in a state of considerable material comfort. But before the close of his reign the labouring classes became impoverished, and tenant farmers were ruined with high rents exacted by the new nobility. The landed gentry and nobility, however, profited by this, and the merchants grew rich by their accumulations in foreign trade. But those who depended directly upon the cultivation of the land for their living suffered severely. There had been for some years past a steady rise in the price of wool for export, partly because the manufacturers of the Netherlands were so flourishing, and partly owing to a general rise of prices on the Continent since the great discoveries of silver in South America. Land-owners saw that it was more immediately profitable to turn their arable land into pasture, and go in for sheep farming on a large scale. They therefore did three things. They evicted as many as possible of their smaller tenants, and as Sir Thomas More tells us : " in this way it comes to pass that these poor wretches, men, women, husbands, orphans, parents with little children—all these emigrate from their native fields without knowing where to go." Then they raised the rents of the larger tenants, the yeomen and farmers, so that, as Latimer mentions, land for which his father had paid £3 or £4 a year, was in 1549 let at £16, almost to the ruin of the tenant. Thirdly, the large land-owners took from the poor their common lands by an unscrupulous system of enclosures. Wolsey had in vain endeavoured to stop their doing this, for he had sagacity enough to perceive how it would pauperize the labourers and others who had valuable rights in such land. But enclosures and evictions went on in spite of his enactments, with the inevitable result of social disorders.

The most important of these risings took place in Norfolk, where enclosures had been made upon a tremendous scale. Ket, a wealthy tanner of Norwich, took the lead (in 1549) of a large body of some 16,000 tenants and labourers, who demanded the abolition of the late enclosures and the reform of other local abuses. The Earl of Warwick defeated the petitioners in a battle, put down the rising, and hanged Ket at Norwich Castle. The farmers and peasantry were thus cowed into submission.

§ 7. **Other economic changes**—From these facts it became evident that the old mediæval industrial system was breaking up in England. The new life created by the Renaissance caused a keener and more eager spirit among all classes of men. Competition began to operate as a new force, and men made haste to grow rich. The merchants were becoming bolder and more enterprising in their ventures. The discoveries of America by Columbus (1492) and by Cabot (1497), and of the sea-route to India by Vasco da Gama (1498), had kindled a desire to share largely in the wealth of these newly accessible countries. At home the lords of the manors no longer remained in close personal relationships with their tenants. The tenants were no longer villeins, but were nominally independent, and had certain rights. But the lords of the manors had small respect for rights that were only guarded by custom; and evicted or oppressed their tenants to such an extent that multitudes of dispossessed and impoverished villagers flocked to the towns. In fact Sir Thomas More tells us that the tenants "were got rid of by fraud or force, or tired out by repeated wrongs into parting with their property."

Many labourers, too, could be found wandering from place to place, begging or robbing. The old steady village life, with its isolation and strong home ties, was undergoing a violent transition. Constant work and regular wages were becoming things of the past. The labourer's wages would not purchase the former quantity of provisions under the new high prices caused by the debasement of the currency, and the discoveries of silver from 1540–1600; for wages, though they ultimately follow prices, do so very slowly, and not always even then proportionately.

§ 8. **Summary of the changes of the sixteenth century**—Such were the events which caused so great an economic transition in this period. They resulted in the pauperization of a large portion of the working classes, and the impoverishment of the small farmers. On the other hand, the nobles and land-owners gained considerable wealth. The merchants also were exceedingly flourishing, and foreign trade was growing. In summing up, then, we may say that the suppression of the monasteries, and the creation of a new nobility from the adventurers of Henry VIII.'s court, who obtained most of the monastic wealth; the debasement of the coinage and the exaltation in prices, aided largely (1540–1600) by the discovery of new silver mines in South America; the rise in the price of wool both for export and home manufacture, coupled with the consequent increase in sheep farming and the practice of enclosure of land—all produced most important economic changes in the history of English labour and industry. To these we must add, towards the end of the sixteenth century, the great immigration of Flemings, chiefly after 1567, owing to the continual persecutions of Alva and other Spanish rulers. This gave a great impetus to English manufactures, its effects, however, being chiefly felt in the seventeenth century, when another immigration took place. Finally, in the sixteenth century were laid the foundations of our present commercial enterprise and maritime trade, by the voyages of Drake and other great sea-captains of Elizabeth's reign. Their expeditions, it is true, were mainly buccaneering exploits, but they created a spirit of maritime enterprise that bore good fruit in the following reigns. Nor indeed was trade even in the previous centuries entirely insignificant, but had considerably developed, as the following chapter will show.

CHAPTER II

THE GROWTH OF FOREIGN TRADE

§ 1. **The expansion of commerce. The new spirit**—Just as the beginning of the sixteenth century marks what may be called an economic revolution in the home industries of the country, so too it marks the beginning of international commerce upon the modern scale. The economic revolution, of which the new agricultural system and the practice of enclosures was the most striking feature, was a change from the old dependent, uncompetitive, and regulated industrial system, to one under which Capital and Labour grew up as separate forces in the form in which we recognize them now. Labour had become nominally independent after the Peasants' Revolt of 1381, and at the same time it consciously felt that it was in opposition to capitalist and land-owning interests. In its desire for freedom it had also begun to shake off even its self-imposed restrictions, and the power of the gilds had rapidly waned. A new and eager spirit came with the Renaissance and the Reformation, a spirit which on the economic side showed itself in the development of competition, the shaking off of old restraints, and in more daring and far-seeing enterprises. Especially was this the case among the merchants, fired as they were by the great discoveries of the latter end of the fifteenth century, and hence we notice, throughout the sixteenth century and especially at its close, that our foreign trade becomes more extensive than it had ever been before, and the foundations of our present international commerce were securely laid.

§ 2. **Foreign trade in the fifteenth century**—At this point we must look back for a moment at our foreign trade before this new epoch. Although our enterprises were by no means large, there was yet a fairly considerable trade done with the countries in the west of Europe—*i.e.* France, Spain, and the Baltic lands, and especially with the Low Countries. As England was then almost entirely an agricultural country, our chief export was wool for the Flemish looms to work up ; but there was also other agricultural produce exported ; and likewise some mineral products. In fact England supplied nearly all Western Europe with two most important metals, tin and lead ; the former coming chiefly from Cornwall and the latter from Derbyshire, though in neither case exclusively from those counties. Bodmin was, however, the staple town for the export of tin. Our huge mineral wealth in coal and iron was hardly yet touched, even for home use, and none was exported. Our imports were numerous and varied, their number being balanced, as they must always be, by the greater bulk and value of our exports of wool and lead.

A fair amount of trade was done with Portugal and Spain, which sent us iron and war-horses ; Gascony and other parts of France sent their wines ; rich velvets, linens, and fine cloths were imported from Ghent, Liège, Bruges, and other Flemish manufacturing towns. The ships of the Hanse merchants brought herrings, wax, timber, fur and amber from the Baltic countries ; and Genoese traders came with silks and velvets and glass of Italy. And all met one another, as we saw before, in the great fairs, as at Stourbridge, or in the great trading centre of the Western world, London.

§ 3. **The Venetian fleet**—But our most important trade in the fourteenth and fifteenth centuries centred round the annual visit of the Venetian fleet to the southern shores of England. This was a great company of trading vessels, which left Venice every year upon a visit to England and Flanders.[1] Our English vessels did not at this time venture into the Mediterranean, and so all the stores of the Southern European countries, and more especially the treasures of the East, came to us through the agency of Venice. Laden with silks, satins, fine damasks and cottons, and other then costly garments, together with rare Eastern spices and precious stones, camphor and saffron, this fleet sailed slowly along the shores of the Mediterranean, trading at the ports of Italy, South France and Spain, till it passed through the Straits of Gibraltar, and at length came up the Channel, and

[1] Hence the Venetians themselves called it the "Flanders fleet."

reached our southern ports. When it had reached the Downs, the fleet broke up for a time, some vessels putting in at Sandwich, Rye, and other towns, and a large number stopping at Southampton. Others went on to Flanders. Several days, sometimes weeks, were spent in exchanging their valuable cargoes for English goods, chiefly wool, the balance being paid over in gold, and then the various portions of the great fleet would reunite again, and set sail for Venice, from which they were often absent for nearly a twelvemonth. This annual visit was very convenient for English traders, before our own merchants ventured far away from our coasts. But it is a sign of the increased commercial enterprise of England in the sixteenth century that this visit then became unprofitable, and the last time the Venetian fleet came to our shores was in 1587.

§ 4. **The Hanseatic League's station in London**—While our commerce was, however, not yet so greatly developed, there existed another important institution carried on by foreign merchants, this time from Germany. The Hanse, or Hanseatic League, was started in the twelfth century by some of the leading trading towns of Germany, such as Hamburg and Lübeck, and after a time these towns formed themselves into a League for mutual protection among the constant Continental wars, and became a sort of republic (1241). In another century (by 1360) it had grown so large and powerful that ninety cities belonged to the confederacy, and it had branches or depots in every important town of Northern Europe. Of course there was also a branch at London, in the "Steelyard," on which spot the Cannon Street Station now stands. This branch had existed from very early times, and a warehouse was there in which the German merchants stored their goods. In Richard II.'s time this building was enlarged, and so it was again in the reign of Edward IV. Round it dwelt the foreign merchants who formed quite a little colony in the very heart of mediæval London. Here they held a kind of chamber of commerce, presided over by an alderman, with two co-assessors, and nine council-men, and meeting regularly on Wednesday mornings in every week. The Steelyard colony existed for some hundreds of years, and taught many valuable commercial lessons to our English merchants. It provided for us a regular supply of the produce of Russia, Germany, and Norway, especially timber and naval stores, and also corn when our English harvest fell short. But as our own merchants grew more prosperous and their commerce extended, they became jealous of the German colony. Attacks were made upon it by London mobs, and Edward VI. actually rescinded its charter. That was the beginning of the end. Mary restored it for a time, but towards the close of Elizabeth's reign (1597) it was finally abolished. This, too, was another sign of the growth of our own foreign trade.

§ 5. **Our trade with Flanders. Antwerp in the fifteenth and sixteenth centuries**—We have mentioned before how the eastern ports and harbours of England used to swarm with small, light craft that plied all the summer through between our own country and Flanders. We have seen too that this continuous trade was due to the fact that we supplied the Flemish looms with wool. Up to the fifteenth century the great Flemish emporium, to which our English ships plied, was Bruges, but in the sixteenth century this town quite lost its former glory, and Antwerp took its place. The change was due to the action of Maximilian, the Emperor of Germany, to whom Henry VIII. was allied, and who, in revenge for a rebellion in which Ghent and Bruges took part, caused the canal which connected Bruges with the sea to be blocked up at Sluys (1482), and thus English and other ships were compelled to direct their course to Antwerp, which then became a great and flourishing port. Antwerp remained without a rival till near the close of the sixteenth century, and every nation had its representatives there. Our own consul, to use a modern term, was, at the close of the fifteenth century, Sir Richard Gresham ; and later, in the reign of Henry VIII., his celebrated son, the financier and economist, Sir Thomas Gresham. The fact of our having these representatives there is again a proof of the growth of trade in the sixteenth century. An Italian author, Ludovico Guicciardini (who died in 1589), gives a very precise account of our own commerce with Antwerp at this period, and it is interesting to note how varied our commerce has by this time become. This is what he says as to our *imports* : "To England Antwerp sends jewels, precious stones, silver bullion, quicksilver, wrought silks, gold and silver cloth and thread, camlets, grograms, spices, drugs, sugar, cotton, cummin, linens fine and coarse, serges, tapestry, madder, hops in great quantities, glass, salt, fish, metallic and other merceries of all sorts ; arms of all kinds, ammunition for war, and household furniture." As to our *exports* he tells us : "From England Antwerp receives vast quantities of coarse and fine draperies, fringes and all other things of that kind to a great value ; the finest wool ; excellent saffron, but in small quantities ; much lead and tin ; sheep and rabbit skins without number, and various other sorts of the fine peltry (*i.e.* skins) and leather ; beer, cheese, and other provisions in great quantities ; also Malmsey wines, which the English import from Candia. It is marvellous to think of the vast quantity of drapery sent by the English into the Netherlands."

This list is sufficient to show an extensive trade, and we shall comment upon one or two items of it in the next chapter. Here we need only remark upon the great growth of English manufactures of cloth.

§ 6. **The decay of Antwerp and rise of London as the Western emporium**—But the prosperity of Antwerp did not last quite a century. Like all Flemish towns it suffered severely under the Spanish invasion, and the persecutions of the notorious Alva. In 1567 it was ruinously sacked, and its commerce was forced into new channels, and the disaster was completed by the sacking of the town again in 1585. Antwerp's ruin was London's gain. Even in 1567, at the time of the first sacking, many Protestant Flemish merchants fled to England, where, as Sir Thomas Gresham promised them, they found peace and welcome, and in their turn gave a great impulse to English commercial prosperity. Throughout Elizabeth's reign, in fact, there was a continual influx of Protestant refugees to our shores, and Elizabeth and her statesmen had the sagacity to encourage these industrious and wealthy immigrants. Besides aiding our manufactures, as we shall see later, they aided our commerce. In 1588 there were 38 Flemish merchants established in London, who subscribed £5000 towards the defence of England against the Spanish Armada. The greatness of Antwerp was transferred to London, and although Amsterdam also gained additional importance in Holland, London now took the foremost position as the general mart of Europe, where the new treasures of the two Americas were found side by side with the products of Europe and the East.

§ 7. **The merchants and sea-captains of the Elizabethan age in the New World**—It is thus of interest to note how the great Reformation conflict between Roman Catholic and Protestant in Europe resulted in the commercial greatness of England. Interesting, also, is the story of the expansion of commerce in the New World, owing to the attacks of the great old sea-captains, Drake, Frobisher, and Raleigh, upon the huge Catholic power of Spain. These attacks were perhaps not much more than buccaneering exploits, but the leaders of them firmly believed that they were doing a good service to the cause of Protestantism and freedom by wounding Spain wherever they could. And possibly they were right. Their wondrous voyages stimulated others, likewise, to set out on far and venturesome expeditions. Men dreamt of a northern passage to India, and although Willoughby's expedition failed, one of his ships under Richard Chancellor reached Archangel, and thus opened up a direct trade with Russia; so that in 1554 a company was formed specially for this trade. It was, too, in Elizabeth's reign that the merchants of Southampton entered upon the trade with the coast of Guinea, and gained much wealth from its gold-dust and ivory. Sir John Hawkins engaged in the slave-trade between Africa and the new fields of labour in America. Bristol fishermen sailed across the dreaded Atlantic to the cod-fisheries off Newfoundland, and at the close of Elizabeth's reign English ships began to rival the Portuguese in the Polar whale-fisheries.

This reign witnessed also the rise of the great commercial Companies. The company of Merchant Adventurers had indeed existed since Henry VII.'s time, having been formed in imitation of the Hanseatic League. The Russian Company of 1554 was formed upon the model of this earlier company; and then came the foundation of the great East India Company. It was due to the results of Drake's far-famed voyage round the world, which took three years, 1577–80. Shortly after his return it was proposed to found " a company for such as trade beyond the equinoctial line," but a long delay took place, and finally a company was incorporated for the more definite object of trading with the East Indies. The date of this famous incorporation was 1600, and in 1601 Captain Lancaster made the first regular trading voyage on its behalf. To this modest beginning we owe our present Indian Empire.

§ 8. **Remarks on the signs and causes of the expansion of trade**—Now, if we look at the broad features that mark the growth of sixteenth century trade, we shall see that it was closely connected with England's decision to abide by the Protestant cause. It was that which won her the friendship of the Flemish merchants ; it was the religious disturbances in Flanders that gained for London the commercial supremacy of Europe ; it was our quarrel with Roman Catholic Spain that inspired the voyages of Drake and Hawkins, and thus caused others to venture forth into new and perilous seas, over which in course of time the English merchants sailed almost without a rival. And, as we have shown, the signs of the expansion of England are seen in the fall of the Hanse settlement in London, and the stoppage of the visits of the Venetian fleet. On the other hand the rapid growth of the port of Bristol in the west witnessed to fresh trade with the New World ; and the rise of Boston and Hull [1] on the east coast is significant as showing the development of our Northern and Baltic trade, even to the extent of rivalling the great Hanse towns. A great stimulus had arisen, and England was now taking a leading position among the nations of the world. It is now our business to survey it as it existed in the time of Elizabeth.

[1] They had always been important (cf. p. 64).

CHAPTER III

ELIZABETHAN ENGLAND

§ 1. **Prosperity and pauperism**—The reign of Elizabeth is generally regarded as prosperous, and so upon the whole it was. But she had come to the throne with a legacy of pauperism from her father, Henry VIII., and from her father's counsellors, who guided her weak brother, Edward VI. Nor had Mary helped to alleviate it. Social discontent was at Elizabeth's accession prevalent, and it is to her credit as a sovereign that at her death danger from that source had passed away. This was partly due to the growth of wealth and industry throughout the kingdom, to the great gains of our foreign trade, and to the rapid expansion of our manufactures. But pauperism was now a permanent evil, and legal measures had to be taken for its relief. One abiding cause of it was the persistent enclosures which still went on, together with the new developments in agriculture. Nevertheless, before the close of her reign the bulk of the people became contented and comfortable, owing to the prolonged peace which prevailed. The merchants and landed gentry were rich; the farmers and master-manufacturers were prosperous; even the artisans and labourers were not hopelessly poor, though to call them well-off would be a misstatement. We may now see how the wealth of the first two classes was produced.

§ 2. **The growth of manufactures**—The economic transition before alluded to (p. 55), by which England developed from a wool-exporting into a wool-manufacturing country, had in Elizabeth's reign almost been completed.

The woollen manufacture had become an important element in the national wealth. England no longer sent her wool to be manufactured in Flanders, although a good deal of it was dyed there. It was now worked up at home, and the manufacturing population was not confined to the towns only, but spread all over the country ; and both spinning and weaving afforded direct employment for an increasing number of workmen, while even in agricultural villages it was a frequent bye-industry. The worsted trade, of which Norwich was still the centre, spread over all the Eastern counties. The broad-cloths of the West of England took the highest place among English woollen stuffs. Even the North, which had lagged so far behind the South in industrial development, ever since the harrying it underwent at the hands of William the Norman, began now to show signs of activity and new life. It had, in this period, developed special manufactures of its own, and Manchester friezes, York coverlets, and Halifax cloth now held their own amongst the other manufactures of the country.

§ 3. **Monopolies of manufacturing towns**—One important sign of the growth of manufactures is seen in the fruitless attempts made in the sixteenth century to confine a particular manufacture to a particular town. This is a sure sign that the manufacture of that article was increasing in country districts, and that competition was operating in a new and unexpected way upon the older industries. An example of this may be seen in the monopoly granted by Parliament in Henry VIII.'s reign (1530) to Bridport in Dorsetshire, "for the making of cables, hawsers, ropes, and all other tackling." This monopoly was granted upon the complaint made by the citizens of Bridport, that their town "was like to be utterly decayed," owing to the competition of "the people of the adjacent parts," who were therefore by this monopoly forbidden to make any sort of rope. The only result of this measure, however, was to transfer the rope-making industry from Dorset to Yorkshire, and Bridport was in a worse plight than before.

In the same reign (1534), the inhabitants of Worcester, Evesham, Droitwich, Kidderminster, and Bromsgrove, then the only towns in Worcestershire, complained that "divers persons *dwelling in the hamlets, thorps, and villages* of the county made all manner of cloths, and exercised shearing, fulling, and weaving within their own houses, to the great depopulation of the city and towns." A monopoly was granted to the towns, the only result of which was that they became worse off than before, a great portion of the local industry being transferred to Leeds. A little later (1544) the citizens of York complain of the competition of "sundry evil-disposed persons and apprentices," who had "withdrawn themselves out of the city into the country," and competed with York in the manufacture of coverlets and blanketings. York got a monopoly, but her manufactures gained nothing thereby. Again, in 1552 Edward VI. enacted that the manufacture of hats, coverlets, and diapers should be confined to Norwich and the market towns of Norfolk. Elizabeth granted numerous *trading* monopolies [1] for the sale of special articles, but the monopoly system was opposed to the new competitive spirit of the age. In 1601 a great many of the most obnoxious were withdrawn, and by that time few remained imposed upon the manufacture of goods. The above illustrations, however, are interesting as showing the growth of manufactures in all parts of the kingdom, and in rural districts (cf. p. 65).

[1] See note 11*a*, p. 246, on Monopolies.

They are useful also as glaring instances of the folly of protective enactments.

§ 4. **Our exports of manufactures**—Besides these monopolies we have ample evidence of the growth of our cloth manufactures in the statements made by Ludovico Guicciardini (1523–89), as to our exports to Antwerp. "It is marvellous," he says, "to think of the vast quantity of drapery sent by the English into the Netherlands, being undoubtedly one year with another above 200,000 pieces of all kinds, which, at the most moderate rate of 25 crowns per piece, is 5,000,000 crowns, so that these and other merchandise brought by the English to us, or carried from us to them, may make the annual amount to more than 12,000,000 crowns," which is equivalent to some £2,400,000. One great cause of our progress in manufactures was the immigration of persecuted Dutch and Flemish Protestants, previously mentioned, which formed so important a feature in the new growth of manufactures and agriculture in Elizabethan England.

§ 5. **The Flemish immigration in this reign**—This influx of foreign manufacturers and workmen began to occur soon after Elizabeth's accession, when the death of Mary had relieved men from the fear of Romish persecution. A numerous body of Flemings came over in 1561, and starting from Deal, spread to Sandwich, Rye, and other parts of Kent. Another body settled in Yarmouth, and over Norfolk generally. In 1570 there were 4000 natives of the Netherlands in Norwich alone. And after the sack of Antwerp in 1585, the immigration largely increased. The new arrivals introduced or improved many manufactures, such as those of cutlery, clock-making, hats, and pottery. But the greatest improvements they made were in weaving and lace-making. They greatly developed "every sort of workmanship in wool and flax."

The lace manufacture was introduced by refugees from Alençon and Valenciennes into Cranfield (Beds), and from that town it extended to Buckinghamshire, Oxfordshire, and Northamptonshire; while other immigrants founded the manufacture of the well-known Honiton lace in Devon. It is interesting thus to notice how much we owed to foreign teachers in earlier times, for the reigns of Edward III., Elizabeth, and later of Charles II. were all signalized by large influxes of people from the Low Countries, bringing with them increased skill, and often considerable capital.

An interesting testimony to the influence of these refugees is afforded by Harrison in his *Description of England* (in the time of Elizabeth). He says about our wool: " In time past the use of this commodity consisted for the most part in cloth and woolsteds; but now, *by means of strangers succoured here from domestic persecution*, the same hath been employed unto sundry other uses; as mockados, bays, vellures, grograines, &c., whereby the makers have reaped no small commodity."

§ 6. **Agriculture**—The growth of our manufactures helped of course to promote sheep farming, not only on the part of great land-owners, but even of ordinary moderate farmers. Upon this point also Harrison mentions an important fact: " And there is never an husbandman (for now I speak not of our great sheep-masters, of whom some one man hath 20,000) but hath more or less of this cattle (sheep) feeding on his fallows and short grounds, which yield the finer fleece." Besides sheep farming, however, which had long since risen into importance, our agriculture had improved in several respects. Here foreign influence is again visible. Already a change in the mode of cultivation had been brought about, not so great as that which took place in the two succeeding centuries, but still quite perceptible. A larger capital was brought to bear upon the land, the breed of horses and cattle was improved, and more intelligent use was made of manure and dressings. It was said that one acre under the new system produced as much as two did under the old. In addition to these improvements, the coming of the Flemings and Dutch introduced several new vegetables. The refugees cultivated in their gardens, carrots, celery, and cabbages, which were previously either unknown or very scarce in this country. The most important service to agriculture, however, was the introduction of the hop, which is said to have been brought to England by some Flemish, as early as 1524, and later in the century, in Elizabeth's reign, the hop-gardens of Kent had already become famous, and have remained so ever since. The introduction of hops of course led the way to a better method of brewing beer, and from this time forward beer became a national beverage.[1]

§ 7. **Social comforts**—All this increase of the national wealth, in commerce, manufactures, and agriculture, produced important changes in the mode of living. The standard of comfort became higher. Food became more wholesome. As agriculture improved, and animals could be kept through the winter with greater ease, salt meat and salt fish no longer formed the staple food of the lower classes for half the year. Brickmaking had been rediscovered about 1450; and by the time of Elizabeth the wooden, or wattled houses (p. 19) had generally been replaced, at least among all but the poorest class, with dwellings of brick and stone. The introduction of chimneys and the lavish use of glass also helped to im-

[1] The malt liquor, of course, had been in general use at a much earlier period.

prove the people's dwellings; and indeed the houses of the rich merchants, or the lords of the manors, were now quite luxuriously furnished. Carpets had superseded the old filthy flooring of rushes; pillows and cushions were found in all decent houses; and the quantity of carved woodwork of this period shows that men cared for something more than mere utility in their surroundings. The lavishness of new wealth was seen, too, in a certain love of display, of colour, of "purple and fine linen," which characterizes the dress of the Elizabethan age. The old sober life and thought of mediæval England had been entirely revolutionized by the sudden opening of the almost fabulous glories of the New World, and men revelled joyously in the new prospects of the wealth of the wondrous West. But yet there were the seeds of pauperism in the land, and all the wealth of the merchants and the adventurers of Elizabethan England did not prevent the sure and inevitable Nemesis that followed upon the crimes and follies of Elizabeth's father.

§ 8. **The condition of the labourers**—For it is impossible, in glancing at the condition of labour in the days of Elizabeth, to forget the disastrous economic changes wrought by the criminal follies of Henry VIII. and his followers since the earlier days of the fifteenth century. Compared with the fifteenth century, the poverty of the wage-earners in Elizabeth's reign was great indeed, though even then not so bad as it subsequently became. But the whole of the next two centuries show a steady deterioration in the lot of the English labourer and artisan. Of course the condition of labour will be best seen by taking examples of the wages then given. In Elizabeth's reign, then, we may reckon the yearly wages of an agricultural labourer at about £8, 4*s.*, and the cost of living, which now included house rent, formerly unknown, at £8, thus leaving a very narrow margin for contingencies. Daily wages were (in 1564)—for artisans, *8d.* a day in winter and *9d.* in summer; for labourers, *6d.* in winter and *7d.* in summer, and in harvest-time occasionally *8d.* or even *10d.* This is not very much more than the wages paid at the close of the fifteenth century (viz. artisans *3s.* a week, and labourers *2s.*), but the price of food had risen almost to three times the old average.

§ 9. **Assessment of wages by justices. The first Poor Law**—Wages in husbandry and in handicrafts were now fixed, under the statute 5 Elizabeth, cap. 4 (1563),[1] by the justices in quarter sessions, and of course these employers of labour would hardly fix an unnecessarily high rate of wages; and, what is more, wages did actually conform to their assessments in spite of the continual rise in the price of the necessaries of life. It is not surprising that under these conditions the problem of pauperism in England speedily took a very pronounced form. Even in 1541, under Henry VIII., it was found that some system of relief was necessary; but a system of voluntary contributions was for a time sufficient to meet the difficulty. But in Edward VI.'s reign pauperism began to increase alarmingly, though now we see that it was only natural; and finally Elizabeth found it necessary to institute a regular system of poor-law relief. In 1601, therefore, by Act 43 Elizabeth, cap. 3, it was legally enacted that all property should be duly assessed by regular assessors, in order that rates might be levied for the relief of pauperism. After a few renewals this law was made permanent in Charles I.'s reign (1641), and continued legally in force till 1812; and its general principles lasted till 1835. The effect of this poor law

[1] Commonly known as the *Act of Apprenticeship* (cf. note 12, p. 247).

was to keep the wages of labour at the very lowest possible level, for now the employers (chiefly, at that time, the land-owners) knew that if a labourer's wages could not maintain him, he would have to be relieved from the rates. In other words, part of the labourers' wages would be, and was, paid by the general public, and thus expense would be saved to individual employers. This state of things did not, perhaps, ensue immediately upon the passing of this law, but became more common later. The results of the system were seen more clearly in the seventeenth and eighteenth centuries, to which we shall subsequently refer.[1]

§ 10. **Population**—The marked improvement in agriculture and the increase of wealth brought with them, at the close of the sixteenth century, an equally marked increase of population. We saw that at the time of Domesday the population of England was under two millions. When the poll-tax of 1377 was levied, in the last year of Edward III.'s reign, it had not much increased, being at most not more than two and a quarter millions, according to careful calculations based upon the returns of this tax. But by the end of Elizabeth's reign it had rapidly risen to some 5,000,000 souls, at which figure it remained for some hundred and fifty years longer. The bulk of the population was still in the southern half of the country, although the north was now becoming more prosperous, owing to the extension of manufactures. It will be seen that England was by no means overcrowded, and yet people were found who complained of the increase of population. William Harrison in his *Description of England* (written between 1577–87) remarks: "Some also do grudge at the great increase of people in these days, thinking a necessary brood of cattle far better than

[1] See note 12, p. 247, on *Intention of Act*.

a superfluous augmentation of mankind. But," he adds severely, "I can liken such men best unto the Pope or the Devil," and adds that in case of invasion they will find "that a wall of men is far better than stacks of corn and bags of money." Even without the fear of invasion before our eyes, it is well for us to-day not to forget this latter sentence in the modern international race for wealth.

CHAPTER IV

PROGRESS OF AGRICULTURE IN THE SEVENTEENTH AND EIGHTEENTH CENTURIES

§ 1. **Résumé of progress since thirteenth century**—It will be remembered that great agricultural changes had taken place since Henry III.'s reign. For a century or so after his death (1272) the land-owner was also a cultivator, living upon his land and owning a large amount of capital in the form of stock, which he let out under the stock and land lease system. But after the Great Plague (1348) this method of cultivation by capitalist land-owners ceased, except in the one case of sheep farming; the land-owner became generally a mere rent receiver; and agriculture consequently suffered. Marling, for instance, fell into disuse, and the breed of sheep, it is said, deteriorated somewhat. The great feature of the change was the transformation of large tracts of arable land into pasture for sheep, and the growth of enclosures for the sake of the same animal. The landlords rapidly proceeded to raise their rents, till, in the sixteenth century, extortionate renting became so common that Bishop Latimer, and Fitzherbert, the author of a useful work on surveying, complained about it both in sermons and other writings. Hence English agriculture did not materially improve between the days of Henry III. and of Elizabeth. But in this queen's reign, as we saw, several improvements were made under the influence of foreign refugees. For the inhabitants of the Low Countries and Holland have been our pioneers not only in commerce and finance, but in agriculture also. It was now these people who introduced into England the cultivation of artificial grasses and of winter roots, the want of which, it will be remembered, greatly embarrassed the English farmer in the mediæval winter. The introduction of hops also was of great importance.

§ 2. **Progress in James I.'s reign. Influence of landlords**—Of course the greatest industrial progress of this period was made in the direction of foreign trade, and in James's reign progress in agriculture was slow as compared with that in commerce, but it was substantial—substantial enough, at any rate, for the landlords to exact an increased competitive rent, as we know from Norden's work, *The Surveyor's Dialogue* (1607). It was even complained that the actions of the landlords tended to discourage progress, for when a tenant wished to renew a lease he was threatened with dispossession if he did not pay an increased rent for the very improvements he had made himself. However, from the facts given by Norden, and also by another writer—Markham, the author of *The English Husbandman* (1613)—it is evident that there was considerable improvement, development, and variety now shown in English agriculture. The special characteristic feature of the seventeenth century is the utilization of the fallow for roots, though these had been known in gardens in the previous century. Land was still largely cultivated in common fields, and was, of course, much subdivided. The most fertile land was to be found in Huntingdon, Bedford, and Cambridge shires, the next best being in Northampton, Kent, Essex, Berkshire, and Hertfordshire.

§ 3. **Writers on agriculture. Improvements. Game**—Oxen were still preferred to horses; but a noticeable improvement is the attention now paid to the various kinds of manures, on which subject Markham was the first to write specially. The fact that agriculture was now made the topic of various treatises proves that important development was taking place. Besides the works already mentioned, we have the *Systema Agriculturæ* by Worridge, a farmer of Hampshire, the second edition of which appeared in 1675. He is a strong advocate of enclosures, as against the old common field system, on the plea that the former is more conducive to high farming; but he also is in favour of small enclosed farms. Though at first local and somewhat spasmodic, and hindered by the landlord's power of appropriating the results of increased skill on the part of the tenant, under the head of "indestructible powers of the soil," yet the progress made was sufficient to double the population of England. A curious fact in the agriculture of the seventeenth century may be here mentioned; I mean the existence of a very large amount of waste land, and the use made of it for purposes of breeding game. At that time it is evident that killing game was not the exclusive right of the land-owners, but was a common privilege. Large quantities of game were sold, and at a cheap price, and "fowling" must evidently have been an important item in the farmer's means of livelihood.

§ 4. **Drainage of the fens**—A most important feature in the development of agriculture in the Eastern counties was the drainage of the fens—*i.e.* all that large district which extends inward from the Wash into the counties of Lincoln, Cambridge, Northampton, Huntingdon, Norfolk and Suffolk. This district had been reclaimed by the Romans, and had been then a fertile country. But in the time of the Domesday Book it was once again a mere marsh, owing to incursions of the sea, which the English at that time had not the ability to prevent. Although even in 1436, and subsequently, partial attempts had been made to reclaim this vast area, the first effectual effort was begun only in 1634, by the Earl of Bedford, who got 95,000 acres of the reclaimed land as a reward for his undertaking. The contract was fulfilled in 1649, and a corporation was formed to manage the "Bedford level," as it was now called, in 1688. The reclaiming of so much land naturally increased the prosperity of the counties in which it stood, and their agriculture flourished considerably in consequence, Bedfordshire for instance being now the most exclusively agricultural county in the kingdom.

§ 5. **Rise of price of corn, and of rent**—The price of corn, meanwhile, was now steadily rising. From 1401 to 1540—*i.e.* before the rise in prices and the debasement of the coinages—the average price had been six shillings per quarter; after prices had recovered from their inflation and settled down to a general average once more, taking the price from 1603 to 1702, corn was forty-one shillings per quarter. The average produce had apparently declined since the fifteenth and before the improvements of the seventeenth century. In the former period it was about twelve bushels per acre, and in the fourteenth century eleven bushels; but Gregory King, writing in the seventeenth century, only gives ten bushels as the average of his time. His estimate, however, is doubted. At the same time, rent had risen from the sixpence per acre of the fifteenth century to four shillings, according to Professor Rogers, or even 5*s*. 6*d*. according to King, who says the gains of the farmer of his time are very small, and that rents were more than doubled between 1600 and 1699. We will reserve the topic of the rise of rent, however, for a separate section, and keep to the agricultural developments of the period.

§ 6. **Special features of the eighteenth century. Popularity of agriculture**—As the use of winter roots had been the special feature of the seventeenth century, so the feature of the eighteenth was the extension of artificial pasture and the increased use of clover, sainfoin, and rye-grass ; not, of course, that these had been hitherto unknown, but now their seeds are regularly bought and used by any farmer who knew his business. At first, like all other processes of agriculture, the development was very slow and gradual, but it went on steadily nevertheless. A great stimulus to progress was given by the fact that the English gentlemen of the eighteenth century developed quite a passion for agriculture as a hobby, and it became a fashionable pursuit for all people of any means, citizens and professional men joining in it as a kind of bye-industry, as well as farmers and land-owners who made it their business. Arthur Young, the great agricultural writer of this century, declares that "the farming tribe is now made up of all classes, from a duke to an apprentice." But two important mistakes were made in the eighteenth century, and they have not ceased to exist in the nineteenth, causing very largely the distress under which English agriculture has for some time been labouring. They are the mistakes of occupying too much land with insufficient capital, and of not keeping regular and detailed accounts. Still, between 1720 and 1760, progress was very rapid, and noble land-owners made great efforts to improve their estates, in order thereby to raise their rents and increase their profits, in the hope of outdoing the great merchant princes who had now appeared upon the scene. They thus became in a way the pioneers of agricultural progress, the principal result of their efforts being seen in the increased number and quality of the stock now kept on farms.

§ 7. **Improvements of cattle, and in the productiveness of land. Statistics**—The extended cultivation of winter roots, clover, and other grasses, naturally made it far easier for the farmer to feed his animals in the winter; and the improvement in stock followed closely upon the improvement in fodder. The abundance of stock, too, had again a beneficial result in the increased qualities of manure produced, and the utilization of this fertilizer was scientifically developed. The useful, though costly, process of marling was again revived, and was advocated by Arthur Young; soils were also treated with clay, chalk, or lime. So great was the improvement thus made, that the productiveness of land in the eighteenth century rose to four times that of the thirteenth century, when five bushels or eight bushels of corn per acre was the average. Stock, also, was similarly improved; an eighteenth century fatted ox often weighed 1200 lbs., while hitherto, from the fourteenth to the end of the seventeenth century, the weight had not been usually much above 400 lbs. The weight of the fleece of sheep had also increased quite four times. Population being even then small, a considerable quantity of corn was exported, the British farmer being also protected from foreign competition by the corn laws (made in Charles II.'s reign, 1661 and 1664), forbidding importation of corn, except when it rose to famine prices. Young estimated the acreage of the country at 32,000,000 acres (King put it at 22,000,000 in the seventeenth century); its value (at thirty-three and one-half years' purchase) was, says Young, £536,000,000. The value of stock he places at nearly £110,000,000, and estimates the wheat and rye crop at over 9,000,000 quarters per annum, barley at 11,500,000 quarters, and oats at 10,250,000 quarters. The rent of land had risen to nearly ten shillings an acre.

§ 8. **Wrong done to small land-owners by the Statute of Frauds**—The development and success of English agriculture, from 1700 to 1765 or 1770, was thus remarkable and extensive; but it was not effected without considerable economic changes and great and unnecessary suffering among two important classes of the population—the yeomen or small freeholders, and the agricultural labourers. The decay of the yeomanry, indeed, forms a sad interlude in the growing prosperity of the country. The position of many small land-owners had been greatly and disastrously affected by the Statute of Frauds, passed in the time of Charles II. By this extraordinary and high-handed Act it was decreed that after July 24th, 1677, all interests in land whatsoever, if created by any other process except by deed, should be treated as tenancies at will only, any law or usage to the contrary notwithstanding. The intention, apparently, of those who passed this law—an intention which resulted successfully—was to extinguish all those numerous small freeholders who had no written evidence to prove that they held their lands, as they had done for centuries, on condition of paying a small fixed and customary rent. This Act certainly succeeded in dispossessing many of the class at which it was aimed; but there were yet a certain number against whom it was inoperative; hence, at the end of the seventeenth century, twenty years or so after this Act, Gregory King is able to estimate that there were 180,000 freeholders in England, including, of course, the larger owners. But by the time of Arthur Young these also had disappeared, or at least were rapidly disappearing, and he sincerely regrets "to see their lands now in the hands of monopolizing lords."

§ 9. **Causes of the decay of the yeomanry**—The cause was partly political and partly social. After the revolution of 1688, the landed gentry became politically and socially supreme, and any successful merchant prince—and these were not few—who wished to gain a footing sought, in the first place, to imitate them by becoming a great land-owner; hence it became quite a policy to buy out the smaller farmers, and they were often practically compelled to sell their holdings. At the same time, the custom of primogeniture and strict settlements prevented land from being much subdivided, so that small or divided estates never came into the market for the smaller freeholders to buy. It is also certain that this result was accelerated by the fact that small farms no longer paid under the old system of agriculture, and the new system involved an outlay that the yeoman could not afford. Farming on a large scale became more necessary, and this again assisted in extinguishing the smaller men, for large enclosures were made by the landed gentry in spite of feeble opposition from the yeomen, who, however, could rarely afford to pay the law costs necessary to put a stop to the encroachments of their greater neighbours. Thus the yeomen lost their rights in the common lands, and at the same time the new agriculture involved a breaking up of the old common field system, which could not possibly hold its own against the modern improvements.

§ 10. **Great increase of enclosures**—The abolition of

the old system was necessary, but the manner in which it was carried out was disastrous. The enclosures of the landed gentry were often carried on with little regard to the interests of the smaller tenants and freeholders, who, in fact, suffered greatly; and in this present age English agriculture is, in a large measure, still feeling the subsequent effects of the change, while many people are advocating a partial return to small holdings, cultivated, however, with the improved experience given by modern agricultural progress. Apparently, this was not the first occasion on which the land-owners had made enclosures and encroached upon the common lands of their poorer neighbours, and not merely upon the waste; but the rapidity and boldness of the enclosing operations in the eighteenth century far surpassed anything in previous times. Between 1710 and 1760, for instance, 334,974 acres were enclosed; and between 1760 and 1843 the number rose to 7,000,000.

§ 11. **Benefits of enclosures as compared with the old common fields**—The benefits of the enclosure system were, however, unmistakable, for the cultivation of common fields undei the old system was, as Arthur Young assures us, miserably poor. The arable land of each village under this system was still divided into three great strips, subdivided by "baulks" three yards wide. Every farmer would own one piece of land in each strip—probably more—and all alike were bound to follow the customary tillage; this was to leave one strip fallow every year, while on one of the other two wheat was always grown, the third being occupied by barley or oats, pease, or tares. The meadows, also, were still held in common, every man having his own plot up to hay harvest, after which the fences were thrown down, and all householders' cattle were allowed to graze on it freely, while for the next crop the plots were redistributed. Every farmer also had the right of pasture on the waste. This system produced results miserably inferior to those gained on enclosed lands, the crop of wheat in one instance being, according to Young, only seventeen or eighteen bushels per acre, as against twenty-six bushels on enclosures. Similarly, the fleece of sheep pastured on common fields weighed only 3½ lbs., as compared with 9 lbs. on enclosures. It is noticeable, too, that Kent, where much land had for a long time been enclosed and cultivated, was reckoned in Young's time the best cultivated and most fertile county in England. Norfolk, also, was pre-eminent for good husbandry, in its excellent rotation of crops and culture of clover, rye-grass, and winter roots, due, said Young, in 1770, "to the division of the county chiefly into large farms," and, it must be added, to unscrupulous enclosure.

§ 12. **The rise in rent**—The farmer himself, however, was heavily taxed for his land, and though the high prices he got for his corn up to the repeal of the corn laws enabled him to pay it, his rent was certainly at a very high figure. The rise had begun after the dissolution of the monasteries in the sixteenth century, though in that period the rise was slow. But Latimer asserts that his father only paid £3 or £4 for a holding which in the next generation was rented at £16, the increased figure being only partially accounted for by the general rise in prices. In the seventeenth century, according to King, rents were more than doubled, and the sixpence per acre of mediæval times must have seemed almost mythical. The Belvoir estate, the property of the Dukes of Rutland, who are spoken of as indulgent landlords, forms a good example of the rise of rent in the two following centuries. In 1692 land is found rented at 3*s.* 9¼*d.* an acre, and a little later at 4*s.* 1½*d.* By the year 1799 the same land had risen to 19*s.* 3¾*d.*, with a further rise in 1812 to 25*s.* 8¾*d.* In 1830 it was at 25*s.* 1¾*d.*, but in 1850 had risen to 38*s.* 8*d.*, that is about ten times the seventeenth century rent. This enormous rise was not by any means due solely to increase of skill in agricultural industry, but was largely derived from increased economy in production, or, in other words, from the oppression and degradation of the agricultural labourer.

§ 13. **The fall in wages**—This degradation was brought about by the system of assessment[1] of wages which we noticed in Elizabeth's reign, a system by which the labourer was forced by law to accept the wages which the justices (generally the landed proprietors, his employers) arranged to give him. It is not the business of an historian to make charges against a class, but to put facts in their due perspective. Therefore without comment upon the action of the justices in this matter I shall merely refer to one or two of these assessments and show their effect upon the condition of labour, especially of agricultural labour, which occupied more than one-third of the working classes. Speaking generally, we may quote Professor Rogers' remark, that "if we suppose the ordinary labourer to get 3*s.* 6*d.* a week throughout the year, by adding his harvest allowance to his winter wages, it would have taken him more than forty weeks to earn the provisions which in 1495 he could have got with fifteen weeks' labour, while the artisan would be obliged to have given thirty-two weeks' work for the same result." To give details, we may first quote, as an example, the Rutland magistrates' assessment, in April 1610. The wages of an ordinary agricultural labourer

[1] As to the alleged futility of these assessments see *Industry in England*, p. 257.

are put at *7d.* a day from Easter to Michaelmas, and at *6d.* from Michaelmas to Easter. Artisans get *10d.* or *9d.* in summer, and *8d.* in winter. Now, the price of food was 75 per cent. dearer than in 1564, while the rate of wages are about the same; and compared with (say) 1495, food was three, or even four, times dearer. Another assessment, in Essex in 1661, allows 1*s.* a day in winter, and 1*s.* 2*d.* in summer, for ordinary labour. But, in 1661, the price of wheat (70*s.* 6*d.* a quarter) was just double the price of 1610 (35*s.* 2½*d.*). The labourer was worse off than ever. Another typical assessment is that of Warwick, in 1684, when wages of labourers are fixed at *8d.* a day in summer, *7d.* in winter; of artisans at 1*s.* a day. At this period Professor Rogers reckons the yearly earnings of an artisan at £15, 13*s.*; of a farm labourer at £10, 8*s.* 8*d.*, exclusive of harvest work; while the cost of a year's stock of provisions was £14, 11*s.* 6*d.* It is true that at this period the labourer still possessed certain advantages, such as common rights, which, besides providing fuel, enabled them to keep cows and pigs and poultry on the waste. Their cottages, too, were often rent free, being built upon the waste, while each cottage, by the Act of Elizabeth, was supposed to have a piece of land attached to it, though this provision was frequently evaded. But yet it is evident that, even allowing for these privileges, which, after all, were now being rapidly curtailed, the ordinary agricultural labourer—that is, the mass of the wage-earning population—must have found it hard work to live decently. By the beginning of the eighteenth century his condition had sunk to one of great poverty. The ordinary peasant, in 1725, for instance, would not earn more than £13 or about £15 a year; artisans could not gain more than £15, 13*s.*; while the cost of the stock of provisions was £16, 2*s.* 3*d.* Thus the husbandman who, in 1495, could get a similar stock of food by fifteen weeks' work, and the artisan who could have earned it in ten weeks, could not feed himself in 1725 with a whole year's labour. His wages had to be supplemented out of the rates; and there was but little alteration in these rates till the middle of the eighteenth century. But about that time (1750) he had begun to share in the general prosperity caused by the success of the new agriculture and the growth of trade and manufactures. The evil, however, had been done, and although a short period of prosperity, chiefly due to the advance made by the new agriculture, cheered the labourer for a time, his condition after the Industrial Revolution again rapidly deteriorated, till we find him at the end of the eighteenth century and for some time afterwards in a condition of chronic misery.

CHAPTER V

COMMERCE AND WAR IN THE SEVENTEENTH AND EIGHTEENTH CENTURIES

§ 1. **England a commercial power**—In glancing over the progress of foreign trade in the time of Elizabeth, we noticed that our war with Spain was due to commercial as well as religious causes. The opening up of the New World made a struggle for power in the West almost inevitable among European nations; the new route to India *viâ* the Cape of Good Hope, discovered by Vasco da Gama, made another struggle for commercial supremacy as inevitable in the far East. In the reign of Henry VIII. we find, from one of his Statutes, that Malaga had been the farthest port to which at this time English seamen yet ventured. For a century or more after the discoveries of Columbus and da Gama, Spain and Portugal, and a little later on Holland, had practically a monopoly both of the Eastern and Western trade. But now a change had come. The Englishmen of the Elizabethan age cast off their fear of Spain, entered into rivalry with Holland, and finally made England the supreme commercial power of the modern world. The history of the seventeenth and eighteenth centuries is a continuous record of their struggles to attain this object.

§ 2. **The beginnings of the struggle with Spain**—In the last quarter of the sixteenth century Elizabeth had entered (1579) into an alliance, offensive and defensive, with Holland against Spain. The motive of the alliance was partly religious, but the shrewdness of the queen and her statesmen no doubt foresaw more than spiritual advantages to be gained thereby. After the alliance, Drake and the other great naval captains of that day began a system of buccaneering annoyances to Spanish commerce. The Spanish and Portuguese trade and factories in the East were considered the lawful prizes of the English and their allies the Dutch. The latter, as all know, were more successful at first than we were, and soon established an Oriental Empire in the Indian Archipelago. But at the very end of her reign England had prospered sufficiently for Elizabeth to grant charters to the Levant Company, and its far greater companion the East India Company. Then, when a fresh war with Spain was imminent, England wisely began to plant colonies in North America, at the suggestion of Sir Walter Raleigh; and after one or two other abortive attempts, Virginia was successfully founded by the London Company in 1609, and became a Crown colony in 1624.

After this, as every one knows, colonies grew rapidly on the strip of coast between the Alleghany Mountains and the Atlantic. Meanwhile, on the other side of the world the East India Company was slowly gaining ground, and founding English agencies or "factories," that of Surat (in 1612) being the most important. As yet we had not come into open conflict with Spain or Portugal; and indeed we owed the possession of Bombay to the marriage of Charles II. with Katherine of Braganza (1661). Then the company gained from Charles II. the important privilege of making peace or war on their own account. It had a good many foes to contend with, both among natives and European nations, among whom the French were as powerful as the Portuguese.

§ 3. **Cromwell's commercial wars**—The monopoly of Spain was first really attacked by Cromwell. James I. had been too timid to declare war, and Charles I. was too much in danger himself to think of trusting his subjects to support him if he did so. But Cromwell was supported both by the religious views of the Puritans and the desires of the merchants when he declared war against England's great foe. He demanded trade with the Spanish colonies, and religious freedom for English settlers in such colonies. Of course his demands were refused, as he well knew that they would be. Whereupon he seized Jamaica (1655) and intended to secure Cuba; and at any rate succeeded in giving the English a secure footing in the West Indies. He seized Dunkirk also from Spain (then at war with France), with a view to securing England a monopoly of the Channel to the exclusion of our old friends the Dutch. Dunkirk, however, was a useless acquisition, and was sold again by Charles II. Not content with victory in the West, Cromwell with the full consent of mercantile England declared war against the Dutch, who were now more our rivals than our friends. It would have been perfectly possible for the English and the Dutch to have remained upon good terms; but the great idea of the statesmen and merchants of the seventeenth and eighteenth centuries was to gain a sole market and a monopoly of trade, and so the Dutch had to be crushed. It was a mistake, but mistakes have frequently been made, owing to a lack of that indispensable concomitant of statesmanship, accurate economic knowledge. Cromwell succeeded in his object. He defeated the Dutch and broke their prestige in the two years' war of 1652–54, and designed to ruin their trade by the Navigation Acts of 1651 (p. 130). The contest between the Dutch and English for the mastery of the seas was already practically decided, and the capture of New Amsterdam (New York as we called it afterwards) in 1664, and the subsequent wars of Charles II.'s reign, completed the discomfiture of Holland.

§ 4. **The wars of William III. and of Anne**—The continental wars in which England was engaged after the deposition of James II. were rendered necessary to some extent by the tremendous power of France under Louis XIV. William III. saw it was inevitable for the interest of England that Louis XIV. should be checked, and the war of the Spanish Succession (1702–13) was carried on with the object of preventing that king from joining the resources of Spain to those of his own kingdom. For had he done so two disastrous results would have happened. The Stuarts would by his help have been restored to the English throne, and the struggle against absolute monarchy and religious tyranny would unfortunately have been fought over again. Secondly, the growth of English commerce would have been checked if not utterly annihilated. As it was we were preserved from the

Stuarts; and when the war was finally over in 1713, found ourselves in possession of Gibraltar, now one of the keys of our Indian Empire, and of the Hudson's Bay Territory, Newfoundland and Nova Scotia (then called Acadia) — the foundations of our present Canadian dominion. England was also allowed by Spain to trade —in negroes—with Spanish colonies, and to send one ship a year to the South Seas. The war, as far as we were concerned, was a commercial success, though we had to pay rather heavily for it, and were involved in further difficulties in America thereby.

§ 5. **Expansion of English trade after these wars**[1]— Even during the above wars English trade had been spreading. English merchants now did business in the Mediterranean with Turkey and Italy, in the North with Holland, Germany, Russia and Norway, in the East with India, Arabia and Africa, in the West with America and the Spanish colonies. Many companies were started, too numerous to mention here, for those who had hoarded their money during the war were now anxious to make profitable use of it. Of these new companies the most famous was the South Sea Company, formed in 1711 to trade with South America. The directors anticipated enormous profits, and offered to advance the Government £7,500,000 to pay off part of the National Debt. Everyone knows the story of their collapse (1721), and the ruin it brought upon thousands of worthy but credulous shareholders. It was a time when all the accumulated capital of the country seemed to run riot in hopes of gaining profits. Hundreds of smaller companies were started every day, and an unhealthy excitement prevailed. One company, with a capital of £3,000,000, was

[1] See note 16, p. 249, on Union with Scotland, Darien Scheme, and Methuen Treaty.

started "for insuring to all masters and mistresses the losses they may sustain by servants"; another "for making salt-water fresh"; a third for "planting mulberry trees and breeding silk-worms in Chelsea Park." One in particular was designed for importing "a number of large jackasses from Spain in order to propagate a larger kind of mule in England," as if, remarks a later writer with some severity, there were not already jackasses enough in London alone.

All this mania for investing capital, however, shows how prosperous England had now become, and how great a quantity of wealth had been accumulated, partly by trade, but also by the growth of manufactures and improvements in agriculture. Englishmen now felt strong enough to have another struggle for the monopoly of trade, with the result that fresh wars were undertaken, and the country was heavily burdened with debt. But the wars were on the whole a success, though the wish for a monopoly was a mistake.

§ 6. **Further wars with France and Spain**—All the wars in which England now engaged had some commercial object in view. People had yet to learn that the best way to extend a nation's trade is to promote general peace. In default of that, however, it seemed well to provoke a general war. Mistaken as England's policy was, it was no more so than that of her neighbours, for all believed, as many do still, in the sole market theory. Moreover, England was provoked into war by the secret "Family Compact" between the related rulers of France and Spain, by which Philip V. of Spain agreed to take away the South American trade from England, and give it to his nephew, Louis XV. of France. The result was a system of annoyance to English vessels trading in the South Seas, culminating in the mutilation of an English

To face p. 127

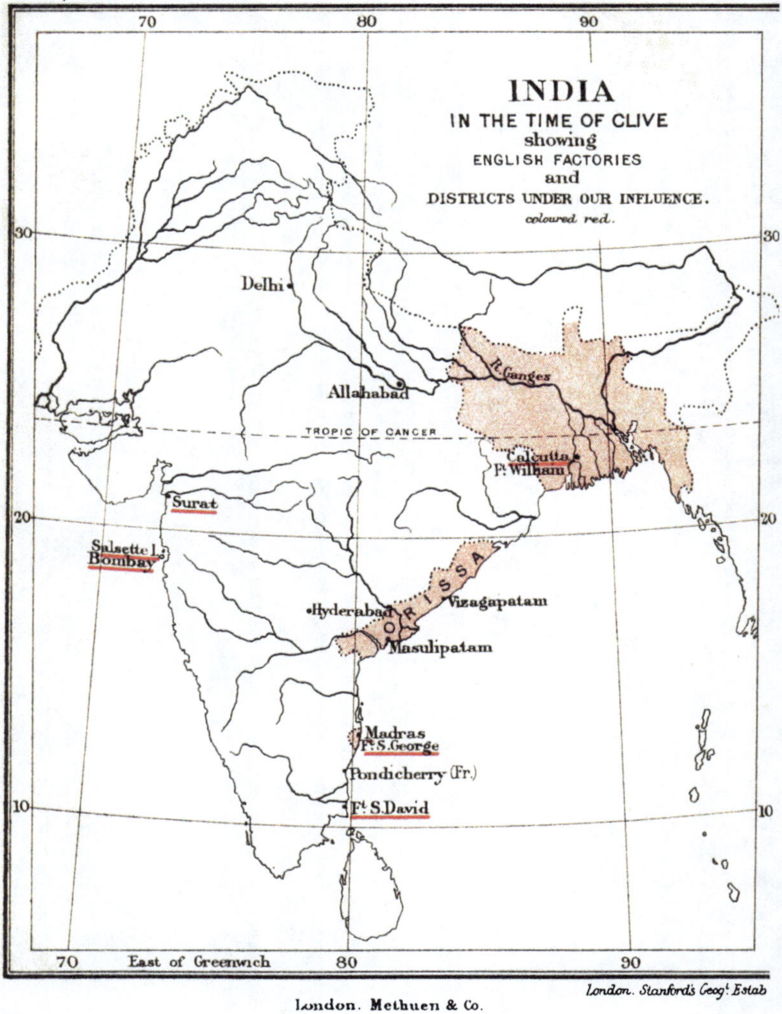

London. Methuen & Co.

captain, one Jenkins, and war was declared openly in 1739. This war merged into the war of the Austrian Succession, which lasted for eight years (1740–48), a matter with which England was in no way concerned, but which afforded a good excuse to renew the struggle against the commercial growth of France as well as Spain. We gained nothing by it except the final annihilation of the hopes of the Stuarts, and a small increase of British power upon the high seas.

After a few years, however, we entered upon another war, the Seven Years' War (1756–63), in which England and Prussia fought side by side against the rest of Europe, and attacked France in particular in all parts of the world. The war was largely caused by the quarrels of the French and English colonists in America, and of rival traders in India. We cannot here go into the details of it. It is sufficient to say that, after a bad beginning, we won various victories by sea and land, and at the close (1763) found ourselves in possession of Canada, Florida, and all the French possessions east of the Mississippi except New Orleans, and had gained the upper hand in India. We held almost undisputed sway over the seas, and our trade grew by leaps and bounds. Unfortunately we afterwards engaged in other wars of a less necessary character, and wasted a great deal of our wealth before the end of the century. But the short peace which ensued after 1763 gave us an opportunity which we did not neglect of increasing our national industries, and practically gave us the great start in manufactures to which we owe our present wealth. In this war, too, we gained our Indian Empire and Canada, to which we must devote a few short remarks.

§ 7. **The struggle for India**—Since the founding of Surat and the acquisition of Bombay, the East India

Company had also founded two forts or stations, which have since become most important cities, namely, Fort St George in 1640 (now Madras), and Fort William in 1698 (now Calcutta). They had become powerful, and each of the three chief stations had a governor and a small army. The French, however, had also an East India Company, whose chief station was Pondicherry, south of Madras; and the two companies were by no means on friendly terms. When their respective nations were at war in 1746-48, they too had some sharp fighting, but it was only when Dupleix, the French Governor of Pondicherry, had gained almost absolute power over Southern India after the death of the Great Mogul and the Nizam of the Dekkan in 1748, that matters became serious. The English traders feared with justice the loss both of their lives and commerce, and open war broke out. The magnificent exertions of Clive and Lawrence defeated the French, and finally Dupleix was recalled in 1754 and quiet was restored. But two years afterwards the Seven Years' War broke out, and India was disturbed again. Suraj-ud-Daula, the ally of the French, took Calcutta and committed the Black Hole atrocity (1757), and he and his allies did their best to drive the English out of Bengal. This province, however, was saved by Clive at the battle of Plassey; Coote defeated the French at Wondiwash (1760); and Pondicherry was captured by the English in 1761. Finally in 1765 the East India Company became the collector of the revenues for Bengal, Behar, and Orissa, and thus the English power was acknowledged and consolidated. Our future struggles in India were not with the French but with native princes.

§ 8. **The conquest of Canada**—There was, however, a great struggle for commercial supremacy to be waged against the French in America. It began in 1754. The

English had now thirteen flourishing colonies between the Alleghany Mountains and the sea. Behind them, above them, and below them, all was claimed by France as French territory. It was inevitable that the growth of our colonies should lead to war, and such was the case. The French began by driving out English settlers from land west of the Alleghany Mountains; the English retorted by driving French settlers out of Nova Scotia, and tried to make a colony in the Ohio valley. In this latter object they were foiled by Duquesne, the French Governor of Canada, who built Fort Duquesne there in 1754. Shortly afterwards, the next Governor, Montcalm, conceived the idea of linking together Forts Duquesne, Niagara, and Ticonderoga by lesser forts, so as to keep the English in their narrow strip of eastern coast-line. Then the English Government at home took up the matter, and sent out General Braddock and 2000 men to help the colonists. Braddock was defeated and killed (1755), but when the Seven Years' War broke out in the next year, Pitt sent ammunition, men, and money to help the colonists to attack Quebec and Montreal. The war was renewed in Canada with fresh vigour; Fort Duquesne was captured in 1758, Quebec in 1759, and Montreal in 1760; and when peace was made in Europe in 1763, England had gained all the French possessions in America, and her colonies were enabled to extend as far as they desired. We foolishly lost them by a mistaken policy a few years afterwards.

§ 9. **Survey of commercial progress during these wars**—The reign of James I. was noticeable for the rapid growth of the foreign trade which had developed from the somewhat piratical excursions of the Elizabethan sailors. Trading companies were formed in considerable numbers, and among them the Levant Company may be noticed, as having made "great gains" in the East in 1605. The mercantile class was now growing both numerous and powerful, and a proof of their advance in social position and influence is furnished by the new title of nobility, that of baronet, conferred by James I. upon such merchant princes as were able and willing to pay the needy king a good round sum for the honour.[1] It is interesting, by the way, to notice the figures of trade in his reign. In 1613 the exports and imports both together were about £4,628,586 in value, and a sign of a quickly developing Eastern trade is also seen in the fact that James made attempts to check the increasing export of silver from the kingdom. At this time English merchants traded with most of the Mediterranean ports, with Portugal, Spain, France, Hamburg, and the Baltic coasts. Ships from the north and west of Europe used in return to visit the Newcastle collieries, which were rapidly growing in value. The English ships were also very active in the new cod fisheries of Newfoundland, and the Greenland whale fisheries. Commerce was further aided by the Navigation Acts of 1651, which provided that no merchandise of Asia, Africa, or America should be imported in any but English ships. Previously, the carrying trade had been in the hands of the Dutch, but Holland had now entered upon the period of its decline, and the short war with England which followed these Acts contributed to hasten it. The development of English trade is signalized in this century by the appearance of numerous books and essays on commercial questions, of which the works of Mun, Malynes, Misselden, Roberts, Sir Josiah Child, Worth, and Davenant may be mentioned as among the most important. The increase in the wealth of the country is shown by the rapid rebuilding of London after the Great

[1] See note 13, p. 247, on Banking and the Stop of the Exchequer.

Fire, when the loss was estimated at £12,000,000; and Sir Josiah Child, writing in 1670, speaks of the great development of the commerce and trade of England in the previous twenty years. We know from Gregory King that rents had been doubled in this period, and that is always a sure sign of prosperity. The East India Company was so flourishing that in 1676 their stock was quoted at 245 per cent. Trade with America was equally prosperous. New Amsterdam, now New York, was taken from the Dutch in 1664, and in 1670 the Hudson's Bay Company received their charter. But the main commercial fact of the latter half of the seventeenth century, and of the eighteenth, was the development of the Eastern trade, and, as a consequence, of the home production of articles to be exchanged for Eastern goods. The cloth trade especially was greatly increased, and imports of cloth from Spain were quite superseded. This improvement in English manufactures led to increased trade with our colonial possessions, especially in the West Indies. It was partly, perhaps, this great development of English trade[1] with both the Western and the Eastern markets that stimulated the genius of the great inventors to supply our manufacturers with machinery that would enable them to meet the huge demands upon their powers of production, for, by 1760, the export trade had grown to many times its value in the days of James I. Then, as we saw, it was only £2,000,000 per annum; in 1703, nearly a hundred years later, it was, according to a MS. of Davenant's, £6,552,019; by 1760 it reached £14,500,000. The markets, too, had undergone a change. We no longer exported so largely to Holland, Portugal, and France, as in the seventeenth century, but instead one-third of our exports went to our colonies. In 1770,

[1] See also my *Commerce in Europe*, pp. 137-147.

for example, America took three-fourths of the manufactures of Manchester, and Jamaica alone took almost as much of our manufactures as all our plantations together had done in the beginning of the century. The prosperity and development of modern English commerce, as we know it, had now begun. It was due, of course, not to the great wars we had waged for the right of a sole market, but to the fact that we were able to supply the markets of the world with manufactured goods that no other country could then produce. How we were able to do so will shortly be seen when we come to speak of the Industrial Revolution of the last half of the eighteenth century.

CHAPTER VI

MANUFACTURES AND MINING

§ 1. Circumstances favourable to English manufactures—I have frequently remarked in previous chapters that Flanders was the great manufactory of Europe throughout the Middle Ages, and up to the sixteenth century. Her competition would in any case have been sufficient to check much export of manufactured goods from England, though we had by the sixteenth century got past the time when most of our imports of clothing came from Flanders. Now, at the end of the sixteenth century, Flemish competition was practically annihilated, owing to the ravages made in the Low Countries by the Spanish persecutions and occupation. But England did not merely benefit by the cessation of Flemish competition: she received at the same time hundreds of Flemish immigrants, who greatly improved our home manufactures, and thus our prosperity was doubly assisted. The result is seen in the fact that our export of wool diminished, and our export of cloth increased.

§ 2. **Wool trade. Home manufactures. Dyeing**—In the reign of James I. the wool trade is even said to have declined, and certainly we know that little wool can have been exported, for nearly all that produced in England was used for home manufacture. On the other hand, however, the same fact shows that the manufacturing industry was rising in importance, for it required all the home-grown wool that could be got ; and, in 1660, the export of British wool was for this reason forbidden, and remained so till 1825. The woollen trade was now very largely in the hands of the Merchant Adventurers,[1] whose methods caused many complaints ; but the manufacturing industry flourished steadily, and a considerable part of the population was now engaged in it. It seems to have received some impetus, also, from the Acts 4 and 5 James I. (1607 and 1608), carefully regulating and guarding the quality of cloth exported, and by the end of the seventeenth century no less than two-thirds of our exports were woollen fabrics. The usefulness of our climate, too, for this particular manufacture had been discovered, and was now recognized, while the manufacturing industry was likewise aided by the impetus given to dyeing by the exertions of Sir Walter Raleigh. Previously to James I.'s reign most English goods had to be sent to the Netherlands to be dyed, as I explained above ; but Raleigh, in his *Essay on Commerce*, called attention to this fact, and proposed to grant a monopoly for the art of dyeing and

[1] This Company, by charters from James I. in 1604 and 1617, had the exclusive privilege of exporting the woollen cloths of England to the Netherlands and Germany. It included some 4000 merchants.

dressing, and by his advice the export of English white goods was prohibited (1608), but the monopoly granted to Sir W. Cockayne caused such an outcry that it was revoked.

§ 3. **Other influences favourable to England. The Huguenot immigration**—But other influences were at work in the seventeenth century in favour of our home industries. It becomes more and more apparent that our insular position was specially fitted for the development of manufactures as soon as they made a fair start. Except for the Parliamentary War, which did not disturb the industry of the country very much—for there is no sign of undue exaltation of prices, or anything else that points to commercial distress—England was free from the terrible conflicts that desolated half Europe in the Thirty Years' War. Our own Civil War was conducted with hardly any of the bloodshed, plunder, and rapine that make war so disastrous. But the Thirty Years' War (1619-1648) did not cease till the utter exhaustion of the combatants made peace inevitable, and till every leader who had taken part in the beginning of the war was in his grave. Germany was effectually ruined, and with Germany and Flanders laid low, England had little to fear from foreign competition. And just at this moment the folly of our neighbour, the French King Louis XIV., induced him to deprive his nation of most of its skilled workmen, by the Revocation of the Edict of Nantes. His loss was our gain. The Edict in question, passed nearly a century previously, had insured freedom of worship to the French Huguenots, who comprised in their ranks the *élite* of the industrial population. Louis XIV. set to work to exterminate the Protestant religion in France, and began by revoking this Edict (1685). Once more England profited by her Protestantism, and, owing

To face p 131

The majority of the population was in the west and south central counties *(dark green)*; but Lancs. and the West Riding of Yorks. were increasing. The chief manufacturing centres in (1) Eastern counties, (2) Wilts, (3) Yorks, &c., are shown thus [symbol] but it must be remembered that manufactures were very scattered and carried on side by side with agriculture. Several other counties are therefore marked with slanting lines.

to the religious opinions of her people, received a fresh accession of industrial strength. Some thousands of skilled Huguenot artisans and manufacturers came over and settled in this land. They greatly improved the silk, glass, and paper trades, and exercised considerable influence in the development of domestic manufactures generally. It is said that the immigrants numbered 50,000 souls, with a capital of some £3,000,000.[1] Everyone knows how they introduced the silk industry into this country, and how Spitalfields long remained a colony of Huguenot silk weavers. Their descendants are to be found in every part of England.

§ 4. **Distribution of the cloth trade**—From this time forward the cloth trade, in especial, took its place among the chief industries of the country, largely owing to the fresh spirit infused into it, first by Flemish, and afterwards by French weavers. It became more and more widely distributed. The county of Kent, and the towns of York and Reading made one kind of cloth of a heavy texture, the piece being thirty or thirty-four yards long by six and one-half quarters broad, and weighing 66 lbs. to the piece. Worcester, Hereford, and Coventry made a lighter kind of fabric, while throughout the eastern counties of Norfork, Suffolk, and Essex were made cloths of various kinds—plunkets, azures, blues, long cloth, bay, say, and serges; Suffolk, in particular, made a "fine, short, white cloth." Wiltshire and Somerset made plunkets and handy warps; Yorkshire, short cloths. Broad-listed whites and reds, and fine cloths, also came from Wiltshire, Gloucestershire and Oxfordshire; and Somerset was famous in the eastern part for narrow-listed whites and reds, and in the west for "dunsters." Devonshire made kerseys and grays, as also did York-

[1] Anderson's *Chron. of Commerce*, ii. 569.

shire and Lancashire. The Midlands furnished "Penistone" cloths and "Forest whites"; while Westmoreland was the seat of the manufacture of the famous "Kendal green" cloths, as also of "Carpmael" and "Cogware" fabrics. It will be seen that the manufacture was exceedingly extensive, and that special fabrics derived their names from the chief centre where they were made. It may be mentioned here, too, that the value of wool shorn in England at the end of the seventeenth century was £2,000,000, from about 12,000,000 sheep (according to Youatt); and the cloth manufactured from it was valued at £6,000,000 or £8,000,000. Nearly half-a-century later (1741) the number of sheep was reckoned at 17,000,000, the value of wool shorn at £3,000,000, and of wool manufactured at £8,000,000, showing that progress in invention had not done much to enhance the value of the manufactured article. But in 1774, when the Industrial Revolution may be said to have fairly begun, the value of manufactured wool was £13,000,000, the value of raw wool (£4,500,000) being smaller in proportion.

§ 5. **Coal-mines**—Turning now from textile manufactures to mining and working in metals, we find that in the seventeenth and eighteenth centuries we were just upon the eve of the most important changes in these industries—changes which, in many places, have entirely transformed the face of the country. But it cannot be too clearly understood that none of our mining and mineral industries attained any proportions worth speaking of till what is known as the Industrial Revolution. Englishmen seem to have had hardly any idea of the vast wealth of coal and iron that has placed us in the forefront of Europe as a manufacturing nation. Nevertheless we may just glance at the imperfect methods which our forefathers used up till the eighteenth century. Coal-mining had been carried on fairly extensively by the Romans, as for instance the discovery of huge cinder-heaps at Aston and other places testifies. Then, like all our industries, it was almost entirely given up, and it was due to the Norman Conquest that coal-mining was revived. That it was practised to some extent in the North is seen from an entry in the *Boldean Book* (a kind of Domesday of the county of Durham, composed in 1183), in which a smith is allowed twelve acres of land for making the ironwork of the carts, and has to provide his own coal. But collieries were not opened at Newcastle till the thirteenth century, in the year 1238. In the next year we find notice of the first public recognition of coal as an article of commerce, and from a charter of Henry III. to the freemen of Newcastle, we may date the foundation of the coal trade. In 1273 this had become sufficiently extensive for the use of coal to be forbidden in London, as there was a prejudice against it and in favour of wood as fuel. In the fourteenth century, again, the monks of Tynemouth Priory engaged in mining speculation, and (1380) leased a colliery for £5. In the fifteenth century trade was sufficiently important to form a source of revenue, for a tax of twopence per chaldron was placed upon sea-borne coal, and in 1421 an Act had to be passed to enforce this tax. In fact in the fourteenth and fifteenth centuries coal-mining became general in Great Britain.

§ 6. **Development of coal trade: seventeenth and eighteenth centuries**—By the seventeenth century it had also become important—important enough for the needy Stuart monarch Charles I. to see in it a chance of revenue. This king gave to Sir Thomas Tempest and his partners the monopoly of the sale of Newcastle coal for twenty-one years, beginning in 1637; and next year he allowed a syndicate to be incorporated which was to buy up all the coal from Newcastle, Sunderland and Berwick, and sell it in London for "not more than 17*s*. a ton in summer, and 19*s*. in winter"—an extravagant price for those times. The king got a shilling a ton out of this ingenious scheme. However, the Long Parliament finally put a stop to this outrageous monopoly.

But although the coal trade was fairly extensive for that period, it was utterly insignificant compared with its present dimensions, and that for a very good reason. There was no means of pumping water out of the mines, except by the old-fashioned air-pump, which was of course utterly inadequate. Nor was a suitable invention discovered till the very end of the seventeenth century, when Thomas Savery in 1698 invented a kind of pump, worked by the condensation of steam. This rather clumsy invention, however, was soon superseded in 1705 by Newcomen's steam pump. But it was not till after the commencement of the Industrial Revolution that steam power was scientifically applied to coal-mines by the inventions of Watt and Boulton (1765 and 1774), which we shall notice in their proper place. Up to that time, also, it was difficult to transport coal into inland districts by road, Newcastle coal being carried to London in ships, and then carried up inland rivers in barges. But these barges could not go high up many rivers at that time, and canals were not yet made. It was difficult for instance to get coal to Oxford, for it had to come to London, and then part way up the Thames, which was not then navigable so far. But at Cambridge it was easily procurable, for barges could come right up to the town from eastern ports. Hence it was much cheaper at Cambridge than at Oxford.

§ 7. **The iron trade**—As it had been with coal, so with iron. Only very small quantities of it were mined in the

Middle Ages ; it was smelted only by wood, as a rule, and was manufactured only in a very rude way. We saw that at the great fairs foreign iron, chiefly from the Biscay coast, was much in demand, as our own supply was utterly insufficient. It was naturally not until we learnt to mine and use our coal properly that we learnt also how to mine and manufacture our iron. Before learning this, English workmen used wood as fuel, and it is to this cause that we owe the destruction of most of the forests which, at the time of Domesday, occupied so large an area. "The waste and destruction of the woods in the counties of Warwick, Stafford, Hereford, Monmouth, Gloucester, and Salop by these iron-works is not to be imagined," a speaker said in Parliament as late as the beginning of the eighteenth century. And as wood was used as house-fuel also, it will readily be understood what a vast destruction of timber took place. In 1581 the erection of iron-works within certain distances from London and the Thames was prohibited "for the preservation of the woods."

But early in the seventeenth century (1619) Dud Dudley, son of Lord Dudley, began to make use of sea and pit coal for smelting iron, and obtained a monopoly "of the mystery and art of smelting iron-ore, and of making the same into cast works or bars, in furnaces, with bellows." Dudley sold this cast-iron at £12 a ton, and made a good profit out of it. He actually produced seven tons a week, which was considered a large supply, and shows the comparative insignificance of the industry then. However, it was only comparatively insignificant, for before the close of the century it was calculated that 180,000 tons of iron were produced in England yearly ; and in the eighteenth century (1719) iron came third in the list of English manufactures, and the trade gave employment to 200,000 people. There was, however, still great waste of wood, since a great many ironmasters did not use coal, and therefore the export and even the manufacture of iron was discouraged by legislation to such an extent that by 1740 the output had been reduced to 17,350 tons per annum, barely a tenth of the previous amount quoted. The waste of timber was most noticeable in the Sussex Wealden, the forests of which owe their destruction almost entirely to the iron and glass manufactures.

But about this time another inventor, Darby, discovered the secret of the large blast furnace in which pit coal and charcoal were used. He began his experiments as early as 1730, but did not do much for some twenty years. In 1756, however, his works were "at the top pinnacle of prosperity; twenty and twenty-two tons per week sold off as fast as made, and profit enough."

After Darby came Smeaton, and other inventors, and the Industrial Revolution spread to the iron trade. We shall see it in operation in our next period.

§ 8. **Pottery**—As with all other manufactures, so too the development of pottery was reserved for the Renaissance of industry in the eighteenth century. Of course pottery of a kind had always been made in England, especially where the useful soil of Staffordshire formed a favourable ground for the exercise of this art. But the pottery hitherto manufactured had been rude and coarse, and its manufacture was a strictly domestic and not very widespread industry. We owe its improvement, as in so many other cases, largely to the efforts of the Dutch and Huguenot immigrants of the sixteenth and seventeenth centuries. For the Dutch had been great among the potters of Europe, as the renown of Delft-ware still testifies, and France had the honour of being the land of Palissy. The factories at Burslem owed their origin to the industry of two Germans, called Elers, from whom an Englishman, Astbury, learnt the secret of producing the red unglazed Japanese ware, and the black Egyptian ware. Burslem, too, was the birthplace of Josiah Wedgwood, born 1730, who first began business in 1752 as manager for a master-potter, but started in business on his own account in 1759, the eve of the Industrial Revolution. His efforts and experiments were magnificent and untiring, and they can be read at leisure in various biographical works. It is sufficient here to say that Wedgwood was the man who first made the art of pottery a science, and before his death in 1795 he had brought this manufacture to such a pitch of excellence, that few improvements have been left for his successors to make, and it rose to be one of the chief industries of the country.

§ 9. **Other mining industries**—There remain one or two industries that require a passing mention, but which were not in the eighteenth century of much importance. As to the metals, the foreign trade in tin and lead has been already mentioned. In the reign of John the tin-mines of Cornwall were farmed by the Jews, and the tin and lead trade must have attained considerable proportions in the fourteenth century, for the Black Prince paid his own expenses in the French wars by the produce of his mines of those metals in Devonshire. Copper, also, was mined in the northern counties, and in a statute of 15 Edward III. (1343) we find grants of mines given at Skeldane, in Northumberland; at Alston Moor, in Cumberland; and at Richmond, in Yorkshire; a royalty of one-eighth going to the king, and one-ninth to the lord of the manor. Keswick was at that time a centre of this industry; but there cannot have been any great output, for copper had to be imported from Germany in the fifteenth century. The mines were also very primitive, the approaches being made not by shafts, but by adits in the side of a convenient hill. Another mineral, which is very abundant in England, especially in Worcestershire and Cheshire, was at this period hardly utilized. Salt was a necessary of life to the English householder, for he had to salt his meat for the winter ; but he did not know how to mine it himself, and either got it imported from south-west France or contented himself with the inferior article evaporated on the sea-coast, until the end of the seventeenth century.

In this place, too, we may mention that brickmaking was a lost art from the fifth to the fifteenth century, and bricks were not even imported. The first purchase of bricks to be recorded was at Cambridge, in 1449 ; but before the end of the fifteenth century it became a common building material in the eastern counties, and in the sixteenth century was generally used in London and in the counties along the lower course of the Thames.

§ 10. **The close of the period of manual industries**—We have now reached a turning-point in English industrial history, and are about to study a period that is in every way a violent contrast to the centuries which preceded it. We have come to the time when machinery begins to displace unaided manual labour. Hitherto all our manufactures, our mining, and of course our agriculture, had been performed by the literal labour of men's hands, only slightly helped by a few simple inventions. Industry, too, was not organized upon a vast capitalistic basis, though of course capitalists existed ; but it would be more correct to say that hitherto industry had been chiefly carried on by numbers of smaller capitalists who were also manual workmen, even when they employed other workmen under them. Only in agriculture had the capitalist class become very far removed from the labourers. There was certainly no such violent contrast as now exists between a mill-owner and a mill-hand in the realm of manufacturing industry, though of course this contrast existed between the rich land-owner who received rents, and the poor agricultural labourer whose labour helped to pay them. But, speaking of industry generally, it may be said that the absence of machinery kept employers and workmen more upon a common level, and as large factories of course did not exist, industry was carried on chiefly in the workmen's homes, and the workman was not merely a unit among hundreds of unknown "hands" in a mill, but a person not hopelessly removed in social rank from his employer, who was well acquainted with him, and like him worked with his own hands.

But now this old order of things passes away, and a new order appears, ushered in by the whir and rattle of machinery and the mighty hiss of steam. A complete transformation takes place, and the life of England stirs anew in the great Industrial Revolution.

PERIOD V

THE INDUSTRIAL REVOLUTION AND MODERN ENGLAND

CHAPTER I

THE EVE OF THE REVOLUTION

§ 1. **Industry and politics. Land-owners and merchant princes**—We are, of course, mainly concerned in this book with industrial facts ; but as these underlie all politics and national history, we must pause for a moment to see how the growth of commerce had by this time affected the relations of two great classes : the land-owners and their new rivals, the great merchants and the commercial classes generally. Up to the time of the deposition of James II., or the Whig Revolution of 1688, as it is sometimes called, the land-owning class had been practically supreme in social and political influence. But from that time forward, although they still held this high position, their influence was heavily counterbalanced by that of the mercantile classes. The capitalist and the commercial magnates were all favoured by the great movement which divided the nation into the two historic parties of Whigs and Tories, for it was that movement which first accentuated their importance in the political life of the nation. That importance was still more accentuated by a series of significant economic events which took place shortly after the Revolution ; namely, the foundation of the Bank of

England (1694),[1] the new and extended Charter granted to the East India Company in 1693, the beginning of the National Debt in the same year, and the Restoration of the Currency in 1696. The commercial and industrial section of the community was becoming more and more prominent, and the great Whig families who occupied themselves with endeavouring to rule England in the eighteenth century, relied for their support upon the middle and commercial classes. The old reverence, however, for the position of a land-owner had not yet died out, and the men who had gained their wealth by commerce strove for a higher social position by buying land in large quantities. The time had not yet come when a merchant was on equal terms with a landlord.

In fact there has always been an extraordinary sentimentalism as regards land among all classes of the English people ; and for some reason that has never been fully explained a man who has merely inherited a large amount of land (even if he has never attempted to cultivate it) is regarded as being superior to one who has amassed a fortune in the industrial or commercial world. And this feeling was stronger in the eighteenth century than it is at the present time. Hence commercial magnates bought land, and with it social prestige. The James Lowther who was created Earl of Lonsdale in 1784 was the descendant of a merchant engaged in the Levant trade ; the first Earl of Tilney was the son of that eminent man of business, Sir Josiah Child. The daughters of merchant princes were even allowed to marry—and maintain—the scions of a needy aristocracy. Defoe actually discovered the amazing and revolutionary fact that a man engaged in commerce might be a gentleman, though no doubt this

[1] See notes 13 and 14, pp. 247, 248, for details.

bold supposition of his was at first looked upon with incredulity. He says: "Trade is so far from being inconsistent with a gentleman that in England trade makes a gentleman; for, *after a generation or two*, the tradesman's children come to be as good gentlemen, statesmen, parliament men, judges, bishops, and noblemen as those of the highest birth and the most ancient families." Dean Swift remarked "that the power which used to follow land had gone over to money." Dr Johnson announced oracularly that "an English merchant was a new species of gentleman."

Now, the Industrial Revolution went still further to gain social and political influence for the commercial classes. It succeeded in destroying the foolish idea that the land-owners alone were to be looked upon as the leaders of the nation. It gave the capitalists and manufacturers a new accession of power by enormously increasing their wealth. Moreover, it helped to undermine the landed interest by making the manufactures of England at first equal, and afterwards superior, to her agriculture, so that a rich mill-owner or ironmaster became as important as a large land-owner. The monopoly of the landed interest was broken by capital. Nowhere is the contrast between the old and new classes in the last century seen more closely than in Scott's *Rob Roy*, where the old Tory squire who held fast to Church and king is contrasted with the new commercial magnate who supported the House of Hanover. One good we enjoyed from the rise of the commercial classes, and that was the final overthrow of the Stuarts, with all the follies which that unfortunate race represented.

§ 2. **The coming of the capitalists**—Now, although the commercial capitalist was fast coming into prominence as the rival of the land-owner, he was becoming still more prominent as the master of the workmen whom he employed. For before the Industrial Revolution the capitalist had occupied a comparatively subordinate place. The vast enterprises of modern industry, such as railways or mills, which often require so large an expenditure of capital before they can begin to be in any way remunerative, were practically unknown a century ago. The industrial system was, moreover, far less complicated, far less international, far less subdivided. Instead of the great capitalist manufacturers of to-day, who can control the markets of a nation, England possessed numbers of smaller capitalists, with far less capital, both individually and in the aggregate, than what is now required by a man who undertakes even a moderate business. The large capitalists of the last century were chiefly the foreign trading companies. For English home manufactures, although greatly developed, were still largely conducted upon the domestic system, and the small capitalist-artisan was a conspicuous feature of that time, just as the large mill-owner or ironmaster is of our own day. Manufactures were carried on by a number of small master-manufacturers, who gave out work to be done in the homes of their employés; and who often combined agricultural with manufacturing pursuits. But nevertheless there were signs of the approach of modern capitalist methods, of production upon a large scale. It was becoming increasingly the custom to employ a large number of workpeople together under one roof, or at least under the direction and supervision of one great manufacturer. Arthur Young, for instance, mentions a silk mill at Sheffield with 152 hands—a large number in the eighteenth century; a factory at Boynton with 150 hands; and a master-manufacturer at Darlington who ran above fifty looms. Work was also given out by capitalist manufacturers or merchants to workmen to do at home in the villages and towns. These workmen were, like the employés of the present day, entirely dependent upon their employer for work and wages. Thus, at Nottingham in 1750 we find fifty master-manufacturers who "put out" work in this way for as many as 1200 looms in the hosiery trade.

§ 3. **The class of small manufacturers**—But although the coming of the capitalists was now near at hand the old order of things was not seriously disturbed till the application of steam power to machinery some years later. There were still many small manufacturers who lived on their own land and worked with their workpeople in their own houses. Defoe in his *Tour through Great Britain* (made in 1724–26) gives an interesting account of this class at a time when they were in the height of their prosperity, before machinery and steam had even begun to cause their disappearance. Speaking of the land near Halifax, in Yorkshire, he says: "The land was divided into small enclosures from two acres to six or seven each, seldom more, every three or four pieces of land having a house belonging to them; hardly a house standing out of speaking distance from another. We could see at every house a tenter, and on almost every tenter a piece of cloth or kersie or shalloon. At every considerable house there was a manufactory. Every clothier keeps one horse at least to carry his manufactures to the market; and every one generally keeps a cow or two or more for his family. By this means the small pieces of enclosed land about each house are occupied, for they scarce sow corn enough to feed their poultry. The houses are full of lusty fellows, some at the dye-vat, some at the looms, others dressing the cloths; the women and children carding or spinning; being all employed, from the youngest to the oldest." And Defoe adds a remark which is certainly not applicable either to Halifax or any other manufacturing town of the present day, for he concludes his description with the words : "not a beggar to be seen, or an idle person."

§ 4. **The condition of the manufacturing population**—For it is a significant fact that under the old domestic system, simple and cumbrous as it was, the manufacturing population was very much better off than it was for some time after the Industrial Revolution. For one thing, they still lived more or less in the country and were not crowded together in stifling alleys and courts, or long rows of bare smoke-begrimed streets, in houses like so many dirty rabbit-hutches. Even if the artisan did live in a town at that time, the town was very different from the abodes of smoke and dirt which now prevail in the manufacturing districts. There were no tall chimneys, belching forth clouds of evil smoke; no huge, hot factories with their hundreds of windows blazing forth a lurid light in the darkness, and rattling with the whir and din of ceaseless machinery by day and night. There were no gigantic blast furnaces rising amid blackened heaps of cinders, or chemical works poisoning the fields and trees for miles around. These were yet to come. The factory and the furnace were almost unknown. Work was carried on by the artisan in his little stone or brick house, with the workshop inside, where the wool for the weft was carded and spun by his wife and daughters, and the cloth was woven by himself and his sons. He had also, in nearly all cases, his plot of land near the house, which provided him both with food and recreation, for he could relieve the monotony of weaving by cultivating his little patch of ground, or feeding his pigs and poultry. Work too was more regular than it often is at present, for there were fewer commercial fluctuations; fashions did not change so quickly, and the market for home-spun fabrics was always steady and assured. The relations between employers and employed were far closer; even the distribution of wealth was comparatively more equal. Wages were of course less in money value than at present, but then prices of food and rent were only about half what they are now. Arthur Young gives 9*s.* 6*d.* as the average weekly wages of an artisan in the North and Midland counties, while the average rent for a cottage in the same counties he puts at 28*s.* 2*d.* a year, or only 6½*d.* per week. And it must be remembered that this included a piece of land round the cottage. Meat, also, was cheap, being from 2½*d.* to 3¼*d.* per pound; and bread 1¼*d.* a pound. In fact we may confidently say that artisans, especially spinners and weavers, were well off about 1760. Adam Smith testifies to this in the *Wealth of Nations.* "Not only has grain become somewhat cheaper," he says, "but many other things from which the industrious poor derive an agreeable and wholesome variety of food have become a great deal cheaper." And the healthy condition of industry in general is shown by the fact that at the close of the wars with France by the Peace of 1763, when more than 100,000 men accustomed to war were thrown upon the country and had to find work or else be supported somehow or other, "not only no great convulsion, but no sensible disorder arose."

§ 5. **Condition of the agricultural population**—Nor was that convenient plenty which was the lot of the manufacturing portion of the people confined only to that section. The condition of the agricultural labourer, who was generally the worst off of all classes from being so much under the direct supervision of his master, had considerably improved, together with the general improvement of agriculture spoken of in a previous chapter. The price of corn had fallen, while wages had risen, though these were less than an artisan's, being, according to Arthur Young's average estimate for the North and Midland counties, about 7*s.* a week. But it was generally 8*s.* or 10*s.*, while the board of a working man may be placed at about 5*s.* or 6*s.* a week. Cottages were occasionally rent free, or at any rate only paid a low rent, never more than 50*s.* or 60*s.* per year. There was an abundance of food, clothing, and furniture. Wheat-bread had entirely superseded rye-bread. Every poor family now drank tea, which had formerly been a costly luxury. The consumption of meat was, says Arthur Young, "pretty considerable," and that of cheese "immense." Indeed he states that the labourers "by their large wages and the cheapness of all necessaries enjoyed better dwellings, diet, and apparel in England than the husbandmen or farmers did in other countries." Certainly Arthur Young must have been struck with the difference between the agricultural population of England and that of France, which latter country he visited shortly before the Revolution, when the misery of the labourers was at its lowest depth, thanks to the extortions of the privileged noblesse.

§ 6. **Growth of population**—But not only had the condition of the industrial population improved in the period 1700–1750, but their numbers had also considerably increased. And now too was beginning that great shifting of the centres of population from the South to the North of England, which is so important a feature in the new industrial epoch. The most suggestive fact of this period is the growth of the population of Lancashire and of the West Riding of Yorkshire, which were rapidly becoming the seats of the cotton and coarse woollen manufactures. Similarly also Staffordshire and Warwickshire, the pottery and hardware centres, were growing in numbers, and so, too, were Durham and Northumberland, whose coal-fields were now far more developed than before. On the other hand, the population of the Western and Eastern counties, still large manufacturing centres, had increased very little. But in the North and North-west the increase was enormous. Between 1685 and 1760 the people of Liverpool had increased tenfold, of Manchester fivefold, of Birmingham and Sheffield sevenfold. The total population of England had increased from the five millions or so of Elizabeth's time, to not much less than eight millions in Arthur Young's time, and far more of these were in the northern portions of the country than was the case even in Defoe's time. Defoe said in 1725, "the country south of the Trent is by far the largest, as well as the richest and most populous." But forty or fifty years later the shifting towards the North had already made itself felt. The cause of the great increase of population between 1700 and 1760 is to be found in the rapid increase of national wealth gained by foreign commerce, in the progress of home manufactures and of agriculture. Increased wealth means increased comfort in living, increased command of food, and consequently better chances of survival among children born of poor parents. And in this period the increase in national wealth was, in spite of foreign wars, enormous; for if England had to pay heavily for these wars other countries had to pay more heavily still, and were, moreover, the battle-grounds of contending armies, while our own land was at least free from invasion.

§ 7. **England still mainly agricultural**—Of the population of the country at this time the majority were still engaged in agriculture, and the agricultural labourers alone formed one-third of the working classes, and a large number even of the manufacturing classes still worked in the fields for a portion of the year, especially in harvest-time. In 1770 England was still mainly an agricultural country, and Arthur Young estimates that the income of the agricultural portion of the nation was larger than that of all the rest of the community. But it must be remembered that by far the largest portion of this income was in the hands of large land-owners and the farmers, the share of the labourer being of course much smaller. Arthur Young's estimates must be taken with a certain amount of caution, but they are probably approximately correct, and are certainly interesting as giving us a very fair idea of the distribution of occupations and national wealth just before the Industrial Revolution. Hence I append a small table, giving in round numbers the figures of his estimates. It will be noticed that the number of the population is rather too high, but the proportion of one class to another is probably correct.

INCOMES OF VARIOUS CLASSES[1]

IN MILLION POUNDS

Bar	Class
5	Interest on capital 5
1·5	Paupers 1·5
5	Military and official 5
5	Professions 5
10	Commercial 10
27	Manufacturing 27
66	Agricultural 66

Total = £119,500,000.

[1] This table is drawn to scale.

POPULATION

IN MILLIONS

·5	Paupers ·5
·5	Military and official ·5
·2	Professional ·2
·7	Commercial ·7
3	Manufacturing 3
3·6	Agricultural 3·6

Total = 8,500,000.

It will be perceived that the agriculturists, though only about half a million more in numbers than the manufacturing classes, had a far larger proportionate income, in fact more than double. This was of course partly due to the agricultural improvements of this period, and to the fact that manufactures were still carried on almost solely by hand, thus giving only a small production from a good many workmen. But the Industrial Revolution rapidly changed all this, and now agriculture is no longer the staple industry of the country. We may here refer to what has been previously mentioned in regard to the agricultural development on enclosed land, and to the superiority of the results of enclosures over common fields. Those farmers and large owners who understood the best ways of raising crops prospered, and more and more land was enclosed every year to grow corn (which by the way was rapidly rising in price), clover, turnips and other root-crops. No less than 700 Enclosure Acts were passed between 1760 and 1774. The old common fields were beginning to disappear, and the working classes also lost their rights of pasturing cattle on the wastes, for wastes now were enclosed. It must be admitted that the old common-field system produced very poor results (cf. p. 41), but the loss of his common rights was very disastrous to the labourer, for it drove him off the land at the same time as the growth of manufactures attracted him off from it, and thus the labourer became in a few years completely divorced from the soil. At present attempts are being made to attract him back to it by offering him small strips of inferior land at a high rent. This is known as the allotment system. It need scarcely be said that, as at present carried out, it is hardly likely to succeed.[1]

§ 8. **The domestic system of manufacture**—But in the period we are now speaking of, the period before the great inventions, neither the agricultural labourer nor the manufacturing operative was quite divorced from the land. The weavers, for instance, often lived in the country, in a cottage with some land attached to it. There had certainly been changes in the industrial system before 1760. At first the weaver had furnished himself with warp and weft, worked it up, and brought it to the market himself; but by degrees this system grew too cumbersome, and the yarn was given out by merchants to the weaver, and at last the merchant got together a certain number of looms in a town or village, and worked them under his own supervision. But even yet the domestic system, as it is commonly called, retained in many if not in most cases the distinctive feature that the manufacturing industry was not the only industry in which the artisan was engaged, but that he generally combined with it a certain amount of agricultural work in the cultivation of his own small plot of land. This fact explains to some extent the comparative comfort of the operative in this cottage industry, for that they were fairly well off is the testimony of Adam Smith, in 1776. Commercial fluctuations were few; the home market was steady;

[1] For recent developments, *v.* p. 231.

employer and employed were more closely knit together than at present; wealth was more equally distributed, and capital existed in smaller amounts but in a larger number of hands. The poet's vision of "contentment spinning at the cottage door" was not altogether imaginary, for women and children shared in the common task brought home by the head of the family. Nor, after all, was trade so restricted and hampered as some writers have seemed to suppose. On the contrary, there was, in spite of bad roads, very frequent and considerable internal communication for manufacturing purposes, and this was facilitated by means of the local markets, the importance of which in those days cannot be easily overrated. Manufacturers would ride a long way to buy wool from the farmers or at the great fairs already mentioned, such as that of Stourbridge (p. 63), which was sufficiently considerable even a hundred years ago, or those of Lynn, Boston, Gainsborough, and Beverley, all four of which were celebrated for their wool-sales. This wool was then brought home and sorted; then sent out to the hand-combers, and on being returned combed was again sent out, often to long distances, to be spun. It was, for instance, sent from remote parts of Yorkshire to Lancashire, or even farther; or again from near London to Kendal and back. When spun, the tops, or fine wool, were entrusted to some shopkeeper to "put out" among the neighbours. Then the yarn was brought back and sorted by the manufacturer himself into hanks, according to the counts and twist. The hand-weavers would next come for their warp and weft, and in due time bring back the piece, which often was sent elsewhere to be dyed. Finally, the finished cloth was sent to be sold at the fairs, or at the local "piece halls" of such central towns as Leeds or Halifax.

Hence it will be seen that there was a considerable diffusion of work under the old system, and it was not necessary for great numbers of people to live close together, or work in factories upon a large scale. Things were done with greater leisure, and more time was taken over them. But with the Industrial Revolution came all the hurry and stress of modern manufacturing life, and a complete change took place in the manner and methods of manufacture. And now, having seen how things stood immediately before this great change, we can proceed at once to the means by which it was brought about.

CHAPTER II

THE EPOCH OF THE GREAT INVENTIONS

§ 1. **The suddenness of the Revolution and its importance**—The change from the domestic system of industry which has been briefly sketched in the previous chapter to the modern system of production by machinery and steam power, was sudden and violent. The great inventions were all made in a comparatively short space of time, and the previous slow growth of industry developed quickly into a feverish burst of manufacturing production that completely revolutionized the face of industrial England. In little more than twenty years all the great inventions of Watt, Arkwright, and Boulton had been completed, steam had been applied to the new looms, and the modern factory system had fairly begun. Nothing has done more to make England what she at present is—whether for better or worse—than this sudden and silent Industrial Revolution, for it increased her wealth tenfold, and gave her half-a-century's start in front of the nations of Europe. The French Revolution took place about the same time, and as it was performed amid streams of blood and flame, it attracted the attention of historians, who have apparently yet to learn that bloodshed and battles are merely the incidents of history. The French Revolution also succeeded in giving birth to one of the world's military heroes, and a military hero naturally excites the enthusiasm of the multitude. But the French Revolution was the result of economic causes that had been operating for centuries, and which had had their effect in England four hundred years before, at the time of the Peasants' Revolt. These economic causes have been rather kept in the background by modern historians, and it was hardly to be expected that they should recognize the operation of such causes in England; more especially as their effects were not accentuated by political fireworks, but were even partially hidden by subsequent events resulting from these effects. Men were blinded too by an increase in the wealth of the richer portion of the nation, not even seeing whence that wealth proceeded, and quite ignoring the fact that it was accompanied by serious poverty among the industrial classes. Nor did historians perceive that the world-famous wars in which England was engaged at the close of the last century and up to 1815, were necessitated by England's endeavour to gain the commercial supremacy of the world, after she had invented the means of supplying the world's markets to overflowing. Economic causes were at the root of them all. We shall discuss later the connection between our foreign politics and our industry; at present we must adhere to the subject of the development of that industry by the great inventors.[1]

[1] There was an Agricultural Revolution as important as the Industrial one, but it is best to treat it separately. I have done so in Ch. vi.

§ 2. **The great inventors**—The transition from the domestic to the factory system was begun by four great inventions. In 1770 James Hargreaves, a weaver of Standhill, near Blackburn, patented the spinning-jenny—*i.e.* a frame with a number of spindles side by side, which were fed by machinery, and by which many threads might be spun at once, instead of only one, as had been the case in the old one-thread hand-spinning wheel. Hargreaves first used this "jenny" for some time in his own house, and was at once enabled to spin eight times as much yarn as before. In 1771 Arkwright established a successful mill at Cromford on the Derwent, in which he employed his patent spinning machine, or "water-frame," an improvement upon a former invention of Wyatt's, which derived its name from the fact that it was worked by water power. A few years later (1779) both these inventions were superseded by that of Samuel Crompton, a spinner, but the son of a farmer near Bolton. His machine, the "mule," combined the principles of both the previous inventions, and was called by this name as being the hybrid offspring of its mechanical predecessors. It drew out the roving (*i.e.* the raw material when it has received its first twist) by an adaptation of the water-frame, and then passed it on to be finished and twisted into complete yarn by an adaptation of the spinning-jenny. This invention effected an enormous increase in production, for nowadays 12,000 spindles are often worked by it at once and by one spinner. It dates from the year 1779, and was so successful that by 1811 more than four and a half million spindles worked by "mules" were in use in various English factories. Like many inventors Crompton died in poverty in 1827.

These three inventions, however, only increased the power of spinning the raw material into yarn. What was now wanted was a machine that would perform the same service for weaving. This was discovered by Dr Cartwright, a Kentish parson, and was patented as the "power-loom" in 1785, though it had afterwards to undergo many improvements, and did not begin to be much used till 1813. But the principle of it was there, and it was one of the most important factors in the destruction of the old domestic system. For at first only spinning was done by machinery, and the weavers could still do their work by hand in the old methods; and indeed they continued to do so till a comparatively recent period, and many old people in Northern manufacturing districts can still remember the old weaving industry, as carried on in the workmen's own houses. But the improvements on Cartwright's invention did away with the hand-weaver, as the others had abolished the hand-spinner, and the old form of industry was doomed.

Its death-blow, however, was yet to come. Wondrous as were the changes introduced by the machines just spoken of none of them would have by themselves alone revolutionized our manufacturing industries. Power of some kind was needed to work them, and water power, though used at first, was insufficient and not always available. It was the application of steam to manufacturing processes which finally completed the Industrial Revolution. In 1769, the year in which Wellington and Bonaparte were born, James Watt took out his patent for the steam-engine. It was first used as an auxiliary in mining operations, but in 1785 it was introduced into factories, a Nottinghamshire cotton-spinner having one set up in his works, which had previously been run only by water power. Of course the enormous advantages of steam over water power became immediately apparent; manufacturers, especially in the cotton trade, hastened to make use of the new methods, and in fifteen years (1788–1803) the cotton trade trebled itself.

§ 3. **The revolution in manufactures and the factories**—Although these machines of which we have just spoken were intended at first for use in the manufacture of cotton, they rapidly extended to that of woollen and linen fabrics. It is impossible here to describe all the various modifications and adaptations that were thus made ; we can only refer to the general features of the great change. The most remarkable of these features was the sudden growth of factories, chiefly of course at first for spinning cotton or woollen yarn. The old factories had perforce been planted by the side of some running stream, often in a lonely and deserted spot, very inconvenient for markets and the procuring of labour ; but necessarily so placed for the sake of the water. Those of my readers who know Yorkshire or Lancashire fairly well may remember how frequently in the course of some long country walk near Bradford, Halifax, Leeds, or Manchester, they come upon the ruins of some old mill, crumbling beside a rushing stream, a silent relic of the old days before the use of steam. How wonderful must the first rude inventions have seemed to the workers in those old factories, as the strange new machinery rattled and shook in the quiet country hollows, and the becks and streamlets ran down to turn the new spindles and looms that were to revolutionize the face of agricultural England. But the old water-mills gave way to others worked by steam power, and now it was no longer necessary to choose any particular site for the works. So the new race of manufacturers made haste to run up steam-factories wherever they could. "Old barns and cart-houses," says Radcliffe, "outbuildings of all descriptions were repaired ; windows broke through the old blank walls, and all were fitted up for loom-shops; new weavers' cottages arose in every direction." The merchants too, who did not run factories on their own account, but merely purchased yarn, began to collect weavers around them in great numbers, to get looms together in a workshop, and to give out warp themselves to the workpeople. And now the workers began to feel the difference between the old system and the new. Formerly they used to buy for themselves the yarn they were to weave, and had a direct interest in the cloth they made from it, which was their own property. They were in fact economically independent. The new system made them dependent upon the merchant or upon the mill-owner. At first, it is true, they gained a rise in wages, for the increase in production was so great that labour was continually in demand, and every family, says Radcliffe, brought home forty to one hundred and twenty shillings per week. But this did not last very long. The new machinery soon threw out of employment a number of those who had worked only by hand; it enabled women and children to do the work of grown men; it made all classes of workers dependent upon capitalist employers; it introduced an era of hitherto unheard-of competition. The coming of the capitalists had become an accomplished fact, and with it began again the exploitation of labour. Of this we shall speak in another chapter. Other national changes now demand our attention.

§ 4. **The growth of population and the development of the Northern districts**—The two most striking facts of the Industrial Revolution are the great growth and the equally great shifting of the population. Before 1751 the largest decennial increase of population had been about 5 or 6 per cent. But for each of the next three periods of ten years the increase became rapidly greater, till in 1801

To face p. 163

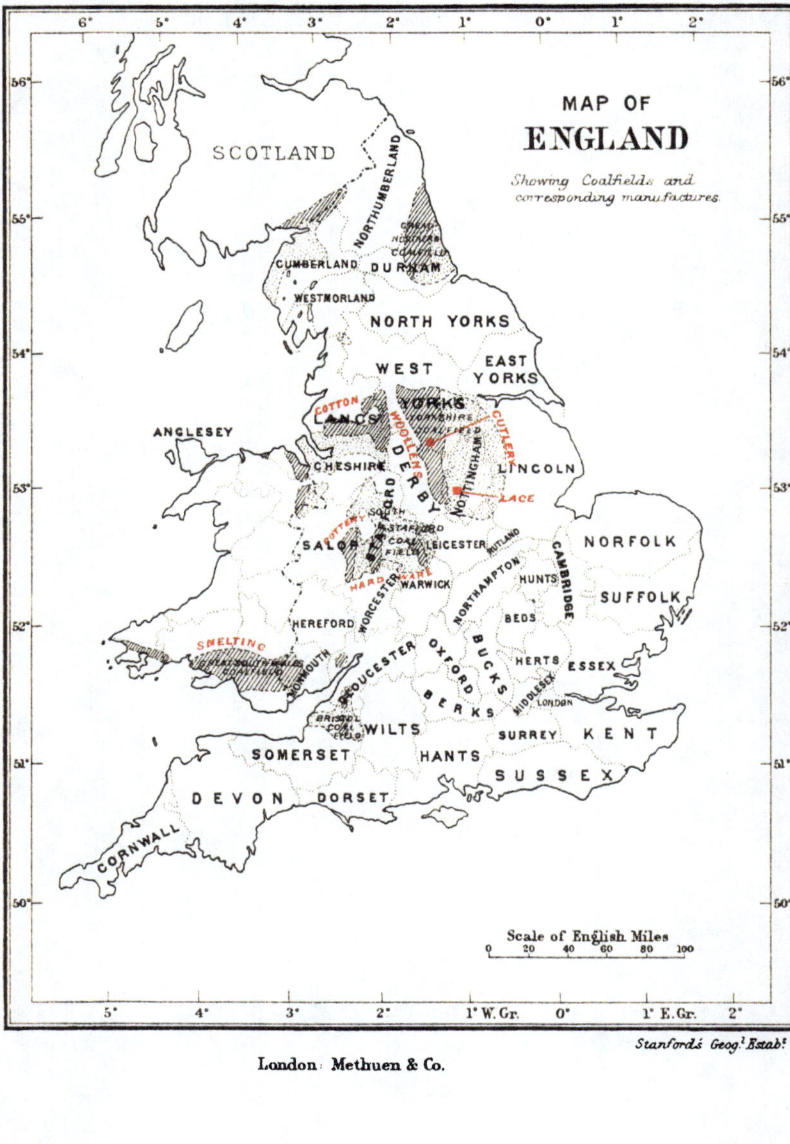

Stanford's Geog.l Estab.t

London: Methuen & Co.

it was 14 per cent. on the previous ten years, and reached even 21½ per cent. in the period 1801 to 1811. This last was the highest rate ever reached in England, and is more than double that recorded in the census of 1881 or 1891. The population of England had been under 8,000,000 in 1760; by 1821 it had risen to nearly 12,000,000; and at the present moment it is certainly nearly treble that number.

At the same time, the great migration to the North, already begun before the Revolution, was now accelerated and completed. The Northern counties, which in the Middle Ages had, as we saw, been comparatively deserted, now became and have since remained the most populous and flourishing of all. The centres of the new factory system were in the North, and thither flocked the workers who had formerly been distributed over England in a much more extensive manner, or who had clustered round the great Eastern and Western centres of industry, which before 1760 had excelled the other centre, the West Riding, in prosperity. But now this was changed. Before the Revolution, the Eastern counties, more especially about Norwich and the surrounding districts, had been famous for their manufactures of crapes, bombazines, and other fine, slight stuffs. In the West of England the towns of Bradford-on-Avon, Devizes, and Warminster had been manufacturing centres noted for their fine serges; Stroud had been the centre of the manufacture of dyed cloth, and so had Taunton been, for even in Defoe's time (1725) it had 1100 looms; and the excellence of the Cotswold wool had done much for the industry of the district. These two centres and their productions, then, were far more famous than the third, the West Riding, including the towns of Halifax, Leeds, and Bradford, where only coarse cloths were made. The cotton trade of Lancashire, too, had previously been insignificant, for it was only incidentally mentioned by Adam Smith, though Manchester and Bolton were then, as now, its headquarters. In 1760 only 40,000 persons were engaged in it, the annual value of the cotton manufacture was comparatively insignificant, while in 1764 the value of our cotton exports was only one-twentieth of our woollen, and only strong cottons, such as dimities and fustians, were made. But now the cotton cities of Lancashire and the woollen and worsted factories of Yorkshire greatly surpass the older seats of industry in wealth and population, while the cotton export has risen to be the first in the kingdom, and the vast majority of the industrial population is now found North of the Trent. These great industrial changes were the direct consequence of the introduction of new manufacturing processes. For the use of steam power in mills necessitated the liberal use of coal, and hence the factory districts are necessarily almost coincident with the great coal-fields, as will be seen from the appended map.[1] Moreover, the coal industry had been developed almost simultaneously with the growth of manufactures, and indeed one reacted upon the other. It will be convenient here to mention the improvements made in coal-mining and in the iron trade.

§ 5. **The revolution in the mining industries**—I have mentioned in a previous chapter that the development of the vast natural resources of our country as regards coal

[1] In this industrial map it will be seen that we have

(1) corresponding to the Yorks. coal-field, manufactrs. of { woollens, &c. / cutlery, &c. / lace & hosiery. / machinery.
(2) ,, ,, Lancs. ,, ,, ... cotton.
(3) ,, ,, Staffs. ,, ,, pottery and hardware.
(4) ,, ,, S. Wales ,, smelting & iron industries.

and iron was retarded by the lack of steam power (p. 137). But with the steam-engines of Watt and Boulton a new era dawned upon coal-mining. In 1774 Watt, after vainly advocating his invention, entered into partnership with Matthew Boulton, a Birmingham man, and their new engine soon produced a vast change in the manner of pumping water from the mines, just as it also produced other changes in every manufacture dependent upon the use of coal. Steam power was used not only to clear the mines of water, but also in sinking shafts, where formerly entrance had often been made only by tunnelling in the side of a hill. It was used too in bringing up the coal from the pit, and in many other necessary processes. The result of this application of steam power was soon seen in the general opening up of all the English coal-fields, and the consequent further growth of towns like Newcastle, Sheffield, and Birmingham, whose industries now depend so greatly upon a large supply of coal.

With the great output of coal came an immediate revival of the iron trade, which it will be remembered had greatly declined about 1737 and 1740, for as coal was not available wood had to be used as fuel, and the consequent destruction of forests, especially the Sussex Wealden, had caused legislative prohibitions. The scientific treatment of iron ore in the various processes of manufacture had indeed been improved, but nothing much could be done without coal. This was seen for instance by an iron-master, Anthony Bacon, in 1755, who obtained a lease for 99 years of a district at Merthyr Tydvil, eight miles long and five broad, upon which he erected both iron and coal works. In 1760 Smeaton's invention of a new blowing apparatus at his works at Carron, near Falkirk, did away with the old clumsy bellows ; and the other inventions of Cranage (1766), of Onions (1783), and of Cort

(1784), for which separate treatises must be consulted, brought the manufacture of iron almost to perfection. Whereas about 1740 we produced only some 18,000 tons of iron annually, and had to import at least 20,000 tons; we produced in 1788 as much as 68,000 tons, and the production has gone on steadily increasing to the present time, when our export alone amounts to four and a half million tons of iron and steel annually.

§ 6. **The nation's wealth and its wars**—Of course these discoveries of new processes in procuring coal and making iron enormously increased the wealth of England, and at the same time entirely changed the conditions of industry. For they helped on the textile manufactures by providing any amount of fuel and machinery, and all these together gave employment to a population that seemed to grow in accordance with the need of the nation for workers. The new textile and mining industries supplied England with that vast wealth which enabled her to endure successfully the long years of war at the close of last century and the beginning of this. The Industrial Revolution came only just in time, for after the repose of 1763 to 1792, during which this silent Revolution matured and took root, England engaged in a struggle which she certainly could never have supported without a far greater national wealth than she possessed in the first three quarters of the eighteenth century. And as it was, the year 1815 found a large portion of her people in poverty and distress, and the industrial classes suffered heavily from the taxation which the war imposed. But owing to her industrial development the war left England at its close, in spite of all her troubles, the foremost nation of Europe in economic matters, and consequently in all other matters also. As is the case with most modern wars, this great war originated in economic causes, even to a certain extent in economic mistakes, but it had important effects upon industry and was largely affected by industrial considerations. Hence we must consider it rather more closely.

CHAPTER III

WARS, POLITICS, AND INDUSTRY

§ 1. **England's industrial advantages in 1763**—If we look at the state of the European powers after the conclusion of the Seven Years' War by the Treaty of Paris in 1763, we shall see that England had achieved a very favourable position for the growth of her internal industries. It is true that along with the rest of Europe she had adopted the policy of endeavouring to secure a sole market for her goods, and though that policy was a ruinous mistake she was not alone in her error, and since other powers were doing the same, it was just as well that she should hold the lead among them. And, as Professor Rogers has remarked, since we are paying interest upon the heavy national bills which we ran up at that time, we may profitably examine what we gained thereby.

In the first place, England had seriously crippled her powerful commercial rival, France, both in her Indian and American possessions. By the Seven Years' War we had gained Canada, Florida, and all the French possessions east of the Mississippi River (except New Orleans); while in India our influence had become supreme, owing to the victories of Clive. French influence in India and America was practically annihilated. Spain, the faithful ally of France, lost with her friend her place as the commercial rival of England in foreign trade. Germany was again being ravaged by the dynastic struggles in which Frederick the Great bore so prominent a part, between the reigning houses of Austria and Prussia. Holland was similarly torn by internal dissensions under the Stadtholder William V., which gave the rival sovereigns of Prussia and Austria a chance of making matters worse by their interference. By 1790 the United Provinces had thus sunk into utter insignificance. Sweden, Norway, and Italy were of no account in European politics, and Russia had only begun to come to the front. Hence England alone had the chance of "the universal empire of a sole market." The supply of this market, especially in our American colonies, was in the hands of English manufacturers and English workmen. The great inventions which came, as we saw, after 1763 were thus at once called into active employment, and our mills and mines were able to produce wealth as fast as they could work without fear of foreign competition.

§ 2. **The mistake of the Mercantile Theory**—But unfortunately our capitalists made a great mistake in their policy. The commercial mind of England was dominated by what is known as the "Mercantile Theory." It was a theory that had grown up naturally out of the spirit of Nationalism, of self-sustained and complete national life, that was our heritage from the Renaissance and the Reformation. It was not altogether wrong, for its object was national greatness, an object laudable and harmless enough. But the believers in the policy of increasing our national greatness also believed that it could only be attained in one way, and that was at the expense of our neighbours. In one form and another the theory frequently crops up even to-day, though we are supposed to have repudiated it. The measures adopted to attain this end were various and not always unsuccessful. True, our commercial forefathers made the mistake—not uncommon even now—of believing that national wealth consisted chiefly in holding large stores of gold and silver, and hence they prohibited the export of bullion, till the East India Company demonstrated the futility of this scheme.[1] They endeavoured, too, to obtain a supply of the precious metals by prohibiting the purchase of foreign manufactures, and encouraging only the imports of raw material, that we might sell our own manufactures for foreign silver and gold. Hence proceeded wars of tariff, as for instance when we prohibited the import of gold-lace from Flanders, and the Flemish in revenge excluded our exports of wool. But the most famous of the restrictions imposed by this theory were the Navigation Acts of 1651, by which it was ordered that no goods from Asia, Africa, or America were to be imported into England or her colonies, except in ships belonging to English subjects, and no goods of any European country were to be imported except in English vessels, or ships belonging to the country from which the goods came. Of course these Acts resulted in collision with Dutch interests, for the Dutch were at that time the ocean carriers of the world. We were driven out of neutral ports, and lost the Russian and Baltic trade, because of the high charges of English ship-owners, to whom this protective scheme gave a monopoly of freights. But at the same time our shipping trade gained a great stimulus, and our commercial supremacy grew with it. Of course, however, this protective measure made the country at large pay a higher price for this privilege than was necessary, and we could probably have done better without it. Nevertheless these Acts, coupled with the development of our Indian and American trade, resulted in giving us a position of undoubted

[1] See note 15, p. 249, on this point.

commercial supremacy. Many other Protective measures, of a worse kind than this, were passed owing to the dictates of this theory, as for instance when in 1750 Parliament forbade the importation of pig and bar iron from our American colonies. But the Nemesis of this Protective policy was sure to come, and come it did in that fatal folly which caused us to lose those very colonies which we had defended against the French in the Seven Years' War.

§ 3. **The loss of the American colonies**—The way in which English statesmen looked upon our colonies in the last century was that they owed everything to England, and that therefore it was only fair that they should be exploited in the interests of the mother-country. Thus all imports to our colonies from any other country of Europe except England were forbidden, in order that our manufacturers might monopolize the American market. The criminal folly of our legislators went even further than this, for every attempt was made to discourage the colonists from starting manufactures at home. The American woollen industry was practically suppressed ; all iron manufactures, as just mentioned, were forbidden in 1750 ; even colonial hatters were not allowed to send hats from one colony into another.

Nevertheless the American colonists evaded the regulations that forbade them to trade with any but the mother-country, and did, for instance, a considerable trade with South America, But in George III.'s reign, Grenville, a Whig minister, was foolish enough to try and stop this. Moreover, he sought to raise money wherewith to pay for the American portion of the Seven Years' War by taxing the colonists upon the stamps on legal papers (Stamp Act, 1765). The idea that the colonists should pay part of the expenses of the war undertaken in their defence was just enough ; but that these expenses should be defrayed by a system of taxation in which they had no voice was exactly the reverse. It is to the credit of Pitt that he protested against this taxation without representation, and exerted his influence for the repeal of this Act (1766). Thus the feelings of the colonists were soothed for a time, and in 1770 Lord North took off all taxes except that on tea. The colonists refused to buy tea: the East India Company, whose trade naturally suffered, tried to force their tea into America, and matters culminated in the celebrated emptying of a shipload of it into Boston harbour by the citizens of that port (1773). North tried to punish the Bostonians by decreeing that their port should be closed, and that the charter of Massachusetts, their colony, should be annulled. Of course war was now imminent. We need not here go into the details of that unfortunate conflict, though we must mention the heroic endeavours of Pitt, now Lord Chatham, to make England give full redress to her offspring. His efforts were in vain. France eagerly took the opportunity of assisting the Americans against the English, and England had to pay very dearly for her adherence to the Mercantile Theory.

§ 4. **The outbreak of the great Continental War**—But although the War of Independence cost us a great deal, it did not greatly affect the development of our home industries. The Industrial Revolution went steadily on, and for just thirty years (1763-93) the country, though not entirely at peace, was yet sufficiently undisturbed to make rapid progress in the new manufacturing methods. But in 1789 the French Revolution broke out, and for over twenty years Europe was plunged into a disastrous and exhausting conflict. At the first outbreak of the Revolution, England looked on quietly. Many men were openly glad that the downtrodden masses of the French nation had overthrown the tyranny of an upper class whose only idea of their duty in life was to extort the last farthing from those below them, in order to spend it in irresponsible debauchery. Statesmen like Fox gloried in it; the younger Pitt was anxious not to interfere. But Pitt was forced into action by the capitalists, who now were equal with the land-owners as the two ruling powers of England. He saw that the conquests which the new French Republic was already beginning to make might help France to secure again her old position as the most formidable rival of English commerce. If now this rival could be finally struck down, England was sure of the control of the world's markets. It was obviously the policy of England to check the power of France, and when war was declared by the young Republic, England was not slow to answer the challenge. After this England was plunged headlong into the great European struggle of Monarchy against Republicanism. Pitt gained the support of all classes at home. The merchants and manufacturers were only too glad to see their old rival ruined; the land-owners and nobility were of course indignant at seeing the "lower classes," even of a foreign nation, rise against their lords, even though their lords perhaps deserved their punishment. It was generally believed, and it was largely true, that England was fighting for the great principles of Monarchy and Religion, exemplified by a foolish king and a corrupted priesthood. For a time everyone supported Pitt's policy. But the French Revolution had found many sympathizers among the working classes, and after the country had felt the first severity of the burdens imposed by the war, a spirit of discontent manifested itself. But the nation at large was against this opposition, and drastic measures were taken to silence it. Pitt was indomitable till his death (in 1805), and under his guidance England often fought single-handed against the world.

At times, as in 1796, she was threatened with invasion by the French, and the Irish, or a certain section of them, assisted her would-be invaders. At another time (1806), English industry was threatened with ruin by Napoleon's Berlin Decree, forbidding Continental nations to trade with us.[1] But at last the great inspiring genius of England's enemies was defeated, and the long years of war came to a close in 1815.

§ 5. **Its effects upon industry, and the working classes**—When peace came at length, it found the resources of the nation sorely tried, but not yet exhausted. All classes had suffered somewhat, but the working classes worst of all. The French Revolution, and the consequent wars, had retarded to some extent the development of our industries, for it took nearly all the wealth produced by the new industrial system to pay for them. But in one thing we possessed a great advantage over Continental nations, for our island was the only country in which war was not actually going on, and hence our manufactures were undisturbed. Consequently England was by no means so exhausted as the other participants in the struggle, and she had, moreover, the ocean-carrying trade left secure to her by our undisputed naval supremacy. But yet her finances had been tried and stretched to an enormous extent. The total cost of the war with France had been £831,446,449, to meet which Pitt was compelled to turn to almost every expedient that his financial ingenuity could suggest. Taxation became more and more heavy, and £600,000,000 was added to the debt which we have since been engaged in paying off. The currency had been placed in the most abnormal condition; cash payments were (in 1797) suspended by the Bank of England; and it became a necessity, as soon as

[1] See my *Commerce in Europe*, p. 177.

the war was over, to put an end to the circulation of a practically inconvertible paper currency by the resumption of them in 1819.

But the working classes had suffered the most, in spite of the fact that our manufactures prospered and exports increased all through the war. In 1793 the exports were officially valued at over £17,000,000; for every year afterwards they were at least £22,000,000, often more; in 1800 over £34,000,000, and in 1815 had quite doubled their value at the beginning of the war, being then over £58,000,000 (official value). But the profits all went into the hands of the capitalist manufacturers, while taxation fell with special severity upon the poor, since taxes were placed on every necessity and convenience of daily life. Even as late as 1841 there were 1200 articles in the customs tariff. The price of wheat, moreover, rose to famine height; from 49*s*. 3*d*. per quarter in 1793, to 69*s*. in 1799, to 113*s*. in 1800, and 106*s*. in 1810. At the same time wages were rapidly falling,[1] and thus the chief burdens of the war fell upon those least able to pay for them. But the poverty of the poor was the wealth of the landowners, who kept on raising rents continually and grew rich upon the starvation of the people; for they persuaded Parliament to prohibit the importation of foreign corn except at famine prices (cf. p. 200), and shifted the burden of taxation, as was not unnatural, upon other shoulders. It was owing to their influence that Pitt raised fresh funds from taxes on articles of trade, manufacture and general consumption. The result was seen in the deepening distress of the industrial classes, and in 1816 riots broke out everywhere—in Kent among the agricultural labourers, in the Midlands among the miners, and at

[1] For further details as to condition of the working classes, see p. 194.

Nottingham among the artisans, who wreaked their vengeance upon the new machines which they thought had stolen their bread. They should have blamed those who did not allow them to participate in the wealth they had helped to create.

§ 6. **Politics among the working classes**—Such were the economic effects of the war upon English society—the enriching of the capitalists and land-owners at the expense of the working classes. So dire was the distress of the workmen that they felt something must be done to make their voice effectively heard in the government of the people. William Cobbett, in his *Weekly Political Register*, taught them to believe that a reform of Parliament would cure their evils. The influences of the French Revolution and the Industrial Revolution also combined to arouse an active political feeling amongst them; for the former excited a sympathetic feeling of revolt against unjust oppression, from what source soever it might come, and the latter brought home to them in their daily lives the new and sharp distinctions between the capitalist autocrat and his hundreds of workpeople bound to him only by a cash nexus, and as yet powerless to resist his endeavours to keep down their wages. Indistinctly, but none the less keenly, the working classes began to feel that they too must be consulted in the councils of the nation, and as a preliminary step must gain an influence over political events. But their early endeavours were sharply and severely repressed, and the legislation following on the (so-called) Manchester Massacre of 1819, crushed them for a time. But the Great War had roused the political feelings of the masses, by the misery it had inflicted upon them and by the industrial conditions which it had brought more fully into play. For although at first it retarded them, it gave a direct stimulus to the new manufactures and to the new manufacturing system, by leaving England the only nation not too exhausted to continue her commerce. During its progress England had definitely become the workshop of the world, her industry had definitely completed its transition from the domestic to the factory system. Of this system, with its enormous advantages but also enormous evils, we must now speak.

CHAPTER IV

THE FACTORY SYSTEM AND ITS RESULTS

§ 1. **The results of the introduction of the factory system**—The great war of which I have just spoken in the preceding chapter found England at its beginning a nation whose mainstay was agriculture, with manufactures increasing, it is true, but still only of secondary importance. At the commencement of the war, English workers spun and wove in their cottages ; at its close they were herded together in factories, and were the servants of machinery. The capitalist element had become the main feature in production, and the capitalist manufacturers the main figures in English industry, rivalling and often overtopping the landed gentry. But a man cannot become a capitalist without capital, and capital cannot be accumulated without labour ; though these remarkably obvious facts are constantly forgotten. The large capitalists of earlier manufacturing days obtained their capital, after the first small beginnings, from the wealth produced by their workmen and from their own acuteness in availing themselves of new inventions. Of the wealth produced by their workmen they took nearly the whole, leaving their employés only enough to live upon while producing more wealth for their masters. Hence it may be said that capital was in this case the result of abstinence, though the abstinence was on the part of the workman and not of his employer, as we shall shortly see.

This, then, was the immediate result of the factory system : the growth of large accumulations of capital in the hands of the new master manufacturers, who with their new machinery, undisturbed by internal war, were able to supply the nations of Europe with clothing at a time when these nations were too much occupied in internecine conflicts on their own soil to produce food and clothing for themselves. Even Napoleon, in spite of all his edicts directed against English trade, was fain to clothe his soldiers in Yorkshire stuffs when he led them to Moscow. It was no wonder that the growth of capital was rapid and enormous. Other results followed. The formerly widespread cottage industry was now aggregated into a few districts, nearly all in Lancashire and Yorkshire. Persons of all ages and both sexes were collected together in huge buildings, under no moral control, with no arrangements for the preservation of health, comfort, or decency. The enormous extension of trade rendered extra work necessary, and the mills ran all night long as well as by day. The machines made "to shorten labour" resulted in many cases in vastly extending it ; while in others again they took away all the means of livelihood from the old class of hand-workers. Hence riots frequently occurred, and the labourers sought to destroy the new machinery ; the struggle of what were called "the iron men" against human beings of flesh and blood long continued to be a source of controversy and complaint, more especially as the workmen saw that the profits made by these iron men went almost entirely into the hands of their masters.

§ 2. **Contemporary evidence of the new order of things**—A very good idea of the effects of the introduction of the factory system upon the operatives may be formed from a resolution unanimously adopted by the magistrates at the quarter sessions of Preston, in Lancashire, dated November 11th, 1779, wherein it was "resolved: That the sole cause of great riots was the new machines employed in the cotton manufacture: That the county [*i.e.* the manufacturers] had greatly benefited by their erection, and that the destroying them in one county only led to their erection in another; and that if a total stop were put by the legislature to their erection in Britain it would only tend to their establishment in foreign countries, to the detriment of the trade in Britain." But better than the cold words of a formal resolution is the description of the country round Manchester published in 1795 by a Dr Aikin. He points out what we have already referred to, that "the sudden invention and improvement of machines to shorten labour have had a surprising influence to extend our trade, and also to call in hands from all parts, particularly children for the cotton mills." He says that domestic life is seriously endangered by the extensive employment of women and girls in the mills, for they had become ignorant of all household duties. "The females are wholly uninstructed in knitting, sewing, and other domestic affairs requisite to make them frugal wives and mothers. This is a very great misfortune to them and to the public, as is sadly proved by a comparison of the labourers in husbandry, and those of manufacturers in general. In the former we meet with neatness, cleanliness, and comfort; in the latter with filth, rags, and poverty." He also mentions the great prevalence of fevers among employés in cotton mills, consequent upon the utterly unsanitary conditions under which they laboured. But nowhere were the evils which accompanied the sudden growth of wealth and of industry so marked as in the case of those miserable beings who were brought to labour in the new mills under the apprentice system. Their life was literally and without exaggeration simply that of slaves.

§ 3. **English slavery. The apprentice system**—When factories were first built there was a strong repugnance on the part of parents who had been accustomed to the old family life under the domestic system to send their children into these places. It was in fact considered a disgrace so to do: the epithet of "factory girl" was the most insulting that could be applied to a young woman, and girls who had once been in a factory could never find employment elsewhere. It was not until the wages of the workman had been reduced to a starvation level that they consented to their children and wives being employed in the mills. But the manufacturers wanted labour by some means or other, and they got it. They got it from the workhouses. They sent for parish apprentices from all parts of England, and pretended to apprentice them to the new employments just introduced. The mill-owners systematically communicated with the overseers of the poor, who arranged a day for the inspection of pauper children. Those chosen by the manufacturer were then conveyed by wagons or canal boats to their destination, and from that moment were doomed to slavery. Sometimes regular traffickers would take the place of the manufacturer, and transfer a number of children to a factory district, and there keep them, generally in some dark cellar, till they could hand them over to a mill-owner in want of hands, who would come and examine their height, strength, and bodily capacities, exactly as did the slave-dealers in the American markets.

After that the children were simply at the mercy of their owners, nominally as apprentices, but in reality as mere slaves, who got no wages, and whom it was not worth while even to feed or clothe properly, because they were so cheap and their places could be so easily supplied. It was often arranged by the parish authorities, in order to get rid of imbeciles, that one idiot should be taken by the mill-owner with every twenty sane children. The fate of these unhappy idiots was even worse than that of the others. The secret of their final end has never been disclosed, but we can form some idea of their awful sufferings from the hardships of the other victims to capitalist greed and cruelty. Their treatment was most inhuman. The hours of their labour were only limited by exhaustion after many modes of torture had been unavailingly applied to force continued work. Children were often worked *sixteen hours* a day, by day and by night. Even Sunday was used as a convenient time to clean the machinery. The author of *The History of the Factory Movement* writes [1]: "In stench, in heated rooms, amid the constant whirling of a thousand wheels, little fingers and little feet were kept in ceaseless action, forced into unnatural activity by blows from the heavy hands and feet of the merciless over-looker, and the infliction of bodily pain by instruments of punishment invented by the sharpened ingenuity of insatiable selfishness." They were fed upon the coarsest and cheapest food, often with the same as that served out to the pigs of their master. They slept by turns and in relays, in filthy beds which were never cool; for one set of children were sent to sleep in them as soon as the others had gone off to their daily or nightly toil. There was often no discrimination of sexes; and disease, misery and vice grew as in a hot-

[1] Samuel Kydd (pseudonym "Alfred").

bed of contagion. Some of these miserable beings tried to run away. To prevent their doing so, those suspected of this tendency had irons riveted on their ankles with long links reaching up to the hips, and were compelled to work and sleep in these chains, young women and girls as well as boys suffering this brutal treatment. Many died and were buried secretly at night in some desolate spot, lest people should notice the number of the graves ; and many committed suicide. The catalogue of cruelty and misery is too long to recite here ; it may be read in the *Memoirs of Robert Blincoe,* himself an apprentice, or in the pages of the Blue-books of the beginning of this century, in which even the methodical dry official language is startled into life by the misery it has to relate. It is perhaps not well for me to say more about the subject, for one dares not trust oneself to try and set down calmly all that might be told about this awful page in the history of industrial England. I need only remark, that during this period of unheeded and ghastly suffering in the mills of our native land, the British philanthropist was occupying himself with agitating for the relief of the very largely imaginary woes of negro slaves in other countries. He of course succeeded in raising the usual amount of sentiment, and perhaps more than the usual amount of money on behalf of an inferior and barbaric race, who have repaid him by relapsing into a contented indolence and a scarcely concealed savagery which have gone far to ruin our possessions in the West Indies. The spectacle of England buying the freedom of black slaves by riches drawn from the labour of her white ones, affords an interesting study for the cynical philosopher.

§ 4. **The beginning of the factory agitation**—The state of things in factories where large numbers of apprentices were employed became so bad, that at last something had to be done. In 1802 an Act was passed "for the preservation of the health and morals of apprentices and others employed in cotton and other mills." It is a significant fact, that the immediate cause of this Bill was the fearful spread through the factory districts of Manchester of epidemic disease, owing to the overwork, scanty food, wretched clothing, long hours, bad ventilation, and overcrowding in unhealthy dwellings of the workpeople, especially the children. The hours of work were "reduced" to only 12 per day. This Act, however, did not apply to children residing near the factory where they were employed, for they were supposed to be "under the supervision of their parents." The result was that, although the apprentice system was discontinued, other children came to work in the mills, and were treated almost as brutally, though luckily they were not entirely in the hands of their master. But the evils of this system of child labour were very great. During the whole of the period of 1800 to 1820, and even to 1840, the results of their sufferings were seen in the early deaths of the majority of children and in the crippled and distorted forms of the majority of those who survived. On the women and grown-up girls the effects of long hours and wearisome work were equally disastrous. A curious inversion of the proper order of things was seen in the domestic economy of the victims of this cheap labour system, for women and girls were superseding men in manufacturing labour, and, in consequence, their husbands had often to attend, in a shiftless, slovenly fashion, to those household duties which mothers and daughters hard at work in the factories were unable to fulfil. Worse still, mothers and fathers in some cases lived upon the killing labour of their little children, by letting them out to hire to manufacturers, who found them cheaper than their parents.

The factory hands in general, and the children in particular, at length found help from a few philanthropists who had not allowed themselves to be dazzled by the glowing eloquence of the agitators against black slavery. Lord Ashley, afterwards Earl of Shaftesbury, and Richard Oastler must in especial be mentioned as the champions of the mill-hands. Long years after Lord Shaftesbury had succeeded in his noble work, he spoke of the sad sights he had seen during his earlier labours in the factory districts. "Well can I recollect," he said in a speech in the House of Lords in 1873, "in the earlier periods of the factory movement, waiting at the factory gates to see the children come out, and a set of sad, dejected, cadaverous creatures they were. In Bradford especially the proofs of long and cruel toil were most remarkable. The cripples and distorted forms might be numbered by hundreds, perhaps by thousands. A friend of mine collected a vast number together for me ; the sight was most piteous, the deformities incredible. They seemed to me, such were their crooked shapes, like a mass of crooked alphabets." A corroboration of his words is found in one of Southey's letters to Mr May (written March 1st, 1833), in which, speaking of factory labour, he remarked with justice : "the slave trade is mercy compared to it."

The companion of the famous Lord Shaftesbury in the factory agitation was Richard Oastler, who was born in 1789 and died in 1861, and at first, especially in 1807, was a great supporter of Wilberforce in his anti-slavery agitation. But, living as he did in the factory districts of Yorkshire, he discovered a worse slavery existing at his very doors, and at once decided to do his best to put a stop to it. From 1829 to 1832 he was the leader of the movement for a "ten hours day," and from 1830 to 1847 he devoted himself especially to stopping the oppression of children in factories, till he caused the Factories Regulation Acts to be passed. A short reference to these Factory Acts will not be out of place.

§ 5. **The various Factory Acts**—After the Act of 1802 already referred to for improving the condition of apprentices, an Act for the regulation of work in cotton mills was passed in 1819, allowing no child to be admitted into a factory before the age of nine, and placing 12 hours a day as the limit of work for those between the ages of nine and sixteen. The day was really one of 13½ or 14 hours, because no meal-times were included in the working day. Then again in 1831 an Act was passed forbidding night-work in factories for persons between nine and twenty-one years of age, while the working day for persons under eighteen was to be 12 hours a day, and 9 hours on Saturdays. But this legislation only applied to cotton factories; those engaged in the manufacture of wool were quite untouched, and matters there were as bad as ever. But a spirit of agitation was fortunately abroad in the country. These were the days of the Reform Bill and of the rise of Trade Unions. These unions of workmen cried out for the restriction of non-adult labour to 10 hours a day, and the Conservative party, who were chiefly interested in the land and not in the mills, supported them readily against the manufacturers, who were mainly Liberals and Radicals. The two most important Acts were those of 1833 and 1847. That of 1833, introduced by Lord Shaftesbury, prohibited night-work to persons under eighteen in both cotton, wool, and other factories; children from nine to thirteen years of age were not to work more than 48 hours a week, and young persons from thirteen to eighteen years were to work only 68 hours. Provision was also made for the children's attendance at school, and for the appointment of factory inspectors. These restrictions in the employment of children led to a great increase in the use of improved machinery to make up for the loss of their labour, and it is probable that they accelerated the use of steam power instead of water power in the smaller and more old-fashioned mills. Then, after one or two minor Acts, the famous Ten Hours Bill (10 Vict. c. 29) was passed in 1847, which reduced the labour of women and young persons to 10 hours a day, the legal day being between 5.30 A.M. and 8.30 P.M. Manufacturers tried to avoid the provisions of this Bill by working persons thus protected in relays, but this was stopped by the fixing of a uniform working day in 1850, so that young persons and women could only work between the hours of 6 A.M. and 6 P.M., and on Saturdays only till 2 P.M. Since the passing of these Acts a great many much needed extensions of their provisions to other industries have been made, and in 1874 the minimum age at which a child could be admitted to a factory was fixed at ten years. The limitation of the labour of women and young persons necessarily involved the limitation of men's labour, because their work could not be done without female aid. Thus the ten hours day at last became universal in factories.

§ 6. **How these Acts were passed**—It is curious to notice how these Acts were passed. They all showed the steady advance of the principle of State interference with labour; a doctrine most distasteful to the old Ricardian school of economists, even when that interference was made in the interests of the physical and moral well-being, not only of the industrial classes, but of the community at large. Hence the economists of the day aided the manufacturers in opposing these Acts to the utmost of their power, and the laws passed were due to the action of the Tories and land-owners. Lord Shaftesbury, Fielden, Oastler, and Sadler were all Tories, though they were accused of being Socialists. They were supported by the landed gentry. But the mill-owners had their revenge afterwards when they helped to repeal the Corn Laws in spite of the protest of the landlords, who did not mind the workmen having shorter hours at other people's expense, but objected to their having cheap bread at their own. The working classes cannot fail to observe that each party was their friend only in so far as they could injure their opponents, or at least do no harm to themselves. John Bright especially distinguished himself (Feb. 10, 1847) by his violent denunciation of the Ten Hours Bill, which he characterized as "one of the worst measures ever passed in the shape of an Act of the legislature."[1] In 1908 a Coal Mines (Eight Hours) Bill was passed into law.

But when we look back upon the degradation and oppression from which the industrial classes were rescued by this agitation, we can understand why Arnold Toynbee said so earnestly: "I tremble to think what this country would have been but for the Factory Acts." They form one of the most interesting pages in the history of industry, for they show how fearful may be the results of a purely capitalist and competitive industrial system, unless the wage-earners are in a position to act as an effectual check upon the greed of an unscrupulous employer.

[1] This extraordinary utterance is to be found in the records of Hansard, third series, volume 89, page 1148.

CHAPTER V

THE CONDITION OF THE WORKING CLASSES

§ 1. **Disastrous effects of the new industrial system**—We have already seen in various preceding chapters that the condition of the labourers deteriorated from the time of Elizabeth onwards, but in the middle of the eighteenth century it had been materially improved owing to the increase of wealth from the new agriculture and from the general growth of foreign trade. But then came the great Continental wars and the Industrial Revolution; and it is a sad but significant fact that, although the total wealth of the nation vastly increased at the end of last century and the beginning of this, little of that wealth came into the hands of the labourers, but went mainly into the hands of the great landlords and new capitalist manufacturers, or was spent in the enormous expenses of foreign war. We saw, too, that the labourer felt far more severely than anyone else the burden of this war, for taxes had been imposed on almost every article of consumption, while at the same time the price of wheat had risen enormously. Moreover, labour was now more than ever dependent on capital, and the individual labourer was thoroughly under the heel of his employer. This, it will be remembered, was the result of the system of Assessment of Wages (p. 107), under which the justices of the peace, including of course chiefly manufacturers and land-owners, fixed the wages of labour for their own districts, and fixed them at so low a figure that they had nearly always to be supplemented out of the rates paid by the general public. The labourer had no redress, for all combination in the form now known as Trade Unions was suppressed, and his condition sank to the lowest depth of poverty and degradation.

§ 2. **The allowance system of relief**—This state of things was aggravated by various misfortunes. The latter part of the eighteenth century was marked by almost chronic scarcity, and after 1790 wheat was rarely below 50*s.* a quarter, and often double that price. The famine was enhanced by the restrictions of the Corn Laws; meanwhile, population was growing with portentous and almost inexplicable rapidity. The factories employed large numbers of hands, but these were chiefly children whose parents were often compelled to live upon the labour of their little ones; and the introduction of machinery had naturally caused a tremendous dislocation in industry, which could not be expected to right itself immediately. Poverty was so widespread that, in 1795, the Berkshire justices, in a now famous meeting at Speenhamland, near Newbury, declared the old quarter sessions assessment of wages insufficient, besought employers to give rates more in proportion to the cost of living, but added that if employers refused to do this they would make an allowance to every poor family in accordance with its numbers. This allowance system succeeded in demoralizing both employers and employed alike, taking the responsibility of giving decent wages off the shoulders of the farmers, and putting a premium upon the incontinence and thriftlessness of the labourers. This method of relief was general from about 1795 to 1834, in fact until the enactment of the New Poor Law. Employers of labour, manufacturing as well as agricultural, put down wages in many parts of the country to what was simply a starvation point, knowing that an allowance would be made to the labourers, upon the magistrates' orders, out of the poor rates. The wages actually paid to able-bodied men were frequently only five or six shillings a week, but relief to the amount of four, five, six, or seven shillings a week, according to the size of the man's family, was given out of the rates. Such a system could not fail to have a permanently disastrous influence upon the moral and social condition of those who suffered from it, taking from them all self-reliance, all hope, all incentives to improving their position in life. And as a matter of fact its ill-effects, especially in agricultural districts, are even yet apparent.

§ 3. **Restrictions upon labour**—What made the condition of the labourers worse still, was the fact that they could neither go from one place to another to seek work, nor could they combine in industrial partnership for their mutual interests. The law of settlement effectually prevented migration of labourers from one parish to another. It began with the Statute of 1662, which allowed a pauper to obtain relief only from that parish where he had his settlement, "settlement" being defined as forty days' residence without interruption. There were many variations and complications of this Statute made in ensuing reigns, but it remained substantively the same till it was mitigated by the Poor Law of 1834. The law of settlement was further strengthened by what are called the Combination Laws, which prevented workmen from coming together to deliberate over their various industrial interests, or to gain a rise in wages. "We have no Acts of Parliament," said Adam Smith, with justice, "against combining to lower the price of work, but many against combining to raise it." Elsewhere he describes the inevitable result of a strike as being "nothing but the punishment or ruin of the ringleaders." The workmen had, of course, no political influence: they could only show their discontent by riots and rick-burnings. Yet the time of their deliverance was at hand.

I have already referred to the sympathy between the French Revolution and the Industrial Revolution. The former, it is true, frightened our statesmen, but it gave courage to the working classes, and made them hope fiercely for freedom. The latter Revolution concentrated men more and more closely together in large centres of industry, dissociated them from their employers, and roused a spirit of antagonism which is inevitable when both employers and employed alike fail to recognize the essential identity of their interests. Now, wherever there are large bodies of men crowded together there is also a rapid spread of new ideas, new political enthusiasms, and social activities. And in spite of the lack of the franchise the artisans of our large towns made their voices heard; fiercely and roughly, no doubt, in riot and uproar, but they had no other means. There were found some statesmen in Parliament, chiefly disciples of Adam Smith, who gave articulation to the demands of labour, and owing to their endeavours the Combination Laws were repealed in 1824. But the following year proved how insecure was the position of the labourers without a vote. The employers of labour were able to induce Parliament in 1825 to stultify itself, by declaring illegal any *action* which might result from those deliberations of workmen which a twelvemonth before they had legalized. But still they were allowed to deliberate, strange as it may now seem that permission was needed for this, and their deliberations materially aided in passing the Reform Bill of 1832. For as soon as a class can make its voice heard, even though it cannot directly act, other classes will take that utterance into account.

§ 4. **Growth of Trade Unions**—But the Reform Bill, though a great step forward, somewhat belied the hopes that had roused the enthusiasm of its industrial supporters. The workmen found that, after all, it merely threw additional power into the hands of the upper and middle classes. Their own position was hardly improved. Then they had to make their voice heard again, and urged on by the misery and poverty in which they were still struggling, they demanded the Charter. The Chartist movement (1838 to 1848) seems to us at the present time almost ludicrously moderate in its demands. The vote by ballot, the abolition of property qualifications for electors, and the payment of parliamentary members were the main objects of its leaders, though they asked for universal suffrage as well. Nevertheless people were frightened, especially when the Chartists wished to present a monster petition at Westminster on April 10th, 1848, and military and police intervention was called in. The movement collapsed, and finally died away when the repeal of the Corn Laws had restored prosperity to the nation. Many have laughed at the working classes for trying to gain some infinitesimal fraction of political power. But the working classes are generally acute, and they saw that this was the ultimate means of material prosperity, nor has the event failed to justify their belief. In the somewhat quieter times which followed the collapse of the Chartists, their influence went on extending, and though the workmen ceased to agitate they were not idle, but continued steadily organizing themselves in Trade Unions. These institutions were not, however, recognized by law till a Commission was appointed, including Sir William Erle,

Lord Elcho, and Thomas Hughes, to inquire into their constitution and objects (February, 1867). Their Report disclosed the existence of intimidation with occasional outrages—as was natural when the men had no other way of giving utterance to their wishes. But Trade Unionism triumphed. The Unions were legalized in 1871, and this Act was further extended and amended in 1876. The old law of master and servant had passed away, and employer and employed were now on an equal political footing. It has remained for the men by silent strength to place themselves on an equal footing in other respects. Meanwhile the employers entered into a like combination by forming the National Federation of Employers in 1873, and the long struggle of the working classes for industrial freedom did not result in any lessening of the feeling of class antagonism. But Trade Unions have done much to gain a greater measure of material prosperity for the working classes, and to give them a larger share than formerly in the wealth which the workers have helped to create. When we look back upon the last half-century we can only wonder that trade unionists have been so moderate in their demands, considering the misery and poverty amidst which they grew up.

§ 5. **The working classes fifty years ago**—For it must continually be remembered that the condition of the mass of the people in the first half of this century was one of the deepest depression. Several writers have commented upon this, and have taken occasion to remark upon the great progress in the prosperity of the working classes since that time. It is true they have progressed since then, but it has hardly been progress so much as a return to the state of things about 1760 or 1770. The fact has been that after the introduction of the new industrial system the condition of the working classes rapidly declined ; wages were lower and prices were higher ; till at length the lowest depth of poverty was reached about the beginning of the reign of Queen Victoria. Since then their condition has been gradually improving, partly owing to the philanthropic labours of men like Lord Shaftesbury, still more owing to the combined action of working men themselves. To quote the expression of that celebrated statistician, Mr Giffen : "it is a matter of history that pauperism was nearly breaking down the country half-a-century ago. The expenditure on poor-law relief early in the century and down to 1830–31 was nearly as great at times as it is now. With half the population in the country that there now is, the burden of the poor was the same." The following table will show the actual figures of English pauperism at a time when the wealth of the nation was advancing by leaps and bounds. It will be noticed that the rate was highest in 1818, which was shortly after the close of the great Continental War, but fell rapidly after 1830, and since 1841 the rate per head of population has not been much more than six or seven shillings.

Year	Population	Poor Rate raised	Rate per head of Population
			s. d.
1760	7,000,000	£1,250,000	3 7
1784	8,000,000	£2,000,000	5 0
1803	9,216,000	£4,077,000	8 11
1818	11,876,000	£7,870,000	13 3
1820	12,046,000	£7,329,000	12 2
1830	13,924,000	£6,829,000	10 9
1841	15,911,757	£4,760,929	5 11¾

But the mere figures of pauperism, significant though they are, can give no idea of the vast amount of misery and degradation which the majority of the working classes suffered. The tale of their sufferings may be read in the Blue-books and Reports of the various Commissions which investigated the state of industrial life in the factories, mines and workshops between 1833 and 1842; or it may be read in the burning pages of Engels' *State of the Working Classes in England in* 1844, which is little more than a sympathetic résumé of the facts set forth in official documents. We hear of children and young people in factories overworked and beaten as if they were slaves; of diseases and distortions only found in manufacturing districts; of filthy, wretched homes where people huddle together like wild beasts; we hear of girls and women working underground in the dark recesses of the coal-mines, dragging loads of coal in cars in places where no horses could go, and harnessed and crawling along the subterranean pathways like beasts of burden. Everywhere we find cruelty and oppression, and in many cases the workmen were but slaves bound to fulfil their master's commands under fear of dismissal and starvation. Freedom they had in name; freedom to starve and die; but not freedom to speak, still less to act, as citizens of a free state. They were often even obliged to buy their food at exorbitant prices out of their scanty wages at a shop kept by their employer, where it is needless to say that they paid the highest possible price for the worst possible goods. This was rendered possible by the system of paying workmen in tickets or orders upon certain shops. It was called "truck"; and has at length been condemned by English law (1887).

But though as a matter of fact the sufferings of the working classes were aggravated by the extortions of employers, and by the partiality of a legislature which forbade them to take common measures in self-defence, yet there was one great cause which underlay all these minor causes, and that was the Continental War which ended in 1815. "Thousands of homes were starved in order to find the means for the great war, the cost of which was really supported by the labour of those who toiled on and earned the wealth that was lavished freely—and at good interest for the lenders—by the Government. The enormous taxation and the gigantic loans came from the store of accumulated capital which the employers wrung from the poor wages of labour, or which the landlords extracted from the growing gains of their tenants. To outward appearance the strife was waged by armies and generals; in reality the resources on which the struggle was based were the stint and starvation of labour, the overtaxed and underfed toils of childhood, the underpaid and uncertain employment of men."[1]

§ 6. **Wages**—And indeed if we examine some of the wages actually paid at the beginning of this century, and again at the beginning of Queen Victoria's reign, we shall find that they were excessively low. The case of common

Year	Weavers' Wages *	Wheat, per qr.*
1802	13*s.* 10*d.*	67*s.*
1806	10*s.* 6*d.*	76*s.*
1812	6*s.* 4*d.*	122*s.*
1816	5*s.* 2*d.*	76*s.*
1817	4*s.* 3½*d.*	94*s.*
	* From Leone Levi.	* From Porter's *Progress.*

weavers was particularly hard in the years of the great war, and affords an interesting example of the extortions of the capitalist manufacturers of the period. For purposes of comparison I give above the price of wheat and

[1] Rogers: *Six Centuries of Work and Wages.*

of weekly wages in the same years; for the price of wheat forms a useful standard by which to gauge the real value of wages, even when it is not consumed in large quantities. It will be seen that wages were at their lowest point just after the conclusion of the war, while, on the other hand, wheat was almost at famine prices. After this, however, and till 1830 the wages of weavers rose again, for the new spinning machinery had increased the supply of yarn at a much greater rate than weavers could be found to weave it, and hence there was an increased demand for weavers, and they gained proportionately higher wages, the average for woollen cloth weavers from 1830–45 being 14*s.* to 17*s.* a week, and for worsted stuff weavers 11*s.* to 14*s.* a week. But even these rates are miserably low.

The wages of spinners were also very poor, the work being mostly done by women and children, though when men are employed they get fairly good pay. The following table will show clearly the various rates, and it will be seen that here wages sink steadily till 1845, owing to the rapid production of the new machinery. The women's

Spinners	1808-15	1815-23	1823-30	1830-36	1836-45
Men	24/ to 26/	24/ to 26/	24/ to 26/	24/ to 26/	24/ to 26/
Women	13/ to 14/	13/ to 14/	11/ to 12/	8/ to 10/	7/ to 9/
Children	4/6 to 5/6	4/6 to 5/6	4/6 to 5/6	4/6 to 5/6	4/6 to 5/6

wages exhibit the fall most markedly, the labour of children being already affected to some extent by the provisions of the Factory Acts. As for the agricultural labourer, he too suffered from low wages, the general average to 1845 being 8*s.* to 10*s.* a week, and generally nearer the former than the latter figure. In fact the material condition of the working classes of England was at this time in the lowest depths of poverty and degradation, and this fact must always be remembered in comparing the wages of to-day with those of former times. Some people who ought to know better are very fond of talking about the "progress of the working classes" in the last seventy years; and the Jubilees of our late Queen of course afforded ample opportunity—of which full advantage was taken—for such optimists to talk statistics. But to compare the wages of labour properly we must go back more than a hundred years, for seventy years ago the English workman was passing through a period of misery which we must devoutly hope, for the sake of the nation at large, will not occur again. It is interesting to note, though it is impossible here to go fully into the subject, that in trades where workmen have combined, since the repeal of the Conspiracy Laws in 1825 and the alteration in the Act of Settlement,[1] wages have perceptibly risen. Carpenters, masons, and colliers afford examples of such a rise. But where there has been no combination it is noteworthy how little wages have risen in proportion to the increased production of the modern labourer, and to the higher cost of living, nor does the workman always receive his due share of the wealth which he helps to create. Of the results of labour combinations we shall, however, have something to say in the final chapter of this little book. But there was one class of people who happened from various causes to obtain a very large share of the national wealth, and who grew rich and flourished while the working classes were almost starving. In spite of war abroad and poverty at home, the rents of the land-owners increased, and the agricultural interest received a stimulus which has resulted in a very natural reaction. The rise in rents and the recent

[1] Page 189, and note 18, p. 251.

depression of modern agriculture will form the subject of our next chapter.

CHAPTER VI

THE RISE AND DEPRESSION OF MODERN AGRICULTURE

§ 1. **Services rendered by the great land-owners**—Although there have been occasions in our industrial history when one is compelled to admit that the deeds of the landed gentry have called for anything but admiration, we yet must not overlook the great services which this class rendered to the agricultural interest in the eighteenth century. I have already mentioned that the development and the success of English agriculture in the half-century or more before the Industrial Revolution was remarkable and extensive ; and this success was due to the efforts of the landlords in introducing new agricultural methods. They took an entirely new departure and adopted a new system. It consisted, as I mentioned before, in getting rid of bare fallows and poor pastures by substituting root-crops and artificial grasses. The fourfold or Norfolk rotation of crops was introduced, the landlords themselves taking an interest in and superintending the cultivation of their land and making useful experiments upon it. The number of these experimenting landlords was very considerable, and in course of time the tenant farmers followed them, and thus agricultural knowledge and skill became more and more widely diffused. The reward of the landlords came rapidly. They soon found their production of corn doubled and their general produce trebled. They were able to exact higher rents, for they had taught their tenants how to make the land pay better, and of course claimed a share of the increased profit. About the years 1740-50 the rent of land, according to Jethro Tull, was 7*s.* an acre ; some twenty years or more afterwards Arthur Young found the average rent of land to be 10*s.* an acre, and thought that in many cases it ought to have been more. It is probable that the landlord would not have done so much for agriculture if he had not expected to make something out of his experiments ; but the fact that he was animated by an enlightened self-interest does not make his work any the less valuable. The pioneers of this improved agriculture came from Norfolk, it being uncertain whether Lord Townshend or Mr Coke, the descendant of the great Chief Justice, was the first. But this much is certain : that Lord Lovell, one of the most distinguished and energetic of the new agricultural school, found that his profits under the new system were 36 per cent., as his accounts, still preserved for the year 1731–32, and a copy of which is extant, bear witness. The new agriculture indeed brought with it a revolution as important in its way as the Industrial Revolution.[1] One of the chief features of the change, the enclosures, has been already commented upon. The enclosure of the common fields was beneficial, and to a certain extent justifiable, for the tenants paid rent for them to the lord of the manor. But it was effected at a great loss to the smaller tenant, and when his common of pasture was enclosed as well, he was greatly injured, while the agricultural labourer was permanently disabled. But it was not unnatural that enclosures should rapidly be made when farming, and especially grain-growing, had become so profitable. The reason for the profits of agriculture at this period we can now examine.

[1] See *Industry in England*, p. 430.

§ 2. **The stimulus caused by the Bounties**—The Government of the year 1660 had imposed heavy protective duties upon the importation of grain from abroad, in fact prohibiting it except when wheat was at famine prices, as it happened to be in 1662, when it was 62*s.* 9½*d.* a quarter, the ordinary price being 41*s.* But it did not reach this price again for many years afterwards. The Government of 1688, not content with the foregoing protective measure, added a bounty of 5*s.* per qr. upon the export of corn from England. But the effect of this bounty was not felt for several years, for happily, soon after the passing of the Bounty Act, a series of plentiful harvests occurred, and corn was very cheap. There were consequently loud outcries from the landlords about agricultural distress, which merely meant that the people at large were enjoying cheap food. The aim of the bounty on corn had been to raise prices by encouraging its export, and thus rendered it scarcer and dearer in England. As a matter of fact, it had the opposite effect, for it served as a premium upon which the wheat-grower could speculate, and thus induced him to sow a larger breadth of his land with wheat. The premium upon production caused producers to grow more than the market required, and so prices fell. Thus, happily for the consumer, the Corn Laws and the bounty were harmless during the greater part of the eighteenth century, for farmers competed one against the other sufficiently to keep down prices. But the inevitable Nemesis of protective measures came at the end of the century, when population was growing with unexampled rapidity and required all the corn it could get. Then the prices of corn rose to a famine pitch, while the duty upon its importation prevented it coming into the country in sufficient quantities. The landlords received enormous rents, and the farmers did not mind paying them, for the profits of both were immense. But meanwhile the mass of the people was frequently on the verge of starvation, and at length the country perceived that things could not be allowed to go on any longer in this way.[1] The manufacturing capitalists of the day supported the leaders of the people in their agitation, for they hoped that cheap food might mean low wages. By their aid the landed interest was overcome, and in 1846 the Corn Laws, by the efforts of Cobden and his followers, were finally repealed. Nevertheless the British farmer and his landlords, forgetting, it seems, the days when they got high prices by the starvation of the poor, still frequently clamour for the re-imposition of the incubus of protection.

§ 3. **Agricultural improvements** — The high prices gained by farmers before the repeal of the Corn Laws had, however, one good effect in increasing the development of agricultural skill and of agricultural improvements. The heavy soils of the London clay had at one time been laid out in pasture lands, as being useless for turnip-growing or for root-crops. The corn duties, however, caused these pastures to be broken up for the sake of growing wheat, barley, and clover; the soil was more thoroughly drained, and mangolds were grown as a rotation crop, so that the

[1] By a law of 1773 importation of foreign wheat was forbidden as long as English wheat was not more than 48*s*. per quarter. In 1791 a duty of 24*s*. 3*d*. was imposed as long as English wheat was less than 50*s*. a qr.; if English wheat was over 50*s*., the duty was 2*s*. 6*d*. The landed interest, however, was not satisfied yet. In 1804 foreign corn was practically prohibited from importation if English wheat was less than 63*s*. a qr.; in 1815 the prohibition was extended till the price of English wheat was 80*s*. a qr. Then came the agitations and riots of 1817–19, after which the country sank into despair till the formation of the Anti-Corn Law League in 1839.

area of bare fallow was much diminished, while the quantity of food, both for men and cattle, was much increased. In recent years much of this very land has reverted to pasture for dairy-farming. Besides the increase of the area under wheat, special attention was given to artificial manures. The use of bones, at first very roughly broken, became recognized. About 1840-41 dissolved bones and Peruvian guano came into use, particularly in growing turnips, and these were followed very soon by mineral phosphates, and more recently by nitrate of soda and sulphate of ammonia. After the repeal of the Corn Laws in 1846 the prospects of English agriculture began to look rather gloomy, or at least the farmers thought so. But the tremendous development of trade and population, the stimulus given to all kinds of commerce by the employment of steam, not only for transit but as a motive power for machinery, had their natural influence upon agriculture, and the farmer did well. Improved agricultural machinery came into use, by which farm work was facilitated, and the outlay for labour was lessened. Makers of these machines showed great enterprise and skill, and many altogether new appliances were placed in the farmer's hands. Steam power has come to be used with advantage in digging, stirring and harrowing the ground, though it has not been such a success in ploughing. Altogether English agriculture made great strides, and was quite prosperous in the years 1870-73, when the general prosperity of the industrial classes was increasing, and people did not mind paying fairly high prices for farm produce. But afterwards a period of depression set in. A succession of bad years, notably the wet and sunless season of 1879 which ruined many a farmer, together with excessive rain and deficient sunshine, most seriously injured the average harvests.

Foreign competition in wheat, imported cattle, and butchers' meat largely increased. The price of wheat fell between 1880 and 1886 from 50*s.* to 30*s.* a qr.; between 1884 and 1887 beef fell from 80*s.* to 55*s.* per cwt.; and other produce also fell in proportion. Thousands of farmers were then ruined, and agriculture generally suffered a severe and prolonged depression, and much arable land was then laid down again as pasture, indeed some went altogether out of cultivation. Meanwhile the political false prophets were going about with their usual nostrums, and the flags of Protection and even of Bimetallism were both waved before the bewildered eyes of the British farmer, as if they were signals of salvation.

§ 4. **The cause of the depression. The rise in rent**—Now it is perfectly obvious to an impartial observer of economic facts, that an industry so flourishing as English agriculture was not very many years ago, could not have suffered so severe a collapse unless there had been some great underlying cause, beside the ordinary complaints of bad harvests and foreign competition. Bad harvests are not peculiar to England, and foreign competition, however keen it may be, has first to overstep a very considerable natural margin of protection in the cost of carriage. It costs, for instance, according to that great authority Sir James Caird, 9*s.* per quarter to transport American wheat from Chicago to London. It is clear that besides these, there must have been other influences of considerable importance, to cause English agriculture to be, in spite of its apparent prosperity, in so insecure a position that it should have sunk to the depressed condition in which it even now remains. We have not to look far for one cause. It is the lack of agricultural capital.

But how, it may naturally be asked, has it come about that the English farmer, after the very favourable period before the depression, should thus suffer from a lack of capital, a lack which renders it almost impossible for him to work his land properly? The answer is simple. His capital has been greatly decreased, surely though not always slowly, by a tremendous increase in his rent. The landlords of the eighteenth century made the English farmer the foremost agriculturist in the world, but their successors of the nineteenth have raised his rent disproportionately. Such, at any rate, is the verdict of eminent agricultural authorities; and the land-owners have been compelled, for their own sake, to reduce the exorbitant rents they received a few years ago. Unfortunately, too, the attention of other classes of the community has been till lately diverted from the condition of our agriculture by the prosperity of our manufactures. But these two branches of industry, the manufacturing and the agricultural, are closely interdependent, and must suffer or prosper together.

It is possible, as I have pointed out elsewhere, that there are certain economic theories which have helped the decline of English agriculture. They are the Ricardian theory of rent, and the dubious "law of diminishing returns." They have made many people think that this decline was inevitable, and have diverted their attention from the prime, though not the only, cause of the trouble—namely, the increase of rent. But putting these doubtful theories aside, we may employ ourselves more profitably in looking at the facts of the case. I have mentioned before that in Tull's time, at the beginning of the eighteenth century, the average rent of agricultural land was 7s. per acre, and by Young's time towards the close of the century it had risen to 10s. per acre. Diffused agricultural skill caused an increase of profits, and the hope of sharing in these profits led farmers to give competitive rents, which afterwards the landlords took care to exact in full and frequently to increase. The farmers were enabled to pay higher rents by the low rate of wages paid to their labourers, a rate which the landed gentry, as justices, kept down by their assessments. In 1799 we find land paying nearly 20*s.* an acre; in 1812 the same land pays over 25*s.*; in 1830 again it was still at about 25*s.*, but by 1850 it had risen to 38*s.* 8*d.*, which was about four times Arthur Young's average. Indeed £2 per acre was not an uncommon rent for good land a few years ago (1885),[1] the average increase of English rent being no less than 26½ per cent. between 1854 and 1879. Now such rent as this was enormous, and could only be paid in very good years. In ordinary years, and still more in bad years, it was paid out of the farmer's capital. This process of payment was facilitated by the fact that the farmer of this century did not keep his accounts properly, a fruitful source of eventual evil frequently commented upon by agricultural authorities; and also by the other fact, that even when he perceived that he was working his farm at a loss, the immediate loss (of some 10 or 15 per cent.) involved in getting out of his holding was heavy enough in most cases to induce him to submit to a rise in his rent, rather than lose visibly so much of his capital.

The invisible process, however, was equally certain, if not so immediate. The result has been that the average capital per acre now employed in agriculture is only about £4 or £5, instead of at least £10 as it ought to be,[2] and the farmer cannot afford to pay for a sufficient supply of

[1] Cf. statistics in my article in *Westminster Review*, December 1888, p. 727.

[2] My calculations on this head will be found in the *Economist* of April 28th, 1888, and they coincide closely with independent statements made by Professor Rogers.

labour, so that the agricultural population is seriously diminishing. Nothing in modern agriculture is so serious as this decline of the rural population, and we must here devote a few words to a consideration of the agricultural labourer and the conditions of his existence.

§ 5. **The labourer and the land. Wages**—It has been previously mentioned that the Industrial Revolution was accompanied by an equally important revolution in agriculture : the main features of the agrarian revolution being the consolidation of small into large farms, the introduction of new methods and machinery, the enclosure of common fields and waste lands, and discontinuance of the old open-field system, and finally the divorce of the labourer from the land. The consolidation of farms reduced the number of farmers, while the enclosures drove the labourers off the land, for it became almost impossible for them to exist on their low wages now that their old rights of keeping small cattle and geese upon the commons, of having a bit of land round their cottages, and other privileges were ruthlessly taken from them. They have retreated in large numbers into the towns and taken up other pursuits, or helped to swell the ranks of English pauperism. Before the Industrial and Agrarian Revolution, Arthur Young in 1769 estimated that out of a total population of 8,500,000 the agricultural class, " farmers (whether freeholders or leaseholders), their servants and labourers," numbered no less than 2,800,000—*i.e.* over one-fourth of the total population. The number of those engaged in manufactures of all kinds he puts at 3,000,000. His figures may be taken as substantially correct, though perhaps not as accurate as a modern census. Now let us look at the agricultural population of to-day. The total number of males and females engaged as agricultural wage-earners is only some 689,000 [1]—that is, very far below the numbers so engaged a century ago, while the proportion has sunk from one person in four to one in twenty-five concerned in agriculture. At the present time our fields have on the average only one man to cultivate twenty-seven acres of land—and that man is very badly paid for his trouble, be he farmer or labourer.

But not only have the numbers of the agricultural population decreased, but the labourer no longer has any share as a rule in the land. Certainly the agricultural labourer, at any rate in the South of England, was much better off in the middle of the eighteenth century than his descendants were in the middle of the nineteenth. In fact in 1850 or so wages were in many places actually lower than they were in 1750, and in hardly any county were they higher. But meanwhile almost every necessary of life, except bread, has increased in cost, and more especially rent has risen, while on the other hand the labourer has lost many of his old privileges, for formerly his common rights, besides providing him with fuel, enabled him to keep cows or pigs and poultry on the waste, and sheep on the fallows and stubbles, and he could generally grow his own vegetables and garden produce. All these things formed a substantial addition to his nominal wages. In 1750 or so his nominal wages averaged 8*s*. or 10*s*. a week ; in 1850 they only averaged 10*s*. or 12*s*., although in the latter period his nominal wages represented all he got, while in the former they represented only part of his total income. Since 1850, however, even agricultural wages have risen, the present average being 13*s*. or 14*s*. a week. The rise, such as it is, is due to some extent to Trade Unions, the leader and

[1] The figures are for 1901 and represent a fall of thirty per cent. since 1881.

promoter of which among agricultural labourers was Joseph Arch. This remarkable man was born in 1826, and in his youth and middle age saw the time when agricultural labour was at its lowest depth. Not only were wages low, being about 10*s*. or 11*s*. a week, but the worst evils of the factory system of child labour had been transferred to the life of the fields. The philanthropists seem to have overlooked the disgraceful conditions of the system of working in agricultural gangs, under which a number of children and young persons were collected on hire from their parents by some overseer or contractor, who took them about the district at certain seasons of the year to work on the land of those farmers who wished to employ them. The persons composing the gang were exposed to every inclemency of the weather, without having homes to return to in the evening, people of both sexes being housed while under their contract in barns, without any thought of decency or comfort, while the children often suffered from all the coarse brutalities that suggested themselves to the overseer of their labour. Their pay was of course miserable, though gangs flourished at a time when farmers and landlords were making huge profits. But the degrading practice of cheap gang-labour was defended as being necessary to profitable agriculture; which means that tenants were too cowardly or too obtuse to resist rents which they could not pay except by employing pauperized and degraded labour. Amid times like these Joseph Arch grew up, and it was not till 1872 (at which time it will be remembered that British farmers were doing very well) that he began the agitation which resulted in the formation of the National Agricultural Labourers' Union. His difficulties in organizing the downtrodden labourers were enormous, but he finally succeeded in spite of the resentment of agricultural employers. His efforts have already done much to improve the material condition of the labourers, and wages have decidedly risen from this and other causes. But they certainly cannot be called high.

§ 6. **The present condition of British agriculture**—It remains to notice briefly the causes which are now influencing our agricultural industry, and to point out in what direction we may expect a revival from the present state of depression. Besides the great fact of the increase of rents we notice an increase of foreign competition, which is of comparatively recent date. Our competitors are mainly Russia, America, and last but by no means least, India. At the time of the Crimean War, and for some years subsequently, Russian competition ceased to exist. When it began it, standing alone, was not very serious, for America had not yet entered the field, and was prevented from doing so by the sanguinary struggles of the Civil War. High prices for grain prevailed therefore till some time after America had ceased her internal conflict, and it was only quite recently that much grain was grown for export in India. But since 1870 or so England has been supplied with grain from these three great agricultural lands, and the English farmer, no longer buoyed up at the expense of the rest of the community by protective measures, has found it impossible to grow wheat at a profit at the old rents. Many farmers have been ruined; and at Sir James Caird's estimate (in 1886) the loss of the agricultural classes of all ranks in spendable income has been nearly £43,000,000 *per annum*. According to this well-known authority rents should therefore have been reduced by £22,800,000 instead of by much less than half that amount. Even now the aggregate rental is higher than it was before the Russian war. In course of time it is certain that the economic action of supply and demand will bring rents down to something like their commercial value; meanwhile the English landlords, as Mr W. E. Bear remarks, have the choice between allowing their old tenants to be ruined first, and then accepting reduced rents, or granting reductions soon enough to save men in whom they have hitherto had some confidence as tenants. It will be necessary also to make important changes in the laws and customs of land tenure, so that our farmers may have complete security for their capital invested in improvements, and freedom of enterprise (*e.g.* in cropping and tilling), in order that they may do their best with the land. An extended system of small holdings and allotments, guaranteed by a thorough measure of Tenant Right, together with free trade in land as well as other commodities, would do much to place moderate farms within the reach of industrious and thrifty yeomen and labourers. Greater facilities for transit, including the abolition of the essentially protective system of preferential railway rates, would enable producers to put their produce with ease upon the home market, for English food requirements guarantee an enormous and steady demand at home for every scrap of food-stuff that the land is capable of producing. The farmer is slow to adapt himself to changed conditions, but a profitable future is open to him even if he gives up wheat-growing and betakes himself more to dairy-farming and market-gardening. But it may not be necessary for him to give up wheat, for it seems probable that the wheat area of the world, except in India, will not increase; since foreign farmers are beginning to find out that they cannot put wheat on the English market at the present low prices. People will see that it is desirable, and that ultimately it will be profitable, to recall capital and labour back to the land which it is evident that it has left;

To face p. 210

Manufacturing districts are shown by slanting lines; large manufacturing towns by black circles; and the most populous counties are coloured darker than the others. It will be noticed that population since 1750 has shifted very much to the North and North West of England, whilst manufactures are far more concentrated than formerly.

and that it is the height of economic folly to rely, as some do, upon the extension of our manufacturing industries to counteract agricultural depression. Prosperous agriculture means for us prosperous manufactures, and from an economic point of view the interests of the plough and the loom are identical. Neither can be served by protective tinkering. Reforms of a totally different character are needed, foremost among which is a widespread reduction of rent, and a general rearrangement of the relations between landlord and tenant. It is on the face of it ridiculous to assert that, with an unequalled demand in the home market for all he can produce, the English farmer cannot find some means of making the land pay and pay well. But before he can do this he must spend more capital upon it than he has lately been able to do.

CHAPTER VII

MODERN INDUSTRIAL ENGLAND

§ 1. **The growth of our industry**—We have now traced the industrial growth of England from the diffused beginnings of manufactures and agriculture in the isolated manors, and have seen how gradually towns grew up, commerce extended and markets arose, while manufacturers became organized in various centres and regulated by gilds. We have seen that for several centuries the back-bone of our national wealth was wool, but that in time we ceased to export it, and worked it up into cloth ourselves, thereby gaining great national wealth. We have seen, too, how our foreign trade, after its petty beginnings in the Middle Ages, took a fresh start in the buccaneering days of the Elizabethan sea-captains and then rapidly developed, by means of the various great Companies, till England became commercially supreme throughout the world. From commercial beginnings we traced the rise of our Indian Empire, and the growth of the American colonies. Meanwhile at home there came an Industrial Revolution which, happening as it did at the moment that was politically most favourable to its growth, gave England a very useful start over all other European nations in manufacturing industries of all kinds, and enabled her to endure successfully the enormous burdens of the great Continental war. Now comes a time of still greater progress, economic as well as commercial, for the old restrictive barriers to trade are to be swept away, and a new economic policy is to be inaugurated.

§ 2. **State of trade in 1820**—If we now endeavour to gain some idea of the trade of the country soon after the war, we may look for a moment at its condition in 1820, just before Free Trade measures were begun. The official value of foreign and colonial imports was declared to be £32,000,000, which with a population of about 21,000,000 was at the rate of about thirty shillings a head. The exports of home produce amounted to some £36,000,000. The tonnage of shipping entering and leaving our harbours was 4,000,000 tons, of which 2,648,000 tons belonged to the United Kingdom and its dependencies. Steamers were, of course, as yet unknown. Professor Leone Levi calculates the trade of the country at not more than one-eighth or one-ninth of what it is at the present time. The wealth and comfort accessible to the people in general was much more limited, the consumption of tea, for instance, being only 1 lb. 4 oz. per head, and of sugar 18 lbs. a head. In fact, if we compare the £244,710,066 worth of our exports in 1889–90 with the £32,000,000 worth in 1820 we see at once how gigantic has been the growth of our trade. In 1889, again, the imports (for the first ten months) were £347,985,087, which is more than nine times their value in 1820. But even at the beginning of the century England was far ahead of her old rival France, for French imports were only worth £8,000,000 in 1815, and her exports only about double that amount, or less than half England's exports, which in that year rose to over £42,000,000 (official value).

§ 3. **The beginnings of Free Trade**—Now the year 1820 is memorable not merely as showing the condition of our trade, but for the great enunciation of Free Trade principles which it witnessed. For in that year the London merchants formulated a noteworthy Petition praying that every restrictive regulation of trade, not imposed on account of the revenue, together with all duties of a protective character, might be at once repealed. At last the teachings of economists were being put into practice by men of business. The Edinburgh Chamber of Commerce sent up a similar petition; a Committee was appointed in Parliament to investigate the wishes of the petitioners of our two capitals; and it brought in a report thoroughly in agreement with the Free Trade principles of the merchants. In the following year Mr Huskisson,[1] the President of the Board of Trade, proposed the first measures of commercial reform, and one by one the restrictions upon our trade were removed. The most important of the new measures was the gradual alteration of the old Navigation Laws (cf. p. 130), finally culminating in their total repeal in 1849.

It is true that in the period 1821 to 1830 the foreign

[1] See more fully note 18, p. 251.

trade of the United Kingdom did not exhibit much material improvement, but still there was a steady increase. The official value of imports rose from £30,000,000 to £46,000,000, and the value of British manufactures exported from £40,000,000 to £60,000,000. But the declared value of exports remained pretty steady at about £37,000,000. Yet in the United Kingdom itself trade was growing rapidly, and the increase of wealth gave an opportunity for a general diminution of taxes, and our sorely strained finances were set in order. Many of the injurious duties upon raw materials and articles of British manufacture—as *e.g.* those on raw silk, coal, glass, paper, and soap—were taken off, to the great advantage of our manufacturing industries.

§ 4. **Revolution in the means of transit**—Now, too, another great industrial revolution was effected. I refer to the introduction of railways, steam navigation, and the telegraph, which have done almost as much as the great inventions of the eighteenth century to revolutionize the commerce of the world. In 1830 the Liverpool and Manchester Railway was opened. In 1838 the first ocean passages to New York by steamship were accomplished by the *Great Western* from Bristol, and the *Sirius* from Cork; although ever since the beginning of the century small steamers and tugs had been used for coasting purposes, and on the River Clyde. In 1837 Cooke and Wheatstone patented the needle telegraph, and the Electric Telegraph Company was formed in 1846 for bringing the new inventions into general use. In 1840 the penny postage came into operation. Yet more recently the Suez Canal (1869) has shortened immensely the distance to the East. It is obvious to all how incalculably all these inventions and appliances have aided the development, not only of English trade, but of the commerce of all the world.

§ 5. **Modern developments. Our colonies**—Now I do not propose, in the limits of a little work like this, to go into a detailed account of the growth of commerce since these great modern inventions. There is ample material for the student in larger works ; and the statistics of our progress may be consulted in the invaluable pages of Mr Giffen's and Professor Leone Levi's books. Here I can only indicate in the broadest outlines the chief features of the recent developments of industry. We have followed the industrial history of England up to a period more prolific in commercial events, and more remarkable for commercial progress than any that preceded it. The experiments and tentative measures of Mr Huskisson and other statesmen paved the way for a bolder and more assured policy on the part of subsequent governments, till at length Sir Robert Peel, urged on by the Anti-Corn Law League (p. 201), and stimulated by great famine in Ireland in 1845, openly adopted the principles of Free Trade. Under his leadership the Corn Laws were repealed (1846) ; the tariff was entirely remodelled, and the old protective restrictions abolished, Mr Gladstone's Budget of 1853 being particularly memorable in this direction. A great increase of trade followed the inauguration of the policy which is always associated with the great name of Cobden,[1] and the wealth of the country was even further developed. The extension of the railway system was at the same time a cause and an effect of this development, and when the great Exhibition of 1851, the precursor of several others, was held, England was able to show to all the world her immense superiority in productive and manufacturing industries.

[1] See note 16, p. 250, on his French treaty.

A further stimulus to trade was supplied by the discovery of gold in California and Australia (1847–51), which supplied a much-needed addition to the currency of the world. Meanwhile, since the war of American Independence, England had been building up a great colonial empire, and she had the sense not to attempt again to levy taxes upon her unwilling offspring. India was taken over from the East India Company (1858). The colonies of Canada and the Cape were gained by conquest; those of Australia and New Zealand were the result of spontaneous settlement. The two former were captured from the French and Dutch, but of the second of them at least we have not made a commercial or even a political success; nor are we likely to do so unless we can contrive to keep on good terms with the original settlers, and to allow no misplaced sentiment about native races to disturb cordial relations between Europeans. As regards our Australasian colonies, they have grown far beyond the expectations of former generations, and gained for themselves entire political freedom, though they have chosen to use it chiefly in carrying on a one-sided war of hostile protective tariffs against their mother-country. As, however, they owe English capitalists a good deal of money, the interest on which is paid in colonial goods, there is a strong commercial bond of union between us and them; a bond which protectionists in England are strangely anxious to break, by placing unnatural obstacles upon the payment in goods of the interest due upon colonial loans.

§ 6. **England and other nations' wars**—But besides the extension of our colonial relations, English trade has benefited by the quarrels of her competitors. The prostration of Continental nations after 1815 precluded much competition till almost the middle of the century, and then the Crimean War broke out (1854–56). As mentioned before, this war gave a great stimulus to our agriculture, and had a similar effect upon our manufactures. The Indian Mutiny which followed it did not much affect our trade, but it rendered necessary the deposition of the East India Company and the assumption of government by the Crown (1858),[1] and thus eventually served to put our relations to that vast and rich empire upon a much more satisfactory and profitable basis. About the same time the Chinese wars of 1842 and 1857, regrettable as they were, established our commercial relations with the East generally upon a firm footing, and since then our trade with Eastern nations has largely developed. Then came the Civil War in America (1861–65), after which there was an urgent demand for English products to replace the waste caused by this severe conflict. The Civil War was succeeded by a series of short European wars, chiefly undertaken for the sake of gaining a frontier, as was the war waged by Prussia and Austria upon Denmark (1864), followed by another struggle between the two former allies (1866). Then in 1870–71 all Europe was shaken by the tremendous fight between France and Germany, and since then the Continental nations have occupied themselves in keeping up an armed peace at an expense almost equal to that of actual warfare. All their conflicts have arrested their industrial development, to their own detriment but to England's great advantage. Not content however with that, they increase their difficulties by a dogged protectionism. As a result, they are far poorer in general wealth than our own land, and only succeed in competing with us by means of underpaid and overworked labour. But the labourer will not

[1] See note 17, p. 250.

always consent to be overworked and underpaid, and signs are not wanting that his discontent is fast ripening into something more dangerous.

§ 7. **Present difficulties. Commercial depressions**—But although English commerce has reached a height of prosperity considerably above that of other nations, it has not been and is not now without serious occasional difficulties. It has been throughout the century visited at more or less periodic intervals by severe commercial crises. In the earlier portion of the century they occurred in the years 1803, -10, -15, -18, -25, and -36; and were short, sharp, and severe. Since 1837 they have occurred at regular periods of about ten years, namely in 1847, -57, -66, -73, and -82; latterly depression has been most persistent, though with short cessations for special industries. In the last year or two, however, trade has again revived, and on the whole we may now (1896) be said to be enjoying a fair measure of prosperity.

The causes of such depressions in trade are various, and not always obvious. They are, so to speak, dislocations of industry, resulting largely from mistaken calculations on the part of those "captains of industry" whose *raison d'être* is their ability to interpret the changing requirements in the great modern market of the civilized world. A failure in their calculations, a slight mistake as to how long the demand for a particular class of goods will last, or as to the number of those who require them, results inevitably in a glut in the market, in a case of what is called (wrongly) "over-production"; and this is as inevitably followed by a period of depression, occasionally enlivened by desperate struggles on the part of some manufacturer to sell his goods at any cost. With such a huge field as the international market, it is not to be wondered at that such mistakes are by no means rare, nor does it seem as if it were possible to avoid them under the present unorganized and purely competitive industrial system. They have been aggravated in England by a belief that our best customers are to be found in foreign markets, and the importance of a steady, well established, and well understood home market is not fully perceived. "A pound of home trade is more significant to manufacturing industry than thirty shillings or two pounds of foreign." Now one of the most important branches of our home trade must be the supplying of agriculturists with manufactures in exchange for food. But when the purchasing power of this class of the community has sunk as much as £43,000,000 per annum, it is obvious that such a loss of custom must seriously affect manufacturers. Again, no small portion of our home market must consist in the purchases made by the working classes, yet it does not seem to occur to capitalist manufacturers that if they pay a large proportion of the industrial classes the lowest possible wages, and get them to work the longest possible hours, while thus obtaining an ever-increasing production of goods, the question must sooner or later be answered: who is going to consume the goods thus produced?

§ 8. **The present capitalist system. Foreign markets**—The answer as far as the capitalist is concerned seems to be: foreign customers in new markets. English manufacturers and capitalists have consistently supported that policy which seemed likely to open up these new markets to their goods. For a long time, as we saw (p. 213), they occupied themselves very wisely in obtaining cheap raw material by passing enactments actuated by Free Trade principles and removing protective restrictions. Cheap raw material having thus been gained, and machinery having now been developed to such an extent as to increase production quite incalculably, England sends her textile and other products all over the world. She seems to find it necessary to discover fresh markets every generation or so, in order that her vast output of commodities may be sold. This policy naturally receives the approval of those engaged in foreign commerce, and most of our wars with countries like China, Egypt, or Burmah, involve commercial interests. But as other foreign nations are also engaging more widely in external trade, the international struggle for new markets is liable to assume at any time a dangerous phase. To-day, indeed, the industrial history of our country seems to have reached a point when production under a purely capitalist system is overreaching itself. It must go on and on without ceasing, finding or fighting for an outlet for the wealth produced, lest the whole gigantic system of international commerce should break down by the mere weight of its own immensity. Meanwhile, English manufacturers are complaining of foreign competition in plaintive tones, which merely means that, whereas they thought some years ago that they had a complete monopoly in supplying the requirements of the world, they are now perceiving that they have not a monopoly at all, but only a good start, while other nations are already catching them up in the modern race for wealth.

§ 9. **Over-production and wages**—With all this, too, we hear cries of over-production, a phrase which economically is meaningless, more especially at a time when a very large number of people in the civilized world are daily on the verge of starvation, when the paupers of every civilized country are numbered by thousands, and plenty of people who never complain have not enough clothes to wear and not enough food to eat. Wages are certainly better than they were fifty years ago, but no one who knows the facts of the case will deny that for the average workman—I am not speaking of skilled artisans and the *élite* of the working classes—it is practically impossible to save anything out of his wages against old age or sickness. It is not the business of a historian to vituperate any particular class, but he may justly point out the mistakes to which classes have as a matter of history been liable. And the great mistake of the capitalist class in modern times has been to pay too little wages.[1] It is an old agricultural saying—I believe of Arthur Young's—that one cannot pay too much for good land, or too little for bad land. The same remark applies to labour. Capitalist employers rarely make the mistake of paying too much for bad labour, but they have constantly, as a matter of history, committed the worse error of paying too little for good labour. At the beginning of this century, as I have shown, the coming of the capitalist and of the capitalist factory system, beneficial as it was ultimately to England, was followed by a time of unprecedented misery and poverty for those whom they employed. The day of the capitalist has come, and he has made full use of it. The day of the labourer will come when he has the wisdom, and, we may add, the self-denial, necessary for a right use of his opportunities.

§ 10. **The power of labour. Trade Unions and Cooperation**—But the labourers of to-day are a very different class from their ancestors of fifty or seventy years ago. They have learnt, at least the most advanced among them, the power of combination, a remedy which at one time was forbidden them, but which is now fortunately once more theirs. The steady growth of Trade Unions and of Co-operative Societies has taught them habits of self-reliance and of thrift, and has made them

[1] This is now not so true as it was some time ago.

look more closely into the economic conditions of industry. These unions and societies do not yet embrace all the workmen of England, but they contain the best and worthiest of them, and their members are able to preserve a certain independence in treating with their employers. The power of capital is now opposed by the strength of united labour, and some of the great strikes of recent years have shown how great this united strength may be. But the power of labour may often in such cases degenerate into what readily becomes its weakness; and in any event, the attitude of mutual distrust and hostility between employer and employed is one which those who have the best interests of labour at heart cannot fail to deplore. It is true that the labourer can look back in his history to times when the power of his employer was used too selfishly and he himself was miserably oppressed. The miseries of the early days of the Industrial Revolution, the pauperism of agricultural labour in the early days of the nineteenth century, the sad conditions of children's employment at the beginning of Queen Victoria's reign—all these show how the greed of gain has rendered masters callous to their workpeople's welfare. But it must be remembered also that in many cases the workpeople themselves were by no means always anxious for the improvement of these conditions; and both masters and men have been slow to recognize the essential identity of interest, and the equal rights, of Capital and Labour. If the great principle of mutual interest and co-operation between employer and employed were more fully acted upon, then the industrial history of our country would enter upon a new era of well-founded prosperity.

CHAPTER VIII

THE NEW AGE, 1897-1911

§ 1. **Industrial Expansion**—It is impossible in the compass of a brief chapter to deal otherwise than in the barest outline with the industrial developments of the last fourteen years. The period opens with the Diamond Jubilee of Queen Victoria, includes the whole reign of her son, King Edward the Seventh, and closes in the Coronation year of her grandson, George the Fifth. From one point of view the country has during this time made marvellous advances in general prosperity. The population, indeed, which according to the returns of 1911 stands at the figure of 36,075,269 for England and Wales, shows a slower rate of progress than for any other decennial period since the institution of the census in 1801; but in so far as the diminished birth-rate is due to a higher standard of living among the people, such a slackening is itself a token of material well-being. And judging by the ordinarily accepted standards neither the accumulated wealth nor the productivity of our nation has ever before attained so great a height.

The gross amount of income brought under the survey of the Inland Revenue Department in 1907–08 (the last year for which returns are available) amounted for the first time to over £1,000,000,000 sterling, while the net amount available for taxation was over £693,000,000 as against £525,000,000 in 1897–98. The public applications for capital registered in London in the year 1910 reached a total of £267,439,100, a vast sum which exceeds all previous records by more than £75,000,000, and (apart from the large number of unrecorded private investments) shows the prosperity of undertakings at home and the amount of surplus capital available for investment abroad.

Wages also, which declined from 1901 to 1905, yet show a marked increase over the whole period under review, though this increase is unfortunately largely nominal, owing to the contemporaneous rise in prices and house-rent.

Both shipping and railway transport have undergone a vast expansion: the statistics for inland traffic are the chief among our few data regarding the advance of home trade. Foreign trade, which the "man in the street" has been led by recent controversy to take as the main criterion of industrial progress, after breaking all previous records in 1907, again surpassed itself in 1910. Our total imports for that year were £678,440,173, and our exports of British produce amounted to £430,589,811. A comparison with 1897, when the value of our imports was £451,028,960 and of our exports £294,174,118, shows how remarkable has been the increase in the volume of our foreign trade. A noteworthy feature is the growth in the re-export figures, which in 1910 for the first time exceeded £100,000,000, thus testifying to the maintenance of our position as the great carrier and transport agent for the world.

§ 2. **Wars, calamities, and the American crisis**—Yet there is another side to this picture of progress and well-being. During the same period the various quarters of the world were visited by a long series of calamities, both natural and artificial, from which our own dominions were not exempt. The Spanish-American War of 1898, the Russo-Japanese War of 1904-05, and the disastrous earthquakes at San Francisco (1906), Jamaica (1907), and Messina (1908) all caused not only loss of life and great physical suffering, but widespread destruction of capital, the effects of which were felt in all industrial countries.

In the earlier years of the period plague and famine in India and a succession of serious droughts in Australia also checked the productive capacity and purchasing power of these great dependencies, and consequently affected our industries at home.

But the closest and most malign influence was that of the South African War (1899–1903), which, after at first giving an apparent impetus to the trades supplying munitions of war, left behind it a legacy of debt, increased military and naval expenditure, and widespread depression in trade, with consequent unemployment during the "lean years" that followed. The National Debt in 1898–99, before the outbreak of war, stood at £638,000,000, but had risen by 1903–04 to £798,000,000, or to the level of 1870, thus wiping out in four years the laborious debt reductions of more than thirty years.

After some years of depression trade again revived, and throughout the world 1907 was a year of abnormally high prices and widespread speculation, which culminated during the autumn in an acute financial crisis in the United States. There practically all the banks suspended cash payments for some months. The effects of this shock to credit were felt far and wide. Vast quantities of gold were shipped to the United States, and although London at the time stood the strain much better than any other financial centre, the Bank of England was forced to raise its rate of discount to seven per cent. In the following year the United States and Japan still suffered from commercial depression, and in India the harvest proved a failure. Hence, as the consuming power of these great areas was checked, their demand for British goods fell off. Thus the volume of our foreign trade was greatly reduced and the average of the monthly unemployment returns by the Trade Unions for 1908 was far the highest for many years past, being 9·1 per cent., as against 4·3 in the preceding year.

§ 3. **The increase of public expenditure**—During the Boer War and since its close there has been an unparalleled growth both in national and municipal expenditure. For every £5 that was required by public departments in 1895 £8 is now expended. The addition to the National Debt, and consequently to the debt charges, has been already noticed, and the following table shows the general figures for the opening and close of the period under review:—

	Expenditure 1897–98	*Estimated Expenditure* 1910–11
Army	£19,330,000	£27,760,000
Navy	20,850,000	40,604,000
Civil Service . .	23,446,000	42,686,000
National Debt and other services . . .	25,000,000	36,945,000
Post Office, Customs and Inland Revenue .	14,310,000	23,852,000
Total	£102,936,000	£171,847,000

These totals represent an expenditure per head of the total population of £2, 11*s.* in 1897–98 and of £3, 16*s.* in 1910–11.

We must remember, however, that the expenses of the Post Office are more than covered by the revenue derived from that institution, and that much of the addition to the Civil Service estimates is due to Old Age Pensions and to the increased provision for education. "The Civil Service charge has risen as the natural result of multiplied and enlarged activities, and advance has been specially heavy in the last two decades, but the Civil Service includes education, poor law, the improvement of roads and health, and many other services which conduce to national well-being. It stands on a very different economic level from armaments, which represent the workings of international discord and jealousy."[1] Yet there is no doubt that in all departments the public money is being expended more freely and extravagantly than was the case some twenty-five years ago.

The portentous increase in naval expenditure must be ascribed partly to the Boer War, but chiefly to our recent rivalry in naval construction with Germany, and our adoption of the *Dreadnought* type of battleship. Army expenditure increased between 1897 and 1899 through a series of "little wars" in Egypt and India, and since the South African War we have been practically maintaining a war establishment in time of peace.

Thus we see that owing to the growth of armaments and fresh expenditure on social needs the taxpayer has to endure a heavy burden, which threatens to grow as the rate of increase among the population slackens. Any expenditure beyond what is required for military efficiency and social well-being is not only wasteful but actually injurious to our industry and commerce, since it diverts capital from productive channels. There is no justification for maintaining taxation at a war level in time of peace. As Mr Gladstone said, money is best left to fructify in the pockets of the people; or, to quote his great opponent, Lord Beaconsfield, who was always in agreement with him on this point, "the more you reduce the burdens of the people in time of peace, the greater will be your strength when the hour of peril comes."

§ 4. **Free Trade and Protection. The Colonies**—Ever since the repeal of the Corn Laws there had been in England a group of agricultural Protectionists, and some thirty years ago a small number of manufacturers began to advocate retaliation against foreign tariffs under the title of "Fair Trade." Towards the close of Queen

[1] *Economist*, Nov. 19, 1910.

Victoria's reign the growth of Imperial sentiment brought into prominence suggestions for a closer political and commercial union between England and her colonies. In 1903 these various strands of thought were combined by Mr Joseph Chamberlain, then Colonial Secretary, in his campaign on behalf of "Tariff Reform." This movement (which thus at first contained the inconsistent elements of protection to the British farmer, retaliation against the foreign manufacturer, and colonial preference) met with some acceptance in that year of depressed trade, and has now been adopted as the programme of the Unionist Party, in spite of the opposition of an important minority. In the General Election of 1906 the Protectionists sustained a crushing defeat, and they have not since been able to secure a majority in the House of Commons.

Although the controversy is still unsettled, it is at present, for various reasons, somewhat in abeyance. Old Age Pensions, which were to have been provided out of the revenues of the tariff, have been granted without recourse to protection, and other questions have occupied the political field at home, while the recent great expansion both in home and foreign trade seems, in the eyes of the public, to have falsified the more gloomy predictions of the "Tariff Reformers."

The supporters of the movement emphasize the growing political and commercial importance of our colonies, and the rapid advances made by Germany and the United States in neutral markets, and they point to the tariff walls which block our trade with foreign nations. Free-traders, in reply, maintain that the progress of Germany and America is due to a combination of many causes apart from their tariffs. They are, for purposes of internal trade, the largest free trade areas in the world.

Since the trade of nations is mutually interdependent we cannot suffer from an increase in commercial prosperity elsewhere, and retaliation has never proved a successful method of fighting hostile tariffs. In conclusion, they declare that an impossible task awaits any statesman who undertakes to frame a British tariff satisfactory alike to farmer, manufacturer, the colonies and India, and one which would not involve an increase in the price of food and other necessaries.

The reader must refer to larger treatises for details of the controversy, which has been much embittered by party spirit. But it seems at least that the war of statistics and arguments has not proved that the position of the working classes in regard to real wages, continuity of employment, and conditions of labour is better in protected countries than among our own people: indeed, as skilled economists constantly remind us, so many other factors are involved and so many qualifications must be made that it is almost impossible to draw trustworthy comparisons of this nature. Nor has the response of the colonies to the suggestions of the Preferentialists been encouraging. They have shown without ambiguity that highly as they value their connexion with the mother-country, they value equally highly their own political and commercial independence. In 1901 the various States of Australia united in a Federal Commonwealth whose tariff is highly protective, and in 1911 Canada began to negotiate mutual tariff concessions with the United States, her nearest and most important market. Our colonies are thus rapidly developing into practically independent States, bound to us, indeed, by ties of filial affection and interest, but determined to shape their own careers. South Africa has just entered upon the most hopeful chapter of her chequered history by the federation of the four colonies in the Union of South Africa. The original settlements of Cape Colony and Natal and the two Boer States conquered in the late war form now a self-governing whole—a happy reconciliation, hardly to have been anticipated at the end of the war, which is a high tribute to the wisdom of statesmen at home and to the healing effects of time in South Africa.

§ 5. **The position of the workers. Social legislation**—Returns recently published by the Local Government Board and other official statistics show that in the last half-century there has been a very marked improvement in regard to public health and social conditions. The rate of infantile mortality (among children less than one year old) is still sadly high in many town areas, yet, though it stood in 1907 at 118 per thousand for the whole of England and Wales, this figure is lower than that for any Continental country except Holland, and the death-rates from many diseases have also fallen rapidly in recent years. Housing accommodation has improved, statistics of overcrowding in 1901 showing a considerable reduction upon those of the previous census, and pauperism has on the average steadily declined. Wage statistics are inadequate and very difficult of interpretation, but they seem to indicate a marked rise during the last forty years, while the level of prices has fallen 24 per cent. during the same period. A detailed consideration of the last five years, however, reveals a less cheerful picture. The depression of trade resulting from the expenditure of capital during the South African War led to a fall in wages and a serious increase in unemployment. The hardships of the workers were aggravated by a period of rising prices and by the reflex effects of the American crisis. The statistics of pauperism in 1907 and

1908 showed a proportion of 24 per thousand inhabitants against an average of 22 per thousand for the preceding decade. In October and November 1908 the Trade Unions returned 9 per cent. of their members as unemployed, whilst amongst unorganized and casual workers the proportion was no doubt higher.

Yet at the same time there is a greatly increased sensitiveness of the public conscience regarding the condition of the vast majority of the population, as has been shown both in Parliamentary legislation and in unofficial movements for social betterment. Among the latter, garden villages and schemes for housing and town-planning bear witness to a recognition by employers and municipalities of a duty to provide workers and their families with some of the necessities for "good life." [1]

Such questions have become all the more urgent with the recent rapid growth of great suburban districts on the borders of our cities. This phenomenon—due to the eagerness of workers to escape into regions of somewhat purer air and lower rates outside the municipal areas—is emphasized in the latest census returns. According to these the boroughs are actually increasing in population less rapidly than their neighbouring counties, and in London itself the overflow is shown by decreases in many of the boroughs and an increase of 33 per cent. in the "Outer Ring."

In another direction the success of the Workers' Educational Association and kindred efforts proves that many among the working classes are eager to grasp opportunities for intellectual growth. But it is in recent legislation that we find the most remarkable testimony both to the power of the labour movement and the awakened

[1] "The State came into being to preserve life, but it continues in being for the sake of good life."—ARISTOTLE.

national conscience to which allusion has just been made.

There was an attempt in 1907 to check the drift townwards by offering the labourer an inducement to remain in the country. The aim of the Small Holdings and Allotments Act of that year was to provide him with a few acres of land at a reasonable rate with security of tenure, and so to re-establish the small cultivator. The Budgets from 1906 to 1908 not only relieved the general taxpayer by debt reduction and the middle classes by a differentiation of the income-tax in favour of earned incomes, but also reduced the tea and sugar duties, which fall most heavily on the working classes. But the Budget of 1908 will be remembered chiefly for the step then taken towards the relief of the aged poor. The institution of Old Age Pensions (already in force for some years in our Australasian colonies) was hotly decried as a Socialistic measure debasing to the recipients. So far, however, the test of experience seems to show none but good results, and since the recent removal of the poor relief disqualification there has been a marked fall in the statistics of pauperism. In 1909 the new Chancellor of the Exchequer, Mr Lloyd-George, introduced his first Budget. Its rejection by the House of Lords, which marked the crisis of the long struggle between the two Houses, has made it famous in constitutional history. But, avoiding its controversial clauses, we may note that this Budget also provided a small sum for the establishment of Labour Exchanges, on the Continental model, throughout the country. These exchanges, which are now working, aim at rendering labour more mobile, at bringing employers requiring workers and workers needing employment into touch with one another, and at publishing reliable information as to the condition of the labour market. The Workmen's Compensation Act of 1897, which placed the liability for industrial accidents on the shoulders of employers, was extended in 1906 to all workers (including domestic servants) whose annual earnings are under £250. Lastly, in 1911, a far-reaching scheme was introduced by which, with State assistance, all wage-earners (under a maximum of £160 per annum) are to be insured against sickness (including for women a maternity benefit) and the experiment of an insurance against unemployment is to be tried in the case of building, shipbuilding, and engineering—the trades which suffer most acutely from periodical lack of work.

We may also notice here the publication in 1909 of the exhaustive Report of the Poor Law Commission appointed in 1905. This is noteworthy both for its wholesale condemnation of the existing poor law system and its drastic proposals for a new method of dealing with the problem of poverty and unemployment. Four Commissioners, led by Mrs Sidney Webb, the well-known social writer, published their own "Minority" report, which contains a still more far-reaching scheme of State control. Both reports have aroused keen interest, they have influenced some of the legislation just described, and one of the schemes or a compromise between them will no doubt form the basis for the expected reform of the Poor Law.

§ 6. **Trade Unionism and the Labour Movement**—It was remarked in the last paragraph that the social legislation recorded was due in part to the pressure of the organized forces of labour upon politicians. The membership of Trade Unions has risen from 1,688,531 in 1898 to 2,426,592 in 1910; while in Parliament the Labour Party consisted in 1911 of about forty members, the majority of whom were nominated by Trade Unions and maintained out of Trade Union funds. Through these representatives Trade Unionists have been able to exert a considerable influence upon legislation. By the decision, on appeal, of the House of Lords, in the Taff Vale Case (1901), the Trade Unions Act of 1871 was so interpreted as to make it possible for a Trade Union to be sued in tort for the acts of its members, and for Trade Union funds to become liable for any damages that might be awarded. Trade Unionists protested against the decision as contrary to the spirit of the legislation of 1871, and sufficient pressure was exerted by the Labour members to ensure the passage of the Trade Disputes Act in 1906. This restored Trade Unions to their original position under the law of 1871.

But in 1909 the "Osborne Judgment" struck a blow at the existence of the Labour Party itself. Osborne, a member of the Amalgamated Society of Railway Servants, sued the officials of that union on the ground that the enforced levy from members for the maintenance of Parliamentary representatives was *ultra vires* and accordingly void. After prolonged litigation the House of Lords gave its final judgment in favour of the plaintiff. The Labour Party in Parliament began to press for the reversal of this decision, and at the same time tried to conciliate opposition by abolishing the "pledge" to which all its members had been forced to subscribe. But the obvious difficulties which handicapped men of moderate means, of whatever party, in their attempts to enter Parliament, led to another movement amongst Liberals, Labour Members, and some Conservatives for the payment of all Members of Parliament out of State funds, and provision for this step was made in the Budget of 1911.

Of recent years there has been considerable unrest in

the labour world and much loss of time and money has accrued to both employers and employed through industrial disputes. The most important stoppages were those in the coal trade (in South Wales in 1898 and 1910 and in the North in 1910), in the Lancashire cotton industry in 1908 and 1910, in the engineering centres on the north-east coast in 1908, and in the shipbuilding trade in 1910. In August 1911 the country had to face stoppages at the London and Liverpool docks, and, closely following, a general railway strike, which occurred at twenty-four hours' notice. The dockers gained their demands ; the railway strike, through the efforts of the Government, only lasted two days, as a small and impartial Commission was immediately appointed to inquire into the working of the Railway Conciliation Boards, the inefficiency of which to remedy grievances was put forward by the railway unions as the cause of the strike. These recent transport difficulties occasioned very serious trade losses and much inconvenience to the general public, and in certain parts of the country were attended by grave rioting and disorder. All the disputes have taxed the powers of skilled arbitrators (Board of Trade officials or distinguished private individuals), but their most disquieting feature has been, in several cases, the tendency of the workers not to comply with the terms of settlement, and the apparent inability of Trade Union officials to enforce such compliance. Action of this kind can only have the effect of alienating popular sympathy even in the case of genuine grievances. However, it is admitted by most observers that the recent increase in the prices of important commodities and the general rise in the standard of life amongst the working classes make the claim for higher wages and shorter hours of work a well-founded one.

§ 7. **Recent inventions and industrial developments**—With regard to industrial machinery recent years have shown rather a greater perfection and rapidity of working than any actually new invention. Perhaps the greatest technical improvements have been made in engineering and steel production, but in many branches of industry the part of the machine constantly increases in importance and that of the individual worker diminishes.

The most striking developments of the last fifteen years have been in connection with transport and communication. The telephone has become a business necessity, and now wireless telegraphy (associated with the name of M. Marconi) has extended our power of rapid intercourse even to mid-ocean. There has been an enormous increase in the size and speed of merchant vessels, the most sensational evidence of which is seen in the vast ocean liners of German and Anglo-American companies plying between Europe and the United States.[1] Not only have these ships reduced the passage between New York and Liverpool to a length of about five days, but they are able to carry much larger cargoes than their predecessors, and thus doubly tend to swell the volume of international trade. On land there has been an extraordinary increase in the use of motor transport both for goods and passenger traffic, and the recent successes of aviation seem to foretell that at no distant time the air will form another highway for human intercourse.

Glancing at the changes in the industrial world we may note the tendency (due to resultant economies of marketing and management) towards an increase in the

[1] The *Lusitania* and *Mauretania* are over 31,000 tons burden; the *Olympic* and the *Titanic*, 45,000 tons.

size of a single business and in the amount of capital invested in it. This tendency is seen in many of the great staple manufactures, such as the textile trades and milling, but also in banking and finance generally, where the huge joint-stock concerns with many branches have swallowed up the old-fashioned private bank with its local connexion. In retail trading, too, the great stores, providing many classes of goods under one roof, prove formidable rivals to the small shopkeepers. These stores are generally run as joint-stock companies and often have branches throughout the country. Nevertheless, thanks mainly to the absence of a protective tariff, which shelters the growth of monopoly, England is comparatively free from the dominance of great Trusts. Some partial or local monopolies exist, of which railways, newspaper combines, and the "tied" public-houses attached to some brewing companies form the most obvious examples. But in the opinion of those qualified to judge, the small trader or manufacturer is holding his own in many branches of industry.

The census returns, which show the shifting of employment in various groups of industry, form a good criterion of their relative importance. Those for 1901 have been analysed as follows by a recent writer :—

"The orders which show the greatest decline are textiles and dress. While metal, ships, pottery, wood, food, etc., show a moderate advance, precious metals and instruments, vehicles, chemicals, printing, show a great increase. A still closer examination into the sub-orders of the census returns shows that the foundational and the staple processes of manufacture are stagnant or declining in importance, while those concerned with the finishing processes of manufacture, especially those concerned with the manufacture of more highly specialized articles, are increasing."[1]

Mr Hobson adds that the most noteworthy advance is shown in two special groups, the trades concerned with the building and furnishing of houses and those which manufacture vehicles for land and water carriage. The growth in the first of these groups tends to corroborate the statistics of improved housing accommodation already mentioned, while that in the second introduces us to the most significant movement of all, the enormous increase in all occupations connected with land and water transport. This again may be correlated with the figures for our re-export trade already given, since both show England's marvellous position as the great market and carrier for the world.

§ 8. **The necessity of studying economic factors in history**—Hitherto our prosperity, great as it is, has frequently had its drawbacks, and has passed through many vicissitudes. Our ancestors and ourselves have made many mistakes, and till recently, as we have seen, the growth of our national wealth has been slow. But a study of industrial history is not without its uses, if it helps us to-day to understand how we have come into our present position, and what faults and follies we must avoid in order to retain it. Unfortunately, few historians have thought it worth their while to study seriously the economic factors in the history of nations. They have contented themselves with the intrigues and amusements of courtiers and kings, the actions of individual statesmen, or the destructive feats of military heroes. They have often failed to explain properly the great causes which necessitated the results they claim

[1] Hobson, *Evolution of Modern Capitalism*, p. 388.

to investigate. But just as it is impossible to understand the growth of England without a proper appreciation of the social and industrial events which rendered that growth possible, and which provided the expenses which that growth entailed, so it will be impossible to proceed in the future without a systematic study of economic and industrial affairs. Many of the great political questions of our day derive most of their difficulty from economic causes; while international politics tend more and more to centre round matters of commercial and industrial importance. After all, the means by which we gain our daily bread form for the majority of mankind the most pressing of problems; and what is true of the individual is true on a larger scale of the nation also. Man is by no means a purely economic animal, but the material wants of human life must be satisfied, and much of human activity must be directed toward their fulfilment. The history of mankind is the history of man's activity, and so long as human nature and men's material conditions are what they are, so long must economic and industrial factors have a potent influence in the course of political and social life. We have seen in these pages how such factors have influenced the growth of our own nation and contributed towards bringing us into our present position; and it is only reasonable to believe that commercial and industrial considerations must weigh more and more heavily with us if that position is to be secured and maintained. And those of us who wish to help in maintaining and advancing our national progress must seek carefully to answer the economic questions that are forcing themselves continually upon us, by looking at them in the light afforded by the industrial history of a great industrial nation.

NOTE ON AUTHORITIES FOR INDUSTRIAL HISTORY

FOR the earlier periods of English industrial history the ordinary student will find Cunningham's *Growth of Industry* and Ashley's *Introduction to English Economic History and Theory* useful. Besides these he should endeavour by all means to read the *Domesday Book*, a translation or copy of which may be found in most public libraries. The well-known histories of Stubbs and Freeman are also a great help. Then, for the whole of the period from Henry III. to the eighteenth century, the large work, *The History of English Agriculture and Prices* (in six volumes) by Professor Thorold Rogers affords a perfect mine of information. The same author's *Six Centuries of Work and Wages* and *Economic Interpretation of History* are absolutely indispensable for anyone who wants to understand, not only our industrial, but our general history. Time spent over these two books is amply repaid. For the eighteenth and nineteenth centuries especially, Toynbee's *Industrial Revolution* and Leone Levi's *History of Commerce* must be read, and the Blue-books of the period should also be consulted.

Besides these works by modern authors, Arthur Young's *Northern and Southern Tours in England*, and Defoe's *Tour* afford a valuable picture of English industries in the last century, as also does the *Wealth of Nations* by Adam Smith. There is likewise a useful little *History of British Commerce*, from the earliest times, by G. L. Craik (published in 1844 by Charles Knight, but now long since out of print), which I have found very helpful and fairly complete.

For the political portion of our history Green's *History of the English People* will probably be sufficient for general readers ; and it contains occasionally a reference to industrial events. Mr George Howell's *Conflict of Capital and Labour* should be read, as affording a clear view of the old gilds and their modern descendants, the Trade Unions ; and no student of modern industrial questions should omit to familiarize himself with the

History of Co-operation, by Mr Holyoake. A little book called *The Romance of Trade* gives a number of interesting industrial facts in a disconnected sort of way, and may be read with advantage when the student knows the general outlines of industrial history. Harrison's *Elizabethan England* (now published in the Camelot Classics Series) might be read in a similar way, as giving a picture of sixteenth century life.

I must acknowledge my indebtedness to all the above works, which I have freely used in this little history, and especially to the works of Professor Thorold Rogers, without which no complete industrial history could have been written. I have also utilized in some places the material already existing in my own *Short Account of the Growth of English Industry* in the *Co-operative Annual* of 1890, and in my article on *English Agriculture* in the *Westminster Review* of December 1888. I have preferred to state in this note the more accessible works that I have consulted, omitting others which are not immediately necessary for ordinary readers, rather than to burden my pages with continual footnotes and references. I trust that the works here indicated may help to guide students of economic history in reading far beyond the limits within which this short outline is necessarily confined.

I have also dealt with this subject more fully in a larger work entitled *Industry in England* (Methuen : London, 1896).

H. de B. G.

Of recent years some standard works on Domesday have been published, including Round's *Feudal England*, F. W. Maitland's *Domesday Book and Beyond*, Vinogradoff's *Villeinage in England* and Ballard's *Domesday Inquest*—the last being an excellent summary. Webb's *Industrial Democracy* and *History of Trade Unionism*, Hobson's *Evolution of Modern Capitalism* and Booth's monumental *Life and Labour of the People of London*, all deal with the modern period. No serious student should fail to consult the publications of Government departments and Royal Commissions concerning questions of trade, industry, and social progress. The census returns and the current Statistical Abstracts are also useful. Bowley's *Elementary Manual of Statistics* affords valuable help in the interpretation of these publications.

M. E. H.

NOTES

1. **Population of Roman Britain** (p. 2)—It is, of course, impossible to state this accurately. Much of the land that supported a large population in Roman times afterwards fell waste—*e.g.* the fens of the eastern counties (p. 111); but the numerous Roman remains still left to us testify to a considerable economic development. (Cf. also the facts given in Cunningham's *Growth of English Industry*, p. 53).

2. **Markets on Boundaries** (p. 3)—A good example of this is Moreton-in-Marsh, an ancient market town situated on the boundaries of the four counties of Oxford, Gloucester, Worcester and Warwick shires. This fact is recorded by a stone, known as "the four shires' stone," and situated about a mile from the town on the London Road. The religious origin of many markets, alluded to in the case of Glasgow, should not be forgotten. (Cf. Cunningham's *Growth of English Industry*, p. 76.)

3. **Danish influence on Commerce** (p. 4)—The Danes, before ever they came to England, were enterprising navigators, as is shown by their very early commerce with Russia, their colonization of Iceland (A.D. 874), and discovery of Greenland (A.D. 985), and the coast of the (now) Eastern United States. They settled chiefly in the north of England, in very large numbers and formed an active industrial population, many of them becoming leading merchants. They were instrumental in causing English trade to develop in the north of Europe, and generally speaking gave a stimulus to navigation. (Cf. Cunningham's *Growth of English Industry*, p. 83 *sqq.*—1890 ed.)

4. **Manorial Courts** (p. 19)—The court baron was composed of a kind of jury of freeholders and was concerned with civil proceedings. The court leet was composed of all tenants, both free and serf, who acted as a jury in criminal cases, minor offences, and so forth. Both courts were presided over by the lord of the manor or his bailiff. Thus local discipline and law was concentrated in the hands of the inhabitants of the parish themselves, and the

manorial courts were a very useful means of education in local self-government. Unfortunately their power, utility, and educational influence declined with the decay of the whole manorial system. (Cf. Rogers' *Work and Wages*, pp. 63 and 420.—1889 ed.)

5. **Decay of Manorial System** (p. 22)—The decay of this social and economic system begins most clearly and markedly with the changes made by the Black Death (1348), and by the social revolution which followed it, of which the Peasants' Revolt was the first and most startling symptom (cf. pp. 73, 74–77). The legislation of Edward I. forms, again, another epoch from which to date the decay of manorial institutions. As Dr Cunningham says (*Growth of Industry*, p. 243), "In regard to commerce, manufactures, and to agriculture alike, the local authorities were gradually overtaken and superseded by the increasing activity of Parliament, till in the time of Elizabeth the work was practically finished." The essentially local and personal relations of the manor gave way to the more general and impersonal relations of national government and national economy.

6. **The Jews** (p. 36)—It appears that this expulsion of the Jews was not absolutely complete, and Jewish tradition gives the year 1358 as the date of final expulsion; but in 1410 a Jewish physician, Elias Sabot, was certainly allowed to practise in England. There seems to have been a certain immigration of Jews to England, when they were expelled from Spain by Ferdinand and Isabella (1492), for there are notices of them recovering debts in English law-courts. Their presence in this country was, however, only first *publicly* sanctioned by Cromwell; and during the Commonwealth and the reign of Charles II. they came back here in considerable numbers. (Cf. Wolf's *Anglo-Jewish Exhibition Papers*, p. 57; and my own *History of Commerce in Europe*, p. 99.)

7. **Commercial relations with Flanders** (p. 49)—We may add to the notices here given the treaty of 1274 between Edward I. and the Countess of Flanders, protecting the export of English wool to Flanders, and the well-known case of Perkin Warbeck. This impostor was supported by the dowager Duchess of Burgundy, and was well received in Flanders, then ruled by the Archduke Philip. As Philip, at the instigation of the Duchess, encouraged Warbeck, Henry VII. took the step of banishing all Flemings from England (1493), and as Philip replied by expelling all the English from Flanders, commercial intercourse between the two countries was almost entirely suspended. The result was, as

Bacon tells us, this interruption "began to pinch the merchants of both nations very sore," and they besought their respective sovereigns "to open the intercourse again." Philip withdrew his support from Warbeck and the impostor was left without resources, so that his subsequent appearance in England was a complete failure. The want of English wool thus altered the policy of the Flemish rulers, and before long the "great treaty," or *Intercursus Magnus*, was made between the two nations (1496), by which trade was once more allowed to proceed unchecked, and "the English merchants came again to their mansion at Antwerp where they were received with procession and great joy."

Henry VII. also made a commercial treaty with Denmark (1490); and one with the Republic of Florence, securing to that city a stipulated supply of English wool every year. (Cf. *Commerce in Europe*, p. 98.)

8. **Other Sources of Income** (p. 50)—Of course we must not forget that the kings who fought against the French got money for their wars by other means as well. Large amounts were extorted from the Jews; enormous debts were contracted by Edward III. with the great Florentine bankers the Bardi; and his repudiation of them in 1345 caused the failure of that firm. Edward III. also pawned his crown and jewels, which were in pledge at Cologne, and could not redeem them, till the Hansa merchants in England came to his rescue and lent him the necessary cash in return for trading privileges in London. (Cf. *Commerce in Europe*, §§ 44 and 62. The question of taxation, etc., may be studied from larger political histories.)

9. **Assize of Bread and Ale** (p. 61)—The best example of such regulation is found, perhaps, in the Act 13, Rich. II., st. 1, c. 8 (1389–90), which ordains: "Forasmuch as a man cannot put the price of corn and other victuals in certain," the justices of the peace shall every year make proclamation "by their discretion," according to the dearth of victuals, how much every mason, carpenter, tiler, and other craftsmen, workmen, and other labourers by the day shall take by the day, with meat and drink or without meat and drink, and that every man shall obey such proclamations from time to time, as a thing done by statute." Finally, provision is made for the correct keeping of the *assize*, or *assessment* from time to time, of the prices of bread and ale. The earliest notice of an "assize" in England is found in the Parliament Rolls for 1203, but the practice is probably much

older; and the most ancient law upon the subject is the 51st Hen. III. (A.D. 1266), "Assisa Panis et Cerevisiæ." The assize of bread was in force till the beginning of the nineteenth century, and was only then abolished in London.

10. **Stourbridge Fair** (p. 63)—This Stourbridge or Sturbridge is now almost in Cambridge itself, the relics of the fair being held in a field near Barnwell, about a mile and a half from the city. In ancient times it was very easy for merchants to come up the River Ouse in barges or light boats, as water-transport was much more used then than now, and even the sea-going ships were very light craft. Probably a Flemish merchant would find no difficulty in sailing all the way from Antwerp to Cambridge in a light ship.

11. **Survivals of Villeinage** (pp. 74, 79)—Of course an ancient and universal custom could not die out all at once, but its decay after 1381 was certainly rapid. Dr Cunningham (*Growth of Industry*, p. 360) quotes cases to prove that villeinage existed in the fifteenth and sixteenth centuries, but he himself says that Fitzherbert (*On Surveyinge*, 1539) "laments over the continuance of villanage as a disgrace to the country"; and Fitzherbert would surely not have spoken thus if it was a recognized institution, instead of a decaying survival. Again, in 1574 Elizabeth enfranchised all bondmen on her estates; and she would hardly have done this if it had been the universal custom to retain villeins in their old bondage. We may readily admit that there were plenty of survivals of villeinage, although the old institutions were practically obsolete.

11*a*. **Monopolies** (p. 102)—These had been used by the crown partly in order to raise money by their sale and partly as a convenient method of paying or rewarding ministers or court favourites. Thus Elizabeth's favourite, Essex, had a monopoly of sweet wines. But by Elizabeth's time they had become so unpopular, and people saw so clearly the taxes which they inflicted on all articles thus monopolized that Parliament demanded (in 1601) their abolition. So determined was the House that the Queen gave way, though she was no doubt within the legal limits of her prerogative. James I., however, used his prerogative to create so many new monopolies that Parliament again protested (in 1609), and he also revoked them all. But after the suspension of Parlamentary government in 1614 monopolies were granted again, till in 1621 their revocation was one of the main points mentioned among the grievances which the House of Commons proceeded to redress, and monopolies were then once more abolished. The three patents (or monopolies) chiefly complained of were those on (1) inns and hostelries, (2) alehouses, (3) gold and silver thread. The Act abolishing monopolies is the 21 Jac. I. cap. 3 (1624). This Parliamentary struggle about monopolies shows very clearly the beginnings of the great fight between Parliament and the Crown, the former trying to regain rights which had for some time (especially under the Tudors) been in abeyance, and the Crown to keep prerogatives which had hitherto been exercised unchecked.

12. **Elizabeth's Poor Law** (p. 107)—There is no doubt that the original intention of the Act was beneficent, and its framers are not to be held responsible for the use made of it in later times.

The **Act of Apprenticeship**, incidentally fixing wages by assessment, was mainly concerned with the relations of masters to their journeymen and apprentices; and enacted also that no person should exercise a craft or trade unless he had been apprenticed to it for seven years.

13. **Banking and the Stop of the Exchequer** (p. 130)—Banking was now becoming a regular business, carried on especially by goldsmiths, who often advanced money to the sovereign upon the security of taxes or personal credit. A pamphlet of 1676, called "The Mystery of the Newfashioned Goldsmiths or Bankers Discovered," shows how banking and money-lending had become a regular business, and gives the year 1645 as about the time when commercial men began regularly to put their cash in the hands of goldsmiths. It also states that "the greatest of them (*i.e.* of the goldsmiths) were enabled to supply Cromwell with money in advance upon the revenues, as his occasions required, at great advantage to themselves." Similarly the famous goldsmith George Heriot had frequently obliged James I. It is well known how the London goldsmiths advanced Charles II. as much as £1,300,000, at 8 to 10 per cent. interest, upon the security of the taxes; and how (in 1672) he suddenly refused to pay them, saying they must be content with the interest, and closed the exchequer, thus causing a serious commercial panic.

The unsatisfactory method of obtaining loans from goldsmiths and other private persons was partly the cause of William Paterson's project, now known as the **Bank of England** (1694). Paterson offered to provide the Government of William III. with £1,200,000, to be repaid by taxation on beer or other liquors and by rates on shipping, while those who subscribed this money were incorporated into a regular company which was to receive 8 per cent. interest and also £4000 a year for management. Thus the matter of loans was first placed upon a proper basis and the Bank thus formed, and supported by Government credit, took at once a leading position in English commerce. (Cf. Rogers' *First Nine Years of Bank of England.*)

14. **National Debt** (p. 145)—This loan, mentioned in the last note, was the beginning of a regular National Debt, the system of contracting loans upon the security of the supplies or upon Government credit, and of paying them off gradually in succeeding generations. (Cf. my *Commerce in Europe*, p. 145, and Grellier's *National Debt.*)

The Restoration of the Currency was due to Montague, the Chancellor of the Exchequer. Up to the time of Charles II. silver money was made by simply cutting the metal with shears, and shaping and stamping it with a hammer. It was thus quite easy to clip or shear the coins again without being detected, and then pass them off to an unsuspecting person for their full nominal value. So the coins became smaller and smaller, and people often found on presenting them at a bank or elsewhere that they were only worth half their nominal value. At first, under Charles II., it was thought sufficient to issue new coins with a ribbed or "milled" edge, but the only result of this was that the good coin was melted or exported and (as is always the case) the inferior money remained at home. It was then seen, by Montague and Sir Isaac Newton (the Master of the Mint), that the only way was to *call in* the old coinage and issue an entirely new and true milled currency. The expenses of this re-coinage, which cost some two and a half millions, were defrayed by a tax on window-panes. (Cf. Rogers' *Economic Interpretation of History*, p. 200.)

The East India Company's New Charter was granted on October 7th, 1693, by William III., and restored all the former powers and privileges of the Company. This Company's monopoly of trade with India had been frequently infringed by private traders, and it was generally regarded with such great hostility that the House of Commons in 1692 requested the King to dissolve the Company upon the ground of mismanagement and conduct injurious to national interests. However, the enemies of the Company failed, and all its privileges were confirmed by the Charter of 1693. Its monopoly was nevertheless still often disregarded, and the validity of it denied by Parliament in spite of the King's favour. A New Company was even formed in 1698, but after a few years the two rival Companies were amalgamated (1708).

15. **Export of Bullion** (p. 169)—"In form the prohibition on the export of gold and silver coin continued to 1816. People were allowed to export gold in bars, foreign coin, and bullion the produce of foreign coin; and an oath had to be taken that exported bars were of this character. People were hired to swear that they were so, and sworn-off gold, as it was called, was worth 1½*d.* an ounce more than other gold was. Three-halfpence an ounce was the bullion-dealer's payment for perjury" (Rogers' *Economic Interpretation of History*, p. 187).

The necessities of their Eastern trade compelled the East India Company to acquire large stores of bullion and export it to India, in spite of any prohibition to the contrary; and their trade, with its enormous profits, was thus a very clear example of the mistaken character of the theory which taught that gold and silver must not be exported for fear of impoverishing the country. This fact, in the case of the East Indian trade, was seen by some economists early in the eighteenth century, and was then clearly stated by a writer in the paper called the *British Merchant* (i. 26), who estimated the export of bullion to India and China at £400,000 or £500,000 a year (in 1764 it was £369,831, and £532,705 in 1790). The *British Merchant* was first published in 1713.

16. **Important Commercial Events** (p. 125)—Among the important commercial events of this period one ought certainly to include the *Darien Scheme* and the *Union of England and Scotland*, although these belong more fitly to a History of Commerce than of Industry. The Darien scheme was a project originated by William Paterson, the founder of the Bank of England, who proposed to colonize the Isthmus of Darien and use it as "the key of the Indies and door of the world" for commerce. English capitalists, however, would not support his scheme and it was denounced by the English Parliament. Nevertheless a company was formed in Scotland, called "The Scottish African and Indian Company," a charter was given it by the Scotch Parliament in 1695, and a capital of £900,000 was ultimately raised, £400,000 coming from Scotland, then a very poor country, and the rest from English and Dutch merchants. The hostility of the East India Company, the Levant Company, and of the Dutch in

general, however, never ceased, and it was owing to their influence that, when the ill-fated colony at last set out for Darien in July 1698, the settlers were left quite unaided against the attacks of the Spaniards, who claimed the monopoly of South American trade. In fact, Spanish attacks and the climate, so utterly unsuited for European colonists, sealed the fate of the expedition, and few who went out ever returned. This failure had the most serious effect in impoverishing the Scotch, who could then ill afford the loss, but there is little doubt that it greatly helped to bring about the subsequent Act of Union between England and Scotland, in which William Paterson was largely concerned (1707). The Union proved of considerable benefit to Scotland, as, by it, trade between the two countries became free, English ports and colonies were thrown open to the Scotch, and Scotland found a large market for woollen and linen goods and cattle in England.

The date of the *Methuen Treaty* is 1703, and it was arranged by John Methuen between England and Portugal. It was agreed that British woollen goods should be admitted into Portugal and her colonies, provided that at all times Portuguese wines were admitted into England at two-thirds of the duty (whatever it might be) levied on French wines. The result was a considerable increase of trade with Portugal, but an even greater decrease of trade with France, while the wine-drinking of our upper classes took a very different direction, for port, which had hitherto been almost unknown in England, became the typical drink of the English gentleman, and more port was sent to the United Kingdom than to all the rest of Europe together. It was not till the time of the commercial treaty of 1860 with France, that the heavy duties on light French wines were reduced, and with them the duties on French manufactures. Till then, as Gladstone said in his speech on the subject in 1862, " it was almost thought a matter of duty to regard Frenchmen as traditional enemies," not only in politics but in commerce. This treaty was only one among the many great services of Cobden to the commerce of his country.

17. **Deposition of East India Company** (p. 217)—In June, 1858, the East India Company ceased to exist, the territories of India were transferred to the Crown of England, and the Queen was proclaimed sovereign of India on November 1st, 1858. The Company's army became part of the Queen's army, and Lord Canning, who had been Governor-General, became the first Viceroy. All the powers hitherto exercised by the East India

Company, or by the Board of Control, were vested in the Secretary of State for India, assisted by a Council of fifteen members appointed by the Crown.

18. **Huskisson's Reforms** (p. 213)—It was Huskisson who in 1823 passed a "Reciprocity of Duties Bill," by which English and foreign ships had equal advantages in England whenever foreign nations allowed the same to English vessels in their ports. He threw open the commerce of our colonies, under certain restrictions, to other nations. He reduced the duties on silk and wool in 1824, and in the same year the Acts fixing wages (cf. p. 107), and limiting the free travelling about of workmen (p. 189) were repealed. So also were all laws controlling combinations of either masters or workmen; though combinations of workmen to intimidate employers were made illegal in 1825.

INDEX

ACCOUNTS, bailiffs' mediæval, 18; modern farmers' lack of, 113, 205
Acreage of England (A. Young), 114
Adam Smith, 150, 189
Agriculture, early combined, 8; before and after Great Plague, 71, 73; mediæval, 40-45; in 16th, 17th, and 18th centuries, 109-117; modern, 198-201; depression of, 202, 209
Agricultural improvements, 104, 113, 201; gangs, 208; labourer, 40, 71, 79, 119, 142, 150, 188, 205, 208; reforms, 210; wages, 79, 119-121; wealth, 152, 209; population, 150, 153, 206; writers, 42, 110; union, 208
Alfred, 4, 5
Allowance system of relief, 188
American War, 170
Anglo-Saxon trade, 3
Antwerp, 59, 95; decay of, 97
Apprentices, in gilds, 29; in factories, 179, 181
Arable land in a manor, 6, 20
Arch, Joseph: his work, 207, 208
Aristocracy: feudal, 32; landowning, 143, 198
Arkwright's inventions, 159
Artisans: mediæval, 29; modern, 174, 190, 221; wages of, 71, 79, 120, 150, 162, 174, 187, 195; Huguenot, 134, 135
Assessments of wages, 107, 119, 187
Aston, manor of, 12
Australian colonies, 216, 225, 229
Aviation, 236

BAILIFFS' ACCOUNTS, 18, 42
Baltic trade, development of our, 99
Bank of England, 144, 173, 225
Barons' wars, 31
Beaconsfield, 227
Beggars (Defoe's remark), 149
Berlin decree, 173
Birmingham, 152
Black Death. *See* Great Plague
Blincoe, Robert, on factories, 181
Bodmin, staple for tin, 92
Bombay, 123, 127
Bordars, 12
Boston, port, 64
Boulton's inventions, 165
Bounties on corn, 200
Bradford, 161, 163, 183
Bread, wheat, 68, 150; price of, 150
Brickmaking, 105, 142
Bristol, 23, 39, 64
Britain in Roman times, 1, 2
Bruges, 95; staple at, 59
Burslem, 140
Bye industries, 155

CALAIS, our staple town, 59
Cambridge, coal at, 138
Canada, 125, 128, 216, 229
Cape Colony, 216, 230
Capital, 223
Capital in agriculture (A. Young), 115; to-day, 205; loss of farmers', 203

Capitalist agriculture, 42; cessation of, 73; artisans, 147; manufacturers, 147, 174, 176
Capitalist manufacture, epoch of, 162; present system of, 219
Capitalists and workmen, 221, 222; the coming of, 146, 162; mistakes of (Mercantile Theory), 168
Captains of industry, 218
Cartwright's inventions, 160
Carucate of land, 16 (*note*)
Castles, growth of towns near, 23
Cattle in mediæval times, 44; improvements in breed of, 114
Census, 237
Chamberlain, 228
Champaign land, 43
Charlemagne, commercial treaty with, 5
Charles I. and coal trade, 137
Charter, the Great, 34
Charters of towns, 25, 28; of companies, 98
Chartism, 191
Cheese, consumption of, 151
Chester a Roman town, 2, 24
Chinese wars, 217
Cistercian monks wool-growers, 42, 49
Civil Service, 226
Civil War in England, its effect, 134
—— in America, 217
Climate, our, useful for manufactures, 133
Closes, 21, 43
Cloth trade, 54, 55, 135. *See* Manufactures
Clover, introduction of, 113
Coal trade, 136, 137; influence on manufactures, 164 and *map*
Cobbett, 175
Cobden, 201, 215
Colonies, our, 122, 128, 167, 170, 215
Combination Laws, 189, 190; power of, 221; of workmen, 191; Combination of peasants in the Peasants' Revolt, 76, 78
Commerce, early, 4; our first treaty of, 5. *See* Trade
Commerce and war, 121-129, 169, 216
Commercial progress, 129; depressions, 218, 225
Common fields, 8, 20; enclosure of, 116, 199; pasture, 20
Communal land, 8, 43
Commutation of services for money payments, 16, 41, 74
Companies, formation of trading, 98, 129, 212
Company, East India, 98; Levant, 129; Hudson's Bay, 131
Competition, appearance of, 92; checked by feudalism, 32; foreign, 209, 220; modern, 219
Condition of the people. *See* Wages and Artisans and Agricultural labourers
Conquest, England after Norman, 37, 39
Continental War, 171, 195
Co-operation, growth of, 221
Corn Laws, 200, 201, 215; Repeal of, 186, 201, 227
Cort's inventions, 165
Cottars, 12
Cotton manufacture, 164
Counties, Eastern, cloth trade in, 57, 135, 163; Northern, desolation of in mediæval times, 38; Northern, shifting of population to, 163, and *map*; Southern most populous, 11, 37, 152
Craft gilds, 27, 29
Crisis (United States), 225
Cromwell's commercial wars, 123
Crusades, 26, 33
Currency, debasement of, 86
Cuxham manor, 17, 18

DAIRY FARMING, 210; dairyman, 43

Debasement of currency, by Henry VIII., 86
Defoe, references to his *Tour*, 64, 145, 148
Demand for labourers after Great Plague, 71
Discoveries of Columbus and others, 89
Dissolution of monasteries, 84
Distress of working classes after 1815, 174, 192
Distribution of wealth before Industrial Revolution, 153, 156
Domesday Book, its historical value, 10; condition of England as shown in, 11, and *map*; towns in, 24; manors in (Cuxham and Aston), 16, 17; population in, 12, 13
Drawbacks of mediæval life, 79, 80
Dreadnought, 227
Dutch, agricultural improvements due to, 105, 110; other improvements, 140; wars with (Cromwell's), 123, 130; carrying trade once in hands of, 130
Dyeing, 55, 133

EARTHQUAKES, 224
East, development of trade with, after Crusades, 33; in James I.'s reign, 129
East India Company, 98, 127, 145, 216
Eastern counties, manufactures in, 57, 135, 163
Economic folly, 170, 203, 211
Economics, importance of, in history, 238
Economist, 226
Edward I. and Edward III., usefulness of wool to them, 49; their alliances with Flanders, 49
Edward III. and Statute of Labourers, 71; and manufactures, 53
Edward VI. and the Hansa in London, 95
Eight Hours' Movement, 186, 235
Elizabethan England, 100-109; sea-captains, 97, 122
Emancipation of villeins, 74
Employers, capitalist, 67, 146, 192, 221; their assessments of wages, 107
Enclosures, 46, 116
England before Norman Conquest, 1-9; after it, 11, 37; in Middle Ages, 68, 81; in Elizabeth's reign, 100; modern, 211 *sqq.*; a commercial power, 121
England and other nations' wars, 216
Estone manor, 16
Expenditure, public increase of, 226
Export of corn, 200
Exports in Roman times, 2; in 12th century, 33; of wool, 36, 48, 51, 92; exports in 15th century, 92, 96; later, 103, 130, 131, 132, 166, 174, 212

FACTORIES set up, 161
Factory Acts, 181-185
Factory children, 179, 182
Factory system, germs of, 66; growth of, 176-181, 186
Fairs, 53, 61-63
Famine of 1315, 70
Farmers, losses of, 209
Fens, the, 38; drainage of, 111
Feudal system, 8; effects of, 31
"Firma Burgi," the, 25
Flanders, its manufactures, 48, 52; our trade with, 95, 132, 169
Flemish weavers in England, 36, 37, 53, 103
Foreign competition, 134, 209, 216, 220
France and England, 123, 126, 157, 167, 172, 213
Frauds, Statute of, 115

Free Trade, 212, 213, 227
Friars, the coming of the, 75

GAME, 111
Gangs, agricultural, 208
Germany, 134, 167, 217, 227, 228
Gilds, 27-30 ; in cloth trade, 54
Gild lands, confiscation of, 86
Gladstone's budget of 1853, 215, (quoted), 227
Glasgow, 3
Gold, discoveries of, 216
Greshams, the, 96
Guicciardini on trade, 96, 103

HANSA, the, factory in London, 94, 95
Hargreaves, 159
Harrison's *Elizabethan England*, 104, 108
Henry of Huntingdon (quoted), 33
Henry II., 31 ; Henry V., 49 ; Henry VIII., 83-91
History, economic questions in, 238
Hobson, 237, 238
Holland, 122, 123, 168, 230. *See* Dutch
Home trade, value of, 219
Houses, mediæval, 19
Housing and town-planning, 230
Huguenots in England, 134
Hull, 64
Huskisson and Free Trade, 213

IMPORTS, 34, 63, 93, 212. *See* Trade
Income-tax, 223
India, 5, 127, 225
Industrial Revolution. *See* Revolution
Industrial transition in 14th century, 55
Industrial villages (mediæval), 65
Industries, manual, 142
Industry, growth of, 212
Infant mortality, 230
Inhabitants of a manor, 12, 13
Inventions, 138, 140, 159, 160, 165, 236
Iron trade, 138, 139, 164

JEWS in England, 35
Jewries, 35
John, King, 39
Joint-Stock Companies, 237

KET'S RISING, 47
King, Gregory, referred to, 112, 114, 116
"Knight's Fee," a, 18

LABOUR, power of, 221
Labour. *See* Agricultural labourer, Manufacturing population, and Artisans ; *also* Wages and Capitalist
Labour Exchanges, 232
Labour Party, 233
Labourer, the "Golden Age" of, 79
Lace, 103
Land, different kinds of, in a manor, 21
Landlords, 73, 77 ; rapacity of, 109, 204 ; their gains, 198 ; services of, 198, 204
Latimer on rent, 118
Leeds, 151, 156, 163
Liverpool, 152, 236
Lloyd-George, 232
London, 2, 24, 39 ; the Western emporium, 97
Lord of the manor, 7, 11

MANCHESTER, 152
Manor, 7, 12
Manufacturers and politics, 56, 145 ; large and small, 147
Manufacture, domestic system of, 155
Manufactures, 36, 51, 100, 135
Manufacturing towns, mediæval, 57 ; decay of, 65 ; monopolies of, 101 ; population, 149, 152, 178, 231

Marconi, 236
Mark, the, 5, 6; mark-moot, 6
Markets, 3, 38, 60; "a sole market," 168; new, 219
Master clothiers, 66
Meadow land valuable, 21
Members, payment of, 234
Mercantile Theory, the, 168
Merchant gilds, 27, 28
Middle Ages, close of, 81
Mining, 141, 164; women in mines, 194
Misery of working classes, 194
Monasteries, dissolution of, 84, 85
Money, 3
Monopolies, 101, 237
More, Sir Thomas, evidence of, 88, 90
Motor transport, 236

NAPOLEON I., 173
National Debt, 145, 173, 225
Navigation Acts, 130, 169, 213
Newcastle (coals), 130, 137
New World, discoveries in, 89
Norfolk, 46, 51, 112; agriculture in, 199
Northern counties, desolation of, 38; growth of, 162
Norwich, 26, 39
Nottingham, 24, 58, 60

OASTLER, RICHARD, 183
Old Age Pensions, 226, 228, 232
"Osborne Judgment," 234
Over-production, 220
Oxford, origin of, 23, 25

PAUPERISM, 100, 192, 193, 232
Peasants' Revolt, 78
Petition, the Merchants', in 1820, 213
Pigs, 45
Pitt, 171
Plague, the Great, 70; its effects, 71, 73
Ploughing, 44
Politics and industry, 49, 55, 144, 175, 222
Poor Law Commission Report, 233
Poor Laws, the, 107, 188. *See* Allowance and Assessments
Poor priests, the, 76
Population of England, 37, 41, 108, 151, 162
Ports, mediæval, 64
Post Office, 226
Pottery trade, 140
Prices after the Plague, 72; mediæval, 80; later, 90, 112, 174, 202; inflation of, 90, 225
Productiveness of land, 41
Protectionism, 169, 216, 227, 237
Protestant refugees to England, 97, 103, 110, 134

RAILWAYS, 214, 224
Reforms, needed agricultural, 210
Rent, mediæval, 15, 22
Rent, rise of, 88, 112, 118, 119, 204, 224
Restrictions on labour, 189
Revolution, the Industrial, 144 *sqq.*, 157, 161, 164, 190; the French, 157, 171, 190,; the Agricultural, 158, 206
Rights of villeins, 13, 43
Rush for new markets, the, 219

SALT, 142
Seamen, the Elizabethan, 91, 97
Serfs, 13
Services due to a lord, 14, 15
Settlement, law of, 189
Shaftesbury, Lord, 183
Sheep, 45
Sheep farming, 46
Sheffield, 58, 152
Silver, discoveries of, 90
Sixteenth century, changes of, 88, 90
Slave, 13; in modern England, 179
Small Holdings, 232
Smith, Adam, 150, 189
Social movements, 68, 75, 142, 146, 190

Social comforts, 105
Soke-men, 15
South Africa, 225, 229
Southampton, 25, 64
South Sea and other Companies, 125
Spain and England, 121, 126, 167
Speenhamland Act, 188
Staple towns, 59
Steam and machinery, 160
Steamers, 214, 236
Steelyard, the, 94
"Stock and Land Lease," the, 42, 85
Stourbridge fair, 63
Strikes, 235

TAFF VALE CASE, 234
Tax on wool, 49, 50
Taxation, 174, 232
Telegraphs, 214
Telegraphy, wireless, 236
Telephone, 236
Ten Hours' Bill, 185
Tenants of a manor, 11; free tenants, 15
Town, life in a mediæval, 30
Towns: in Domesday, 11; origin of, 21; growth in England, 23; charters of, 25; mediæval, 58; staple, 56
Township, 7
Toynbee, Arnold, 186
Trade, Anglo-Saxon, 3, 4, 5; later, 33; expansion of, 91-99, 103, 125, 129, 131, 173, 212, 224
Trade Unions, 191, 207, 221, 231, 233
Trading clauses in the Great Charter, 34
Transit, means of, 214, 224
Truck Act, 194
Trusts, 237
Tyler's Revolt, 78

UNEMPLOYMENT, 230
United States, 225, 228

VENETIAN FLEET, the, 63, 93
Village, a mediæval, 19; industrial, 65
Villeinage, land in, 20
Villeins, 13, 41, 68; emancipation of, 74, 79
Virgate, 12

WAGE-EARNING CLASS, rise of, 40, 69
Wages, 71, 79, 106, 119, 120, 150, 174, 195, 206, 220, 224, 230
Walter de Henley on farming, 42, 44
War, South African, 225, 230
War, the Thirty Years', 134; the Continental, 171, 195
—— cost of, 173
Wars and industry, 81, 122-129, 134, 166, 167-175, 216, 224
"Waste," the, 6, 20
Watt's inventions, 138, 160, 165
Weavers' gilds, 29, 54
Wedgwood, 141
Wheat, prices of, 174, 195, 200, 203; and *see* Wages
Wiklif, 75
Winchester fair, 62
Women and girls in mines, 194
Women's wages, 196
Wool, 47, 50, 104, 136
Workers' Educational Association, 231
Working classes. *See* Artisans, Agricultural labourer, and Manufacturing population; *also* 187-197
Workmen's Compensation, 233
Worsted industry, the, 53
Writers on commerce, 130

YEOMEN, rise of the, 73; decay of, 115-116
Young, Arthur, referred to, 114, 117, 150, 153, 199, 206, 221